KU-612-607

POST-CONTEMPORARY INTERVENTIONS

Series Editors: Stanley Fish and Fredric Jameson

QUESTIONS OF TRAVEL

Postmodern Discourses of Displacement

Caren Kaplan

DUKE UNIVERSITY PRESS   Durham and London 1996

Third printing, 2000
© 1996 Duke University Press
All rights reserved
Printed in the United States of America on acid-free paper ∞
Typeset in Monotype Garamond by Tseng Information Systems, Inc.
Library of Congress Cataloging-in-Publication Data
appear on the last printed page of this book.

For Eric

CONTENTS

PREFACE

For most of my life, travel has been a certainty rather than a question. I grew up in the state of Maine where the license plates read "Vacationland" and the tourists came and went in seasonal waves. And I have been a tourist myself often enough, looking for some relief from the rooted realities of dailiness. But just as important, I grew up with a sense of my family in dispersal across the terrains of the century's immigrations. We had family in Argentina whom we no longer knew how to contact and we had relatives in touch by letter from South Africa and Israel. Always implicit in family narratives but rarely mentioned were the ones who stayed behind in Eastern Europe, now scattered beyond the reach of memory or communications. In the United States we had relatives spread across the continent — in Chicago, Minneapolis, Tucson, Baltimore, and lots of other places; people who gradually lost touch or moved away again. Our closest relatives lived in Boston and New York, ensuring that we made the long drive down (before superhighways) from our ethnic exile way up north to the big metropolitan centers. Travel was unavoidable, indisputable, and always necessary for family, love, and friendship as well as work.

I was also born into a culture that took the national benefits of travel for granted, although in the span of my childhood and adolescence that certainty about the right of U.S. citizens to visit, invade, and invest in any location came under fire. Goodwill ambassadors or imperialists? The calls for Yankees to go home increased and continued to press for an end to U.S. military and economic adventures abroad. Couldn't U.S. citizens travel anywhere they pleased and be assured of a warm welcome? In Istanbul in 1972, as a participant in a liberal student exchange program, I was stunned when I was told "We like you but we don't like your government or your military bases." Military bases? Thus, my education proceeded like that of many people of my class and race and generation; as I learned the difference between official and unofficial stories, I learned that knowledges are invested with social relations, histories, and struggles for representation.

I already knew this lesson from the disjuncture of gender socialization and my generation's fledgling feminist resistance. Like lots of young white people entering what we called the "counterculture," I was learning these lessons through the history of genocides of native American Indians and the enslavement of Africans. Much of this education was based on naive romanticizations and exoticizations, representational legacies that resounded in some aspects of the antiwar movement and many of the so-called new social movements. How to avoid these kinds of objectifications? How to make political coalitions based on material histories rather than mystified fantasies? How to deconstruct the privileges of race, class, and gender supremacy in the United States and rearticulate identities and alliances? This is work that elite and relatively empowered groups and subjects must engage in continually in order to be credible participants in social change.

In my case, asking questions about travel reinforces these lessons. Like most moderns in the West, I was brought up to believe that distance gives needed perspective, that difference leads to insight, and that travel is quite figuratively "broadening." Yet it has also been my experience that travel can be confusing, distance can be illusory, and difference depends very much on one's point of view. Thus travel has not only provoked my questioning of official histories and ideologies (U.S. military bases in Turkey? Why?), but it has produced a profound skepticism toward the terms in which travel is described. Are imperialist travelers' descriptions of cultural differences the ones we want to reproduce in tourist brochures? Who benefits and who suffers from the attitude that distance is the best perspective? As telecommunications and new technologies refigure our sense of distance and travel, why do older ideological formations persist, or in what ways do they shift?

Teaching about travel from this standpoint has helped me come to grips with the pervasiveness of metaphors of travel and displacement in contemporary culture in this country. So many of us desire to travel for fun or for education, even as many of us feel ambivalent about the mobile nature of employment and family organization. How do we sort out these perceptions of travel and come to understand the ways in which they are linked to a more postmodern moment of destabilized nation-states, cultural and economic diasporas, and increasing disparities of wealth and power? "You have ruined my next vacation!" some students complain. But most of the young people with whom I have discussed these ideas at both Georgetown University and UC Berkeley have embraced this project with insightful enthusiasm, and their rigorous questions and innovative readings have greatly aided my studies of this topic.

Questioning travel can be done on many registers and across many disciplines. The contours of this particular study were probably set in my undergraduate and graduate work at institutions that were engaged in pedagogical and curricular "experiments" and where I was encouraged to mix disciplines and methods to address the questions I was learning to pose. I am especially grateful to two of my professors at Hampshire College for giving me invaluable critical tools. Lester Mazor taught me to read closely and rigorously, to integrate teaching with learning, and, in the best anarchist tradition, to question authority. Jill Lewis opened up the world of feminist scholarship to me and provided an example of independence of mind that changed the way I imagined my future. They both gave me a strong sense of how to be radical critics and passionate teachers in conservative times. I could never have grown up to write this book without their faith and care.

I also found educational innovation in the History of Consciousness program at UC Santa Cruz where Hayden White, James Clifford, and Donna Haraway knocked my philosophical socks off, as it were. I am grateful to all three of them for teaching me how to question master narratives (and minor ones, too) and for training me to enter this profession. I must also thank Teresa de Lauretis, Robert Meister, Helene Moglen, Vivian Sobchak, Billie Harris, and Peter Euben, who supported, advised, and worked with me at various times at UCSC. My fellow students were among my best teachers; in particular, I thank Che Sandoval, Katie King, Lata Mani, Ruth Frankenberg, Deborah Gordon, Zoe Sofoulis, Lisa Bloom, and Gloria Watkins. I would like to acknowledge my dissertation chair, James Clifford, who never failed to provide me with things to read and think about that changed the way I approached my work. His patience and generosity continue to sustain me even as the depth and erudition of his own work provide a constant inspiration.

My own desire to travel and, perhaps, to emulate the conventions of modernist expatriation led me to spend two years in Paris after my advancement to candidacy. There I switched gears, learned the language a bit, and "did" the poststructuralist rounds at the various campuses. This book is deeply influenced by the kindness of those professors who admitted me to their seminars and lectures. The kindest and warmest welcome was extended to me by Sarah Kofman. When I was quite overwhelmed by my own displacement, she made me feel at home as a feminist critic.

In its earliest drafts this book profited immeasurably from careful readings and discussions with several of my colleagues in the English Department at Georgetown University, including Michael Ragussis, Leona Fisher, Pam Fox, and Kim Hall. I can't thank them enough for the atmosphere of intellectual support and inquiry that marked our years together. I miss the dailiness of our third-floor confabs in ways for which e-mail simply cannot compensate. I'd also like to thank my former chair, James Slevin, for supporting this book project and its author in every way within his power. Among the many students at Georgetown who helped me work on the questions that make up this book, in particular I'd like to thank Mary Kearney, Gayle Vandenberg, and Michael Magoolaghan for the pleasure of their company. Back in my old neighborhood, Java House kept this project going through many mugs of caffeinated brew.

Moving to Berkeley several years ago affected this project in innumerable ways. The wear and tear of moving and commuting across the continent took up a lot of precious time, but the opportunities to research and write in a new situation were an inspiring compensation. I would like to thank Mary Ryan, Evelyn Glenn, and Carol Stack in the women's studies department for their generous mentoring. Trinh Minh-ha has inspired my work for many years and it is truly delightful to find her across the hall. My warmest thanks to Carla Atkins and Althea Grannum-Cummings for their expert and congenial support. Jillian Sandell has provided this project with imaginative and conscientious research assistance. Among many colleagues at Berkeley and other Bay Area campuses whose advice I have sought and whose work I appreciate, I want to thank Minoo Moallem, Elizabeth Abel, Aihwa Ong, Lydia Liu, Saidiya Hartman, Michael Lucey, Sharon Marcus, Sue Schweik, Parama Roy, Sau-ling Wong, Rosa Linda Fregoso, Irit Rogoff, Rachel Lee, Purnima Mankekar, and Akhil Gupta. Norma Alarcón's brilliant theoretical interventions and institutional vision never fail to inspire me. Carolyn Dinshaw not only teaches me with great patience and tact about widening my narrow "presentist" perspective, she tutors me in the art of academic living with panache and grace.

Along the way I have received generous institutional support from many sources. Many thanks to E. Ann Kaplan and the staff at the Humanities Center at SUNY Stony Brook for their support during my postdoctoral fellowship there. A junior faculty research leave and a summer grant from Georgetown University made a crucial contribution to the completion of this work. Committee on Research grants from UC Berkeley greatly aided my work, as did support for undergraduate and graduate research assistants.

For the kind of support that far surpasses material finances, I reserve my very warmest thanks for my family. My parents, Doris and Arthur Kaplan, showed me that a life of the mind can include principles, humor, and love. Their example as teachers, readers, and writers has been invaluable. For cheering me on through thick and thin, my deepest thanks to Mildred Smoodin. I have appreciated the support of my brother Mitchell and my in-law siblings Roberta Smoodin and Steve Marvin. My cousin Henry Flax knows what it is to burn the midnight oil and I'm proud that soon he'll join me as a Ph.D. Danny Flax keeps me on-line and laughing. The only grandmother I knew, Fanny Brown Flax, was an autodidact, and her room full of interesting books was a true haven for me as a child. To all the ones who didn't get to go to or finish school, who worked so hard so I could grow to this life as a writer, my profound and loving thanks.

For the very great pleasure of their company, I thank Alfred Jessel, Kirin Jessel, Sonal Jessel, Marget Long, Ann Martin, Coca Eckel, Carlo Henschel, Sig Roos, and Ruth Rohde. Colleagues and friends who have read and commented on my work or cheered me up or lured me away from the computer and out to play include Leyla Ezdinli, Bob Stam, Mark Anderson, Lisa Cartwright, Brian Goldfarb,

Heather Hendershot, Elizabeth Young, Tani Barlow, Richard deCordova, Denise Albanese, Cathy Davidson, Elspeth Probyn, Bruce Robbins, Abdul JanMohamed, Sidonie Smith, Julia Watson, Lynne Sachs, Maria Lugones, R. Radhakrishnan, Sneja Gunew, Aurora Wolfgang, and Kamala Visweswaran. Stephen Stein helped me to find my way as a writer, and he gave more to this book than he will ever know. I want to thank Emily Young for encouraging me to speak with her then-new colleague, Ken Wissoker. As an editor, Ken is a writer's dream, someone who understands what you're talking about and who can take the blasted manuscript off your hands and get it into print! I am grateful to two anonymous readers who gave me excellent suggestions at key stages of the project. My thanks to Jean Brady, Judith Hoover, Marc Brodsky, Richard Morrison, and everyone at Duke University Press who has helped this manuscript become a book. My thanks to Jasbir Puar for her help with the index.

It is impossible to work as a feminist and a theorist on the topic of travel without recognizing the contributions of Inderpal Grewal and Ella Shohat. What luck that I have had the immense great fortune to do my work in conversation with them. Ella Shohat pushes me to examine that last notion I would rather ignore. Living out the politics she writes about, she challenges my parochialisms with infinite patience and she practices professional generosity to a fault. If it is sometimes a struggle to keep a hopeful view of the world of academia, Ella's work and her warm presence keep me going.

Finding an ideal intellectual collaborator is rare, but I have found her in Inderpal Grewal. It is my greatest joy to write with Inderpal rather than without her. Although this book has been saved from numerous errors and wrong turns owing to her many conscientious and unstinting readings, often at a moment's notice, it is very much my own book and can't match the luster or scope of her work. For countless conversations of great depth and for all the acts of friendship that kept me sane during trying times, my gratitude is boundless.

This book is dedicated to Eric Smoodin, my spouse and partner in all things. It is somewhat hackneyed to thank someone for all the usual spousal modes of support, but how can such heroics go unmentioned? Who else but Eric would share the late nights over malfunctioning printers and balky software, whip up something hot and nourishing for an exhausted writer to eat, or proofread at the last minute? I also want to thank him for encouraging me to stop working and relax from time to time. But most importantly for this book and the work that comes after it, I want to thank Eric for profoundly shifting my views on critical practice. I came out of graduate school a high theorist without much knowledge about cultural production or reception in any historical specificity despite my interest in colonial discourses. Talking with Eric about his work and reading it closely, observing the immense resistance in the humanities to the study of material cultures and their conditions of production, I became persuaded by his rigorous, interdisciplinary practice of cultural history. It has changed the design of my classes and the formulation of my next book, and I hope that, even in a small way, traces of this passionate discussion between us will be evident in this book.

QUESTIONS OF TRAVEL

An Introduction

Continent, city, country, society:
the choice is never wide and never free.
And here, or there . . . No. Should we have stayed at
home, wherever that may be?
—Elizabeth Bishop[1]

Home or away, "the choice is never wide and never free." In this book, I inquire into categories that are so often taken for granted, asking how and when notions of home and away, placement and displacement, dwelling and travel, location and dislocation, come to play a role in contemporary literary and cultural criticism in Europe and the United States. The prevalence of metaphors of travel and displacement in this body of critical work suggests that the modern era is fascinated by the experience of distance and estrangement, reproducing these notions through articulations of subjectivity and poetics. Yet displacement is not universally available or desirable for many subjects, nor is it evenly experienced.

The historical phenomenon of modern imperialism in the context of European and U.S. industrialization, the economic and cultural annexation of regions into a "Third World" and subsequent decolonizations, as well as the shifts and destabilizations engendered by the deindustrialization of the so-called First World all propose distinct and varied questions for travel. In this book I will argue that the terms of displacement found in Euro-American critical practice rarely admit to these material conditions. Although modern imperialism does not structure every aspect of culture in every site around the globe, I will argue that the emergence of terms of travel and displacement (as well as their oppositional counterparts, home and location) in contemporary criticism must be linked to the histories of the production of colonial discourses.[2]

One way to trace colonial discourses in Euro-American critical practices is to begin to distinguish between historical periods as well as geographical locations. I am particularly interested in the moments that have come to be labeled "modern" and "postmodern" in relation to cultural and artistic movements, because a deconstruction of their apparent "difference" demystifies the history of contemporary aesthetic and critical practices. Thus, while modern and postmodern can be seen as oppositional styles or poetics, they can also be viewed as linked yet distinct responses to questions of cultural representation and expression. I want to demonstrate that metaphors of travel and displacement operate in powerful ways in these representations, especially in articulations of "theory." In this project, then, travel refers not so much to the movements of individuals in the modern era but to the construction of categories in criticism that engender specific ideas and practices.

In focusing on the production of postmodern discourses of displacement in modernity, this study calls attention to the continuities and discontinuities between terms such as "travel," "displacement," and "location" as well as between the particularized practices and identities of "exile," "tourist," and "nomad." All displacements are not the same. Yet the occidental ethnographer, the modernist expatriate poet, the writer of popular travel accounts, and the tourist may all participate in the mythologized narrativizations of displacement without questioning the cultural, political, and economic grounds of their different professions, privileges, means, and limitations. Immigrants, refugees, exiles, nomads, and the homeless also move in and out of these discourses as metaphors, tropes, and symbols but rarely as historically recognized producers of critical discourses themselves. Euro-American discourses of displacement tend to absorb difference and create ahistorical amalgams; thus a field of social forces becomes represented as a personal experience, its lived intensity of separation marking a link with others.[3]

Without rejecting or dismissing the powerful testimony of per-

sonal and individual experiences of displacement, how is it possible
to avoid ahistorical universalization and the mystification of social relations that Euro-American discourses of displacement often deploy?
Beginning with the terms and metaphors of displacement that frequent contemporary criticism, it is possible to begin a history of the
production and reception of "theory" and critical practices. Sorting
through terms, learning their histories of use as well as their conditions of emergence, provides one entry into the study of the production of knowledge. The title of this book refers deliberately to both
"travel" *and* "displacement," raising the question of their rhetorical
relationship. Travel is very much a modern concept, signifying both
commercial and leisure movement in an era of expanding Western
capitalism, while displacement refers us to the more mass migrations
that modernity has engendered.[4] While these terms cannot be viewed
as opposites, it is also impossible to see them as referencing the same
sites and situations. A postmodern reading of the terms might suggest their links as well as their disjunctures, their possibilities of historicized emergence as metaphors in critical practice. But what is at
stake in such a tenuous and site-specific reading?

James Clifford has argued for the efficacy of the term "travel,"
pointing out that "displacement," which appears to some critics to
be more neutral, can too easily homogenize historical experiences.[5]
Although I am deeply influenced by the rigorous work that Clifford
puts "travel" through, in this study I will try to move from travel to
displacement, not in a dialectical synthesis of binary categories where
travel simply signifies modernism and displacement purely articulates
postmodernism, but as a way of querying the construction and proliferation of modernisms from a postmodern critical standpoint. While
Clifford suggests that it is useful to work with and through travel's
"historical taintedness," I propose an allied project that explores similar questions from somewhat different subject positions and, therefore, with specifically constituted investments. *Questions of Travel*, then,
reaches out to a variety of historical constructs of modern displacement: leisure travel, exploration, expatriation, exile, homelessness,
and immigration, to name a few.

Thus I make recourse to both travel and displacement, not as
synonyms but as signs of different critical registers and varied historicized instances. In order to examine the continuities and discontinu-

ities between modern and postmodern critical practices, the terms are not posed in opposition so much as in juxtaposition. In stressing the different material and textual manifestations of displacement, however, I do not mean to suggest that either travel or displacement is ever neutral or utopian—that one or the other proposes a better or more desirable modus operandi. I want to use the term "displacement" to read against the grain of travel, that is, to question the modernisms of representations of movement, location, and homelessness in contemporary critical practices. Yet I do not mean to overvalorize displacement. The task of this book will be to situate these discourses more specifically and to demystify their erasures of history as well as place.

One key question I ask in relation to terms and tropes of travel is why, if the modern experience of forced or voluntary movement has been widespread and diverse, the metaphors and symbols used to represent displacement refer to individualized, often elite, circumstances? In literary criticism, the model for the author or critic is the solitary exile who is either voluntarily expatriated or involuntarily displaced. In *Exiles and Émigrés,* Terry Eagleton argues that the canon of modern British literature has been "dominated" by foreigners and émigrés such as Joyce and Conrad.[6] George Steiner's examination of the phenomenon of multilingualism in contemporary literature, *Extra-territorial,* also employs metaphors of travel and displacement, in particular in reference to the "unhousedness" of such writers as Nabokov, Beckett, and Borges. Few of the writers included in critical assessments of Euro-American high modernism are referred to as immigrants or refugees. Their dislocation is expressed in singular rather than collective terms, as purely psychological or aesthetic situations rather than as a result of historical circumstances.

Can the mystified universalism of such representations be countered by strategies of localization or placement or by expanding the subject from singular to plural? What are the limits and possibilities of representations of immigration and other forms of large-scale displacement?[7] Although immigration does not appear as frequently or in as charged a manner as tropes of exile in contemporary criticism, simply valorizing the term in a binary reversal cannot account completely for the complexities of mass movements in this century. For example, massive troop deployments during imperialist expansion and occupation, the World Wars, and other military projects moved large groups of working-class and middle-class men (and some women) away from their home locales. The twentieth century has also produced unprecedented numbers of refugees as people have fled their homes to avoid famine, genocide, or incarceration. Immigration does not exactly define the situation of so-called guest workers, illegal aliens, or any other workers who spend anywhere from a few months to an entire lifetime in another country without legalization of their residential or national status. Poor people move in large numbers around the globe in search of work either by choice or by circumstance. Although tourism, with its association of leisure time and privilege, is the world's largest growth industry, the numerical majority of people who move in this world do so to work or to survive life-threatening events. Using immigration to read against the grain of modernist exile begins to demystify the construction of specific aesthetic and critical practices, yet immigration should not be universalized as a symbol of displacement.

Thus considering the material histories of immigration is only one way to destabilize modernist myths of travel. Critical examinations of tourism can open up the terms of displacement in modernity as well. For example, in *The Tourist,* Dean MacCannell links modern displacement to the development of mass leisure, international tourism, and sightseeing. MacCannell's study turns sociology upside down, as it were, and proposes the subject as the object. That is, an innocuous and even slightly ridiculous figure—the tourist—becomes the key to social structure in the modern era. In chapter 1 I will argue with MacCannell's effort to pose the tourist as "universal experience," however, and with the structuralist tenor of that project. *The Tourist,* nevertheless, remains a significant text for the study of discourses of displacement, querying high culture's fascination with singular, elite figures of travel.

Obviously, travel generates a complex system of cultural representation. Although Edward Said raised the issue of "traveling theories" some time ago in *The World, the Text, and the Critic,* it is not only theories that can be said to circulate, but the terms, tropes, and subjects of criticism.[8] Because it is arguable that the production of criticism in contemporary transnational cultures is far too vast a field to address in total, I will focus on the particular ways that versions of displacement emerge as primary tropes in several forms of criticism influenced by Euro-American poststructuralist and feminist theories. Just as the concepts of colonial and postcolonial must be grounded in material specificity, poststructuralism can no longer be generalized as a monolithic entity but must be studied as immensely complicated and varied versions. "Feminism" has faced its own legitimation crisis and must be viewed as diverse in its practices as well. My stake in the terms and conditions of such a study stems from my own position as an intellectual who has participated in cultures of Euro-American poststructuralist criticism as well as feminist academic and nonacademic movements. I am, therefore, deeply invested in critiques of the local and global practices of these theories and identity politics as they "travel."

The current version of this book evolved through a long search for a way to query the connections between poststructuralist or postmodern destabilizations of cultural and political authorities and the progressive identity politics that characterized the social movements with which I affiliate myself. Along the way, the formation of colonial discourse studies allied with feminist poststructuralism shifted my work away from two earlier strong influences: Frankfort School social theory and psychoanalytic methodologies. Working on the links between the history of Euro-American imperialism and the construction of gendered and racialized subjects in modernity brought the terms of my inquiry into sharper focus, resulting in a dissertation on travel memoirs written in the post-WWII/decolonization era. I was writing about a "poetics" of displacement at that time, but I became dissatisfied with close readings of literary texts and moved back into my earlier fields of training—political, economic, and social theory— in order to focus my study on questions of representation in the production and reception of Euro-American contemporary criticism. Interdisciplinary cultural studies provides a framework for the pastiche of methodologies and approaches that characterize the modus operandi of this book. Neither literary criticism nor sociology per se, this work stages a number of questions about the way disciplines produce knowledge in order to create "imagined" textual spaces of critical practice.

The title *Questions of Travel* is borrowed from an Elizabeth Bishop poem of the same name. When I first encountered the poem, I was heartened by Bishop's questioning of Western manifest destiny. In Euro-American traditions, at least four centuries of travel writing chronicle the literary styles of various phases of imperialism. Bishop's paradoxical question, whether "lack of imagination" brought about the occupation of "imagined places," is rarely raised in the literature of Western travel. Yet, ten years later, I read the poem in a less charitable light. Posing a question such as "Should we have stayed at home?" can be answered with a futile but emphatic "yes" if "we" are a particular cast of historical agents. In the aftermath of colonialism and in the midst of the advent of diverse neocolonialisms and totalitarianisms, simply destabilizing the notion of home ("wherever that may be") can no longer answer the historical question of accountability. Bishop's subjects (the "us" and "we" of the poem) are not universal although they can be glibly assumed to be transcendental figures of displacement in a modern world of fragmentation. It is one of the tasks of this book to query the mystification of such figures, to historicize the notions of "home" and "away" in the production of both critical and literary discourses.

For many of us there is no possibility of staying at home in the conventional sense—that is, the world has changed to the point that those domestic, national, or marked spaces no longer exist. So I cannot respond to Bishop's more modernist question by "staying put" or fixing my location or promising not to leave my national borders. There is not necessarily a preoriginary space in which to stay after modern imperialist expansion. But identities cling to us, or even produce us, nonetheless. Many of us have locations in the plural. Thus, rather than assuming that we'll never return to these homes again, rather than celebrating the rootless traveler of Bishop's text, I suggest that the fragments and multiplicities of identity in postmodernity can be marked and historically situated. As Iain Chambers argues, historicizing displacement leads us away from nostalgic dreams of "going home" to a mythic, metaphysical location and into the realm of theorizing a way of "being at home" that accounts for "the myths we know to be myths yet continue to cling to, cherish and dream" alongside "other stories, other fragments of memory and traces of time."[9]

Postmodern Question Marks

I promised to show you a map you say but this is a mural
then yes let it be   these are small distinctions
where do we see it from is the question
—Adrienne Rich[10]

The advent of what has been called "postmodernism" in European
and U.S. cultures of criticism has raised numerous questions of location; that is, what position or point of view is occupied by the artist
or author and what happens when those perspectival sites are seen to
be multiple? Questions of space as well as time jostle with destabilizations of master narratives and tropes as various authorities become
delegitimated. Is it a "map" or a "mural"? Adrienne Rich's poem
refers to these generic qualities as "small distinctions," arguing that
the point of view of the active spectator is what is important now. Yet
if postmodernism engenders new agents and discourses, it also remains ambiguously attached to its temporal progenitor, modernism.
In this book I will argue that Euro-American modernisms and postmodernisms are as linked and continuous as they are distinct and discontinuous. Reading theory and criticism as produced, at least in part,
by aspects of imperialism can demonstrate that the modernist experimentations so closely connected to an age of consolidating nationalisms and Western economic expansion are not effaced or superseded
in postmodern articulations so much as they are transmuted or reconfigured. Interpreting versions of travel and displacement as modern
or postmodern, then, does not simply designate styles but links aesthetics to political and economic material practices.

The current age is one characterized by market fragmentation,
flexible accumulation, and increasingly decentered social, political,
and economic forms of organization. The movement of transnational
capital deconstructs traditional modern borders and cultures and re-
constructs new ones, both eroding and consolidating versions of the
nation-state. Permanent refugees have been created during ongoing
territorial conflicts while stable notions of national and cultural identity are increasingly in flux. These are, as Stuart Hall reminds us, dangerous moments.[11] Hall focuses on the constructions of national identity based on newly virulent forms of racism, but we can also identify

the effects of these social processes in the rise of religious fundamen-
talisms of all kinds, the continuing and intensifying violence against
women around the world, and the worsening of economic conditions
for poor people. In this context, theories of identity cannot rely solely
on psychoanalytic or aesthetic categories or modes of explanation.

Just as the solid association between national spaces and identities becomes loosened and, in some cases, dissolves, the attribution
of identity for subjects in modernity is uneven, increasingly differentiated, and, quite often, contradictory. To make this assertion, however,
is not to claim a celebratory hybridity in a world culture of heterogeneity. To put it bluntly, few of us can live without a passport or an
identity card of some sort. Each interaction with the institutional and
cultural and, especially, governmental operates in tandem with our
varied participation in economies of production and consumption
to foster myriad possibilities of identity, not all of them liberating.
These possibilities are not reducible to either "choice" or "freedom"
even as they are not always equal to "coercion" or "imprisonment."
They are the articulated evidence of the limits and possibilities of the
age in which we live.

Examining the status of history in modernist discourses provides an excellent route into the question of how cultures can be
imagined, created, and delimited. Even as Euro-American modernism has celebrated and constructed vanguard movements that rebel
against traditional authorities in the humanities, the gatekeepers of
modernist culture have circumscribed and contained these visions in
the realm of aesthetics. Any effort to link world and text must begin by
deconstructing the opposition between politics and aesthetics. Since
every binary structure hides or suppresses other terms, the question
of travel here signifies the possibilities of multiple figures and tropes
of displacement that might lead us to more complex and accurate
maps of cultural production.

If postmodernism is marked, as Robert Young argues, not only
by a self-consciousness of historical relativity, but also by the "problematic of the place of Western culture in relation to non-Western
cultures,"[12] then there are no better "historical moments" to examine
than those that pertain to modern imperialism. In particular, the interpellation of economic and cultural spheres through the mediation
of modernism requires a closer look. Although the period of "high

colonialism" coincides rather neatly with the era of "high modernism" (the Berlin conference of 1884–85 effectively carved up the land mass of Africa and designated specific portions to particular European nations for economic "development," while studies of modernism frequently begin with the date 1890) the ahistorical, even antihistorical, nature of Euro-American modernisms has suppressed most analyses of possible links between such "events." Yet, as Fredric Jameson has cautioned, the obvious historical parallels between the rise of Western imperialism and the development of Western modernisms should not be read reductively or purely as *content*. If the structure of imperialism made its "mark on the inner forms and structure" of modernism, as Jameson asserts, then the critical project does not consist in determining the reflection of imperialism in modernist representational strategies but in questioning the relationship between form and content, between literature and culture, between art and politics.[13]

From the vantage point of the present, the stakes in mapping the networks of criticism and history are intensified by the currency of modernist technologies and strategies in what is supposedly a postmodern era. The interdependency of modernist and postmodernist techniques of representation suggests that the impact of imperialist social relations must be clearly analyzed in order to avoid further complicities between cultural production and neocolonialism. Whether or not we are in a "post-" or "neo-" colonial era poses a question that can only be answered through critical readings of the legacies of cultures of modernism and postmodernism in diverse locations.

My thoughts on the relationship between modern and postmodern have been influenced greatly by collaborative work with Inderpal Grewal. In the introduction to our book, *Scattered Hegemonies,* we wrote at some length about the distinction between discussions of the postmodern as a literary and cultural style and the notion of postmodernity as a political concept that mediates temporal and spatial relationships in modernity.[14] In this work, we argued forcefully for the strategic analytical value of postmodernity for transnational feminist critical practices. We also questioned the division between "Western high theory" and a "non-Western" antitheoretical stance, suggesting that anticolonial critiques, opposition to Western imperialism, and the struggles to articulate sociopolitical formations from diverse locations have been as influential in formulating postmodernity as Euro-American philosophical reconfigurations. In this sense, we challenged a more Eurocentric view of postmodernism as a debate internal to Euro-American locations, turning the lens, as it were, to view postmodernity as a set of economic and cultural relationships that produce specific discourses of space, time, and subjectivity in a particular time period and in relation to multiple locations. Our approach is echoed in Robert Young's discussion of contemporary theory, particularly in his assertion that colonial discourse analysis is not peripheral to mainstream theory but "itself forms the point of questioning of Western knowledge's categories and assumptions."[15]

Although the discourse on the postmodern has become increasingly politicized and transnational in approach in recent years, throughout the 1980s the critical writing on postmodernity could be roughly summarized as falling into two general schools of thought. The first, more usually represented by concerns about literary and artistic styles and periods, asserted postmodernism as a stylistic break or historical rupture with modernism. This version of the postmodern was interested most often in the activities of twentieth-century avant-gardes in Europe and the United States and in challenging aesthetic classes and distinctions. The second vein of commentary on the postmodern was more concerned with postmodern*ity* in order to mark continuities as well as discontinuities with modernity in the midst of changing social and economic conditions or to track proliferations of modernisms in shifting historical contexts. In these versions of the postmodern, the emphasis lies more in social theories of historical periodization, cultural and political change, and historically specific theories of cultural production.

Although I am in greater sympathy with the latter version of postmodernism, it is important not to reinforce the simplistic notion that there is, then, an "aesthetic" postmodernism to be rejected over a more politicized variant. The very appearance of what could be crudely described as two schools of thought on the critical use of the term "postmodern" as well as the proliferation of slippages between the terms "modernity," "postmodernity," and "postmodernism" strongly suggest that careful delineation and deconstruction of the debates and contests for meaning are increasingly necessary. We would do well to ask why, as Kwame Anthony Appiah puts it, "the modernist characterization of modernity must be challenged."[16]

All versions of the "postmodern" share a distrust or disavowal of master narratives, totalizing systems of explanation, and a recognition of the breakup of formerly hegemonic practices and representations. Equally, an emphasis on local, micro, or regional practices can be found in most varieties of postmodernisms, along with a stress on multiplicity, fragmentation, and difference. But not all postmodern articulations or modes of description and analysis, as we have already seen, function in exactly the same ways or for the same ends. If modernity has produced differentiated effects, then the production and reception of postmodernisms must be structured along those diverse lines. As Appiah so persuasively argues, postmodernity "is the culture in which all postmodernisms operate, sometimes in synergy, sometimes in competition; and because contemporary culture is . . . transnational, postmodern culture is global—though that emphatically does not mean that it is the culture of every person in the world." [17]

Thus, it is fruitless and inaccurate to insist on postmodernism's purely oppositional qualities without specifying which postmodernism is circulating in what context. Questioning the authority of master narratives is certainly revolutionary in some contexts but may only consolidate a new form of hegemony over other interests. For example, literary avant-gardes in Europe in revolt against the burden of influence from earlier generations did not necessarily and inherently challenge the power and practice of Western cultural hegemony in other parts of the world or over Western middle-class women or working-class people. On the other hand, the purely aestheticized struggles within literary cultures in the West could be characterized as extremely local destabilizations of authority that contributed to the ferment and change that mark postmodernity. Therefore, although I am less interested in focusing solely on questions of aesthetic taste and practice, I would resist any absolute polarization between the aesthetic and political in discussions of postmodernity. Rather, I am interested in exploring the links or continuities as well as the distinctions and discontinuities between articulations of modernity and postmodernity.

As both bell hooks and Cornel West point out, if postmodernism is only based upon a process of differentiation from the aesthetic practices of modernism (whose discourses have been largely silent on the cultural productions of non-Western or nonwhite artists and writers of both genders), then postmodernism becomes just another generalized exclusionary theory of what is, in fact, a historically particular phenomenon.[18] Speaking in particular to African American histories of cultural production and reception, hooks and West have argued that modernism has been a primary factor in African American communities from jazz innovators to the Black Power movement. There are, therefore, postmodernisms operating in diverse and compelling ways within African American communities today. Arguing along similar lines but emphasizing the less discussed realm of African American painters and sculptors, Michele Wallace has described the process whereby Euro-American postmodernism emerges as "lily white," systematically denying commonalities and relationships between African American and white Euro-American artists and critics.[19]

When critics seize the term and make it more historically accountable, vibrant alternative usages come to life. For example, Wahneema Lubiano argues that, although she does not wish to endorse every aspect of philosphical postmodernism, the term itself provides an opportunity to "organize a response to modernism's blind spot in regard to people of color."[20] Lubiano identifies a specific postmodern critical practice as historically emergent and contingent: "We can consider African-American postmodernism as not simply a historical moment when modernism's intellectual and cultural hegemony is at least being questioned, but as a general epistemological standpoint for engaging/foregrounding what has been left out of larger discourses, a consideration of certain kinds of difference and the reasons for their historical absences. It theorizes ways that prevent engagement with differences from concretizing into intellectually and politically static categories."[21] Lubiano goes on to argue that postmodernism can be strategically employed to stage particular discussions, challenges, and critiques without serving as the only primary discourse for critics with multiple affiliations.

In a related vein, critics who question Euro-American dominance in cultures of theory also make recourse to the "postmodern" in pragmatic and nuanced ways. For example, Nelly Richard's discussion of the positioning of Latin American theories and cultures both for and against hegemonic formations raises the question of whether or not particular versions of postmodernism can "help the process of decolonization."[22] Rather than reading postmodern theories as cultural imperialism pure and simple, Richard situates Latin America in a world system that is shifting its paradigms of power as its economic and cultural relations realign: "Even though it only finds itself in this position within a theoretical framework formulated elsewhere, Latin American cultural practices are deemed to have pre-figured the model now approved and legitimized by the term 'postmodernism.' The very heterogeneity of the experiences which have created a Latin American space out of its multiple and hybrid pasts creates, at least on the surface, the very qualities of fragmentation and dispersion associated with the semantic erosion characteristic of the crisis of modernity and modernism as its cultural dominant."[23] Although Richard's analysis continues to construct a fairly monolithic "Latin America" through her reliance on center-periphery paradigms, a construction that provokes questions of diversity and complexity within and between cultures, classes, national and ethnic identities, at the very least, her insistence upon the dynamic possibilities of non-European theoretical production and reception is particularly salient to my discussion here. Her stress on "innovative responses" to and "active participation" in postmodern critical rereading strategies echoes the work of other writers and critics who argue that while Western cultural hegemony is as pervasive as its economic base is extensive, its effects are fragmented, contradictory, complex, and intensely diversified by local factors.[24]

Emergent theories of postmodernism, then, argue that the politics of difference are aided and even structured by the international circulation of destabilizing and multiplying cultural elements, events, and instances that "clear a space" for new or previously unheard or unacknowledged narratives. Appiah views postmodernism as a retheorization of the distinctions instigated by modernity. "Modernism saw the economization of the world as the triumph of reason," he writes, while "postmodernism rejects that claim, allowing in the realm of theory the same proliferation of distinctions that modernity had begun."[25] Although these distinctions function on multiple levels, a great deal of critical production concerns itself with theorizations of social identities and political/cultural movements. Such discourses of difference are produced in relation to any number of modern and postmodern agendas, giving rise simultaneously to essentialist and poststructuralist subjects. Postmodernism does not simply delineate the utopian conditions for the production of admirably multicultural and hybrid subjectivities in a brave new world. In postmodernity we can identify a pernicious return of biological determinism with all of its accompanying racisms, sexisms, and terrifying forms of social control in such phenomena as the relentless search for the genetic foundations of "homosexuality" (but not "heterosexuality") and in the reassertion of policies of "ethnic cleansing" as practiced by white supremacists in the United States and South Africa, neofascists in Germany and Italy, or advocates of ethnic "purity" in the Balkans. Biomedical research, reproductive technologies, and transnational communications offer powerful reconfigurations of our representations of what kind of worlds and bodies we inhabit. At the same time, we have seen the "superpowers" lose some of their hegemonic social, economic, and political control over the rest of the world and the proliferation of new social movements that assert progressive notions of identity and alliance.

Thus postmodernity can be seen to have opened up the terms of cultural and political discourse, creating new possibilities for social arrangements and bonds. Yet new forms of exploitation and unequal development have also become possible. Andrew Ross suggests that both the gains in representation and the new structures of oppression "need to be viewed side by side as dual effects of the conditions under which a politics of difference has emerged."[26] The so-called politics of difference (the subject of attacks from both the political Right and Left over representational inclusion, political correctness, identity politics, and theories of liberation and social change) does not constitute a homogeneous or organized social or cultural movement. Modernity, which has mass-produced differentiation and encouraged identity politics, cannot be effectively challenged by the politics of difference alone.

Putting history back into our consideration of "difference" neither erases nor simplifies our ambivalent relationship to the economic systems that we live with, by, and in spite of. Such historicization, in effect, sharpens our abilities to sort through the deadening multiplicities of consumer culture, to better articulate our desires and needs, and to understand the contradictory and productive powers of what Judith Williamson calls *"constructs* of difference." In her studies of colonial discourse and constructions of gendered desires in Western advertising, Williamson analyzes how difference is staged or set up to contain or manage any threatening or deeply subversive conflicts: "The whole drive of our society is toward displaying as much difference as possible within it while eliminating where it is at all possible what is different from it: the supreme trick of bourgeois ideology is to be able to produce its opposite out of its own hat."[27]

While "difference" is a concept that must be treated with as much skepticism as "similarity," the "local" is a related term that requires similar deconstruction. In chapter 4, I will discuss the enthusiastic but uncritical emphasis on the local in postmodern discourses, particularly in geography and feminist theory. How has this emphasis on the local come about? While it can be argued that both structuralism and poststructuralism have stressed the importance of the local meaning of structures and events in the fields of philosophy, anthropology, and linguistics, it is also the case that major changes in relationships between nation-states and colonies and in technologies of communication have created possibilities for the recognition of the value of localized articulations or identities.

Jean-François Lyotard's influential text *The Postmodern Condition* set the terms for philosophy and Euro-American high theory in conceptualizing the postmodern subject as a construction of multiple locations. In arguing against a more idealist notion of the autonomous individual in society, Lyotard writes: "A *self* does not amount to much, but no self is an island; each exists in a fabric of relations that is now more complex and mobile than ever before. Young or old, man or woman, rich or poor, a person is always located at 'nodal points' of specific communication circuits, however tiny these may be. Or better: one is always located at a post through which various kinds of messages pass. No one, not even the least privileged among us, is ever entirely powerless over the messages that traverse and position him at the post of sender, addressee, or referent."[28]

In many ways, Lyotard's observations on the multiple and various particularities that now construct categories and subjects in postmodernity contribute to the progressive arm of the politics of difference that has emerged in recent years. Yet, in portraying master narratives as completely undermined or utterly ineffective, Lyotard constructs sweeping generalizations that cannot account for the lived contradictions of single parents on welfare, immigrants in need of legal papers, or the phenomenon of "ethnic cleansing" now at work in the former Yugoslavia. What infuriates so many people about the philosophical analysis of the postmodern is just such a seemingly callous disregard for the suffering of human subjects who continue to grapple in their daily lives with what appear to be master narratives of racism and sexism, of economic hegemonies, and power inequities of all kinds. How do we account for the persistence of many of the systems of explanation from the Enlightenment in the midst of evidence that there have been reconfigurations or destabilizations of certain authorities or master narratives?

As Nancy Fraser and Linda Nicholson point out, when critique is cast as strictly "local, ad hoc, and ameliorative," no large-scale, systematic problems can be addressed.[29] Fraser and Nicholson, in arguing for a "postmodern-feminist theory," debate Lyotard's contention that master narratives are finished and no macrostructural analysis is any longer possible. Eschewing the essentialist realisms of much of Euro-American feminist theory throughout the last two decades *and* the complete free play of Lyotard's language games, Fraser and Nicholson call for an "explicitly historical" theoretical practice that would be "attuned to the cultural specificity of different societies and periods and to that of different groups within societies and periods."[30] Such a "nonuniversalist" and "pragmatic" critical practice would "tailor its methods and categories to the specific task at hand, using multiple categories when appropriate," avoiding single or total methods and epistemologies.[31]

This kind of dynamic movement between multiple local instances and agendas of social criticism has been advocated by a number of contemporary cultural critics who want to work with postmodern and poststructuralist destabilizations of master narratives while retaining a commitment to progressive political change. For example, Neil Larsen has pointed out that Lyotard's "local determinism" is *not* simply an "anti-'totalitarian' measure" but is part of a "conceptual drive to construct a new locus of postmodern agency."[32] Ernesto Laclau argues that "abandonment of the myth of foundations does not lead to nihilism" nor does it eliminate agency.[33] "Social agents," then, are formed in concrete, historically specific contexts and, Laclau asserts, their "lack of grounding does not abolish the meaning of their acts; it only affirms their limits, their finitude, and their historicity."[34]

Countering the charge of nihilism and ineffective relativism, Gayatri Spivak argues that the postmodern philosophies "notice that we cannot but narrate."[35] That is, such postmodern practices do not so much claim that all narrativity is valueless or the same but recognize "the limits of narration." In such critical intersections between Marxism and postmodern theoretical articulations, then, the local is contingent, historicized, and never separable from larger, macro social forces.

Several critics propose theories of location that do not set up binary oppositions between global and local. For example, Chandra Mohanty theorizes postmodern location as the possibility of retaining "the idea of multiple, fluid structures of domination which intersect to locate women differently at particular historical conjunctures, while at the same time insisting on the dynamic oppositional agency of individuals and collectives and their engagement in 'daily life.'"[36] The notion of "multiple, fluid structures of domination" can also be found in what Inderpal Grewal and I term "scattered hegemonies," a concept that challenges the master narrative of cultural imperialism through specific articulations of transnational identities and relationships.[37] Aihwa Ong's recent research into the labor politics of postmodernity focuses on the flexible policies and strategies that now characterize transnational investment and production. Rather than the older model of exploiting a "single global periphery," corporations are more likely to engage in a "flexible combination of mass assembly and subcontracting systems" that constructs "modern firms and home work as linked units dominated by transnational capital."[38] The modernist master narratives of proletariat revolution, female liberation, racial equality, and nationalist decolonization, among others, cannot adequately address the new structures of inequality and the contemporary resistances and accommodations to these material conditions.

It is precisely these concrete conditions that demonstrate the continuities between modernity and postmodernity. Or, to phrase it more accurately, transnational relations produce postmodernities within the overarching context of modernity. Even Lyotard (who sometimes is cast simplistically as the architect of "aesthetic" postmodernism) argued that the postmodern is part of the modern.[39] Another early commentator on postmodernism, Ihab Hassan, also argued against the view that postmodernism constitutes a total break or rejection of the modern, pointing out nearly twenty years ago that these two social practices "coexist."[40] Ernesto Laclau suggests that postmodernity is not a simple *rejection* of modernity; "rather, it involves a different modulation of its themes and categories, a greater proliferation of its language games."[41] Or, speaking of the emergent political and cultural movements that borrow the terms and programs of modernity, Stanley Aronowitz notes that their postmodernity is evidenced by "new discursive contexts."[42]

Thus I would argue that modernity's stress on fragmentation and change is best read in tension with the grand narratives of holistic systems of explanation, of social cohesion, and of national and other forms of identity. Rather than doing away with the grand narratives entirely (which in many cases have not even gone "underground" into our "collective unconscious," as Jameson has argued, but have resurfaced in recent times in ever more frightening versions of fascism, racism, and totalitarianism), politically invested postmodernisms enact critical practices that produce diverse forms of narrative. That is, if we could do away with all grand narratives in a sort of miraculous fusion of pure social anarchism and an ultra-oedipal elimination of parental and state authority, what kind of micro-isolation of infinite particularity might we find ourselves in? We will always need theories and accounts of social relationships. It is more powerful and persuasive to imagine a multiplicity of dialogues between kinds of Marxisms, nationalisms, identity politics, and feminisms in productive tension with destabilizations of those authoritative challenges to current manifestations of capitalism. We need to know how to account for agency, resistance, subjectivity, and movement or event in the face of totalizing fixities or hegemonic structures without constructing narratives of oppositional binaries.

Some critics who decline to use the term "postmodernity," preferring to reconfigure and reclaim the term "modernity," nevertheless produce theories in sync with critical practices that are already functioning under the rubric "postmodern." For example, in *Modernism and Hegemony,* Neil Larsen "hesitates before the premise that modernism has fully relinquished its intellectual and cultural hegemony."[43] Such a view is not far removed from Fredric Jameson's observation that Lyotard's theory of the postmodern is itself a modernist narrative or a return of the aesthetic of "experimentation or the new."[44] Arguing that the transitory and fragmented nature of the contemporary world is "hypermodern" rather than postmodern, Allan Pred and Michael John Watts raise crucial questions for cultural and political theorists:

> From what vantage points are we to understand the various guises, metamorphoses and reconfigurations of historical and contemporary capitalisms? How might we simultaneously apprehend both the global and transnational forms of capitalist accumulation *and* the symbolic forms, the local discourses and practices, through which capitalism's handmaidens—commodification, massification, and exploitation—are experienced, interpreted, and contested? How are . . . multiple modernities . . . worked and reworked, fashioned and refashioned, against a backdrop of global, transnational forces?[45]

Some of the vantage points that could contribute to this discussion include the subject positions raised by the new politics of difference as well as the spatial and political realignments of the modern world. The recognition of "multiple modernities" (which I would term "postmodernities") requires an understanding of how "new forms of capital make their local appearance" as well as how "difference, connectedness, and structure are produced and reproduced within some sort of contradictory global system."[46] Pred and Watts argue that while attention to the local is crucial, the local cannot be understood without apprehending the global and abstract characteristics of capitalism.

My reading of Pred and Watts situates them as theorists of postmodern articulations precisely through their moving beyond the world system model of an oppositional binary of global and local. The two terms operate in their analysis not to separate into equally distinct fields or zones but to multiply the relationship between them into contradictory, complex, and materially based dynamics. In their study, therefore, Pred and Watts examine a paradoxical configuration: "Communities *separated* by massive physical, cultural, and economic distances, *linked* through the complex circuits of the global electronics industry, are *unified* and yet *differentiated* in their occupation of what Jameson calls a 'hyperspace,' a domain in which local experience no longer coincides with the place in which it takes place."[47] Theorizing separation and linkages, unifications and differentiations may be a modern phenomenon, but this version strikes me as particularly effective in challenging the strictly binary formations of the modern. Rigid national borders, biologically based ethnic, racial, and gendered identities, and traditional modes of explanation become destabilized not in the service of "free play" or a modernist celebration of aesthetic experimentation. Rather, examining "multiple modernisms" underscores the constructed nature of social reality and the historically and geographically particular nature of these constructions. The knowledge produced by this kind of work can also serve contradictory and diverse interests. There is no utopian space of postmodern knowledge. Yet those of us who identify our interests in configurations of alliance can participate in the production and reception of theories and practices that contribute to our lived experience.

The multidimensional quality of Pred and Watts's work can be read as a kind of postmodern production, but I do not think that the issue of labels should overwhelm or determine our dialogues in social theory. The prefix "post-" is less than satisfactory in relation to colonialism as well as modernism, yet I prefer the strategy of deconstructing the term rather than rejecting it. That is, just as "postcolonialism" can be seen to be a homogenizing term that erases historical and geographical specificity, postmodernism serves as a vast, contradictory, and even wildly inaccurate notion.[48] "Post-" will always privilege a temporal language and agenda over a spatial one, and the kind of history staged by the invocation of "post-"ness will tend to be oversimplified, even mystified. But "hyper-" does not address my concerns about the construction and reproduction of contemporary culture in a satisfactory way. "Hyper-" will always seem to connote the speed and intensity of a kind of utopian modernism when some aspects of contempory culture may not be only about speed or even only about displacement. "Neo-" is trapped in the same specular relationship as "post-" (and the underutilized "pre-") to a fixed temporal object. The benefits of both "postcolonial" and "postmodern" as terms is that they have set in motion densely complicated debates and spurred discursive articulations, reconfiguring, straining, and exhausting the terms in ways that are productive and meaningful to critical practice.[49] In choosing to use the term, then, I am not arguing that the "postmodern" must be recuperated or retained in any ideal sense. As long as this term energetically produces the debates and conversations that accurately signify the material conditions of critical practice, it has use value.

Questions of Travel:
Postmodern Discourses of Displacement

The subject of travel is vast—historically, geographically, and cultur-ally. I hope that I have been able to introduce the strands that connect the representation of some kinds of travel to specifically modern and postmodern concerns. Following these strands through their textual peregrinations in this book may require the aid of a map or some fur-ther detail about the contours of the arguments. In shaping chapters out of years of reading and writing on this topic, I am mindful of many directions I was unable to pursue. I chose to focus on examples of contemporary cultural criticism that seem to me to be difficult to reduce to simplistic oppositions in order to illuminate ideological formations in the production of Euro-American theory. The theo-rists and critics whose texts I examine are those whose work has most stimulated and engaged me over time. That there are many others whose texts and work deserve equal or fuller consideration in relation to my topic cannot be understated. References to travel, displace-ment, borders, diasporas, and homelands abound in contemporary criticism. *Questions of Travel* proposes paths of inquiry and only some of the many examples and possible subjects of these vital debates and practices. Each chapter explores a particular binary formation (e.g., exile/tourism) or charged metaphor (e.g., nomad) in order to more fully understand the possibilities and constraints of these terms as they circulate in Euro-American theory, producing subjects of criti-cism in particular historical contexts.

Chapter 1, "'This Question of Moving': Modernist Exile/Post-modern Tourism," examines the production of modernist formations of displacement in a series of linked deconstructions of the oppo-sitions between exile and tourism.[50] First, I explore two paradoxical strands of modernist exilic articulation: the representation of metro-politan communities as celebrations of displacement and the melan-cholic expressions of what Renato Rosaldo calls "imperialist nostal-gia."[51] This tension between an "internationalist aesthetic" and an obsessive regard for the past or for an originary culture articulates modernity's ambivalent relationship to history and geography. I read Malcolm Cowley's midcentury reflections on his generation of Euro-American expatriates in *Exile's Return* as emblematic of the production of specific modernist aesthetic tropes of exile. Next, I examine the links between tropes of exile and tourism in modernity by reading Paul Fussell's popular study of Euro-American literary travel between the two World Wars, *Abroad*. In focusing on both Fussell's and Cowley's texts, I have selected works of criticism that have achieved popular acclaim and widespread circulation beyond the academy. Their "crossover" appeal suggests that these critical narratives of modernism present versions of the history of cultural production that reflect widely held views. To read them against the grain, I draw on Dean MacCannell's and Donald Horne's critical elaborations of displacement in modernity. In the work of these critics, tourism takes the place of exile in the privileging of displacement in critical practice. Finally, I argue that the opposition between exile and tourism itself must be deconstructed in order to recognize the Eurocentrisms that operate in all of these critical representations of modernity.

In Chapter 2, "Becoming Nomad: Poststructuralist Deterritorializations," I argue that the politics of displacement in general and the history of Euro-American imperialism in particular are subsumed in certain strands of poststructuralist thought in favor of mystified notions of exile and nomadism. These modernist figures permeate so-called postmodern theories along with an emphasis on experimental styles, poetics, and a generalized Eurocentric subjectivity. Reading French theorists such as Jean Baudrillard, Gilles Deleuze, and Félix Guattari as producers of modernist tropes of displacement within the social space of postmodernism, I will examine the emergence of a complex field of poststructuralist reception in the United States and the cultural articulations of contested critical practices.

In examining the deployment of modernisms within Euro-American poststructuralist postmodernism, my aim is not to establish that a unified notion of aesthetic postmodernism is false or impure. Rather, the circulation of powerful modernist tropes within postmodern discourses of displacement suggests that postmodernity operates through a contradictory, discontinuous, and uneven process of connection with modernity. More specifically, the legacy of high imperialism in Euro-American poststructuralist theories demonstrates that postmodernisms do not automatically challenge or subvert the terms of modernity. In arguing that poststructuralist "high" theory constructs binary oppositions that produce mystified metaphysics (in

the case of Baudrillard) or ahistorical modernist aesthetics and Eurocentric cultural appropriations (in the case of Deleuze and Guattari),
I am not dismissing or rejecting poststructuralist critical practices out
of hand. Rather, I am arguing for versions of poststructuralism that
destabilize colonial discourses as overtly as they deconstruct logocentrism. I would characterize this effort as an attempt to establish
points of solidarity with "French" poststructuralism even as I would
strenuously argue for a more transnational critical practice that accurately addresses the diverse and asymmetrically related cultures of
postmodernity.

Chapter 3, "Traveling Theorists: Cosmopolitan Diasporas," returns to the trope of exile in order to track more specifically the
production of modernisms in contemporary Euro-American critical
practice, linking the modernist trope of exile to seemingly postmodern articulations of cosmopolitan diasporas. Focusing on Edward
Said's literary and cultural criticism as an extended commentary on
modernist exile, I argue that his engagement with poststructuralist
methodologies as well as contemporary geopolitics destabilizes the
modernist conventions. Over the years, Said's representation of exile
has expanded into a detailed examination of diverse subject positions
in postmodernity. The more monolithic subject of his earlier criticism is challenged by a more complex theory of location and identity,
a theory that is influenced if not determined by Euro-American postmodernism.

Reading exile through Said, as it were, provides a critical map
of the nuanced dynamic between modernist and postmodernist cultural production in a Euro-American context. Similarly, James Clifford's theorizations of travel and cosmopolitan subjectivity reconfigure exile and diaspora in complex ways. Dedicated to destabilizations
of national, cultural, and political borders and boundaries, Clifford's
inquiries into the history of travel in Euro-American modernity move
the discussion into more spatialized and geographically grounded
modalities. In this chapter, I situate both Said and Clifford in a rapidly
expanding field of critical cultural production, reading their works as
well as key responses and critiques as significant reworkings of Euro-
American discourses of exile. Nevertheless, although the tropes of
modernist exile and travel are productively strained in these theorizations, a kind of erasure or suppression of the histories of mass
immigrations and more collective displacements is also evident. Like

tourists, immigrants do not figure largely in modernist discourses of displacement. The "migrant," often referred to in cultural studies texts on diasporic sensibilities, resonates with that earlier singular figure, the "exile." While the two figures cannot be seen as the "same"—different moments and tasks generate different rhetorical tools—an examination of the links between modernist and postmodernist figurations will provide us with a more detailed history of cultural criticism.

Chapter 4, "Postmodern Geographies: Feminist Politics of Location," argues that as postmodern theories of identity have emerged in Euro-American contexts, the politics of placement have become as important as the politics of displacement. In the discipline of geography, debates about the predominance of theories of time or space have produced reassertions of spatialized terms such as "location," "locale," and "place." As cultural studies, feminist theory, and geography borrow and exchange terms and concepts, critiques of such postmodern conditions as flexible accumulation or time-space compression offer new analyses of the ways in which spatial and temporal axes intersect and interact. When a "place on a map" can be seen to be a "place in history" as well, the terms of critical practice have made a significant shift.

In this chapter, I argue that the recent circulation of the term "politics of location"—particularly in Euro-American feminist criticism—depends upon *several* contradictory but linked discourses of displacement. The notion of a politics of location argues that identities are formed through an attachment to a specific site—national, cultural, gender, racial, ethnic, class, sexual, and so on—and that site must be seen to be partial and not a standard or norm. Yet, when a politics of location is imbued with a universalizing "standpoint," a reactionary identity politics is expressed through a seemingly postmodern critical practice. Because the term "politics of location" has gained cultural currency in critical circulation, an analysis of its use clarifies the modernist and postmodernist traditions and conventions at work in the construction of the term itself. For Euro-American feminists, the stakes in the politics of location lie in the effort to address a perceived gap between poststructuralist relativism and rigidly essentialist articulations of identity. Location can be seen to be a place in relation to history, used not to reify gender through nostalgia or authenticity but to unpack the notion of shared or common experience.

Questions of Travel asks how we can pose the question of displacement in such a way as to render it historically and politically viable. How can we theorize the emergence of specific subjects in the midst of vast changes in economic and social orders? In what ways can the links and disjunctures between modernist exile and postmodernist migrancy or nomadism demonstrate that postmodernity is produced and received in diverse and uneven ways? Since we can distinguish between kinds of modernisms and postmodernisms, which continuities continue to produce which critical practices? How do specific terms signal or hail particular ideological formations and how do we account for our critical languages?

To question travel, then, is to inquire into the ideological function of metaphors in discourses of displacement. Metaphors are not unchanging rhetorical monuments nor are they flights of poetic fancy. The metaphors of travel that I query in this book invite and produce their deconstruction through frequent and complex critical usage. The spatialization of travel and displacement in criticism generates references to sites, borders, maps, and diasporas as well as exile, nomadism, and migrancy. To historicize the use of these terms in critical instances rather than simply assuming their value and currency can politicize our critical practices and make them sharper, more meaningful. I do not believe that we are all rootless, existentially adrift, and limitlessly mobile, but if some of us feel that way, if those terms best describe our sense of ourselves or communities, then those terms must be closely examined. Nor do I believe that we are all at home, fixed into neat identities, enjoying stable similarities. What is at stake in feeling exiled or mobile when material conditions might suggest connections and placements in specific geographies, politics, and economic practices? Just as importantly, what is at stake in choosing location over dislocation when the conventions of locating identities and practices are shifting or destabilized? These questions of travel form the agenda of this project, critiquing Euro-American cultures of theory the better to understand the routes we take as critics as well as the sites of our departures and arrivals.

1 "THIS QUESTION OF MOVING"

Modernist Exile/Postmodern Tourism

It seems to me that I would always be better off where
I am not, and this question of moving is one of those
I discuss incessantly with my soul.
—Charles Baudelaire [1]

Modernism looks quite different depending on where one
locates oneself and when.
—David Harvey [2]

The commonsense definitions of exile and tourism suggest that they
occupy opposite poles in the modern experience of displacement:
Exile implies coercion; tourism celebrates choice. Exile connotes the
estrangement of the individual from an original community; tourism
claims community on a global scale. Exile plays a role in Western
culture's narratives of political formation and cultural identity stretch-
ing back to the Hellenic era. Tourism heralds postmodernism; it is
a product of the rise of consumer culture, leisure, and technological
innovation. Culturally, exile is implicated in modernist high art formations while tourism signifies the very obverse position as the mark
of everything commercial and superficial.[3] What is at stake in contemporary Euro-American assertions of oppositional qualities between
these categories? Looking at exile and tourism as cultural representations aids an analysis of the social practices of different kinds of
displacement and travel, moving beyond mystification to more historically and culturally nuanced interpretations.

Like all symbolic formations, Euro-American modernist exile

culls meaning from various cultural, political, and economic sources, including the lived experiences of people who have been legally or socially expelled from one location and prevented from returning.[4] I will argue, however, that the modernist trope of exile works to remove itself from any political or historically specific instances in order to generate aesthetic categories and ahistorical values. The Euro-American formation "exile," then, marks a place of mediation in modernity where issues of political conflict, commerce, labor, nationalist realignments, imperialist expansion, structures of gender and sexuality, and many other issues all become recoded.[5]

Euro-American modernisms celebrate singularity, solitude, estrangement, alienation, and aestheticized excisions of location in favor of locale—that is, the "artist in exile" is never "at home," always existentially alone, and shocked by the strain of displacement into significant experimentations and insights. Even more importantly, the modernist exile is melancholic and nostalgic about an irreparable loss and separation from the familiar or beloved. This said, unlike particular individuals in exile who may experience all or some or none of these qualities, the *formation* of modernist exile seems to have best served those who would voluntarily experience estrangement and separation in order to produce the experimental cultures of modernism.[6] That is, the Euro-American middle-class expatriates adopted the attributes of exile as an ideology of artistic production. Because their displacement has been represented as exile, I see these groups as important sites for deconstructing the binary opposition between exile and tourism in an effort to understand the production of modernisms.

Asserting difference between the cultural representations of exile and tourism maintains the division between "high" and "low" culture, that is, between art and commerce. Deconstructing these binary oppositions demonstrates that Euro-American modernist privileging of exile relies upon a conflation of various kinds of displacement, including expatriation and tourism, while tourism stresses the mystiques surrounding exile and modes of travel associated with the nineteenth and early twentieth centuries. Whether celebrated as the "exploring and mapping" of the "realm of the 'not yet,'"[7] or described as the "desire to seek a place outside the tradition that enables it,"[8] representations of displacement function as powerful tropes in the cultural production of modernisms.

"The Place of Art's Very Making":
Modernist Geographies

For Modernism is a metropolitan art, which is to say it is group art, a specialist art, an intellectual art, an art for one's aesthetic peers; it recalls, with whatever ironies and paradoxes, the imperium of civilization. Not simply metropolitan, indeed, but cosmopolitan: one city leads to another in the distinctive aesthetic voyage into the metamorphosis of form. The writer may hold on to locality, as Joyce did on to Dublin, Hemingway the Michigan woods; but he perceives from the distance of an expatriate perspective of aesthetic internationalism . . . Thus frequently it is emigration or exile that makes for membership of the modern country of the arts, which has been heavily travelled by many great writers—Joyce, Lawrence, Mann, Brecht, Auden, Nabokov. It is a country that has come to acquire its own language, geography, focal communities, places of exile—Zurich during the First World War, New York during the Second. The writer himself becomes a member of a wandering, culturally inquisitive group—by enforced exile (like Nabokov's after the Russian Revolution) or by design and desire. The place of art's very making can become an ideal distant city, where the creator counts, or the chaos is fruitful, the *Weltgeist* flows.
—Malcolm Bradbury[9]

The preceding passage from Malcolm Bradbury's classic study of literary modernism strenuously demonstrates the Euro-American modernist trope of exile. Written in collaboration with James McFarlane for the Pelican Guides to European Literatures series and published in 1976, Bradbury's study of the cosmopolitan world of modernism describes a "country" with its own "landscape, geography, focal communities, places of exile." If modernism is a country, then its capitals are the European and North American metropoles that drew refugees and émigrés during the turn of the century and between the two World Wars. In this narrative, the internationalism of modernism does not extend below the Mediterranean, far into Asia, or south of the U.S. border. Lagos, Buenos Aires, Delhi, and Tokyo are not yet members of the "imperium of civilization" in Bradbury's modernist world order.

In a critical narrative such as Bradbury's, modernist exile is practiced by a "wandering, culturally inquistive group," those who seek metamorphoses in form through the fruitful chaos of displacement.

No matter whether the exile is "enforced" or by "design and desire," the only passport needed to cross the border into the *Weltgeist* is an ability to make the "distinctive aesthetic voyage." Bradbury refers to George Steiner's notion of the modernist writer as "extraterritorial" or "unhoused," but he could just as easily have referred to Harry Levin's discussion of literature and exile or Malcolm Cowley's "lost generation." Euro-American modernist literary histories are replete with references to exiles and expatriates; displacement comes to define modernist sensibilities and critical practices.[10]

While major critics have constructed an imaginary "country" of exiles throughout the twentieth century to house the unhoused, as it were, or to collect and manage the disparate cultural productions that fall under the broad rubric of "modernism," it is interesting to consider the tension between location and dislocation or between nationalism and internationalism in their descriptive narratives. Thus Bradbury imagines an "ideal distant city" for his cosmopolitan subjects. Lifted out of the material political and social conflicts that generated so much displacement in the twentieth century, the exiles who come to live in Bradbury's modernist sites are men without a country.[11] Aesthetic concerns separate these metropolitans from other modern subjects; it is modernist practices that free the artists from the worldly locations of nation-states and bring them together for loftier pursuits.

Benedict Anderson has argued that all communities are imagined and therefore cannot be judged on the level of whether or not they are more false or genuine. Rather, Anderson suggests, communities can be distinguished "by the style in which they are imagined."[12] Following Anderson's lead, then, Euro-American modernisms foster the collective imagining of a condition where national identity matters only in its distance from a present space and time. Or, as Rob Nixon puts it, in such a modernist formation "dislocation" is confused with "detachment," signaling a perceived "freedom from ideology."[13] Throughout recent modernity, at the very least, the idea of an escape from the nation-state into the cosmopolitan and polyglot city underscores most ideologies of modernism. Before we assume that such modernist imaginary communities are utopian refuges from the nationalist conflicts of this century, we would do well to examine the Eurocentric nature of these formulations. The modernist cities of Calvino, Cowley, Bradbury, Eco, Steiner, and others are fashioned more like medieval city-states built to shelter nomadic exiles than sprawling metropoles. That is, the difference between modernist and postmodernist imaginary geographies may be a nostalgia for clear binary distinctions between "country and city" on the one hand and an attachment to less oppositional hybrid cosmopolitanisms on the other. Bradbury's modernist metropolis not only produces unity through heterogeneity but creates specific, invested identities (for example, in Bradbury and McFarlane's *Modernism,* Kafka's identity is "Austrian" while Italo Svevo is labeled "Jewish-Italian"). Modern cities, especially major ports, function as crucibles where identities are formed, transformed, and fixed. Such identities are not always self-chosen, welcome, or advantageous to the newly arrived, but they do play roles in the formation of literary and artistic canons as well as the deployment of political interests on the part of state institutions.

It is difficult to read against the grain of Euro-American modernist romanticizations of the metropolitan experience because the myth of the mixing of peoples and mingling of influences is so powerfully linked to Western ideologies of democracy and nationhood. Yet, following Raymond Williams's suggestion, I would like to take the myth of modernist exile and turn its methods upon itself; that is, I want to "explore it with something of its own sense of strangeness and distance, rather than with the comfortable and now internally accommodated forms of its incorporation and naturalization."[14]

In his posthumously published essays on modernism, Williams called for the historicization of the homogeneous myth of the cosmopolitan modernist city. Challenging the modernist interpretation of its own processes as universals, Williams argued that criticism must look "from time to time, from outside the metropolis; from the deprived hinterlands, where different forces are moving, and from the poor world which has always been peripheral to the metropolitan systems."[15] I would recast this directive, retaining the destabilization of the modernist metropolis as a new formation of Euro-American centrism without reconstituting Williams's nostalgic peripheries. Far better to stretch the imagination further to examine the locations in our communities where the myth is confounded, where the universalizations do not hold true. Williams himself aids this task by proposing studies of the specific locations of the new subjects of modernism, by examining the uneven developments within Europe as well as between

Europe and its former colonies. Contrast the following passage from Williams's "Metropolitan Perceptions and the Emergence of Modernism" to Bradbury's description of the geography of modernism:

> Thus the key cultural factor of the modernist shift is the character of the metropolis: in these general conditions, but then, even more decisively, in its direct effects on form. The most important general element of the innovations in forms is the fact of immigration to the metropolis, and it cannot too often be emphasized how many of the major innovators were, in this precise sense, immigrants. At the level of theme, this underlies in an obvious way, the elements of strangeness and distance, indeed alienation, which so regularly form part of the repertory. But the decisive aesthetic effect is at a deeper level. Liberated or breaking from their national or provincial cultures, placed in quite new relations to those other native languages or native visual traditions, encountering meanwhile a novel and dynamic common environment from which many of the older forms were obviously distant, the artists and writers and thinkers of this phase found the only community available to them: a community of the medium; of their own practices.[16]

While both Williams and Bradbury emphasize the break with national or cultural origins and the formation of a new imagined community through cultural practices, Williams's version of the modernist metropolis pays more attention to historically generated relationships as opposed to Bradbury's transhistorical *Weltgeist*.

Nevertheless, Williams's modernist affiliations cannot be ignored and, thus, the similarities between Williams and Bradbury are as important as the differences. Both critics celebrate a community of artists in search of substantially different forms and methods. Both critics view physical displacement as conducive to groundbreaking insights and experimentations. Finally, both critics formulate European or North American topoi for modernist metropolitan communities. The peripheries in such configurations provide immigrants and exiles but are never the sites of modernist cultural production themselves; that is, they provide the raw materials to be synthesized in the generative locations of the modern, Western metropolis or they offer opportunities for spatial exploration on the part of metropolitans in search of metaphysical displacement.[17]

Williams's perspectives on modern metropoles, then, demonstrate that an emphasis on mass displacement alone does not deconstruct a modernist trope. Nor, as Paul Gilroy has argued, does such an emphasis escape neoconservative affiliations.[18] In order to destabilize the Euro-American myth of modernist exile, it is necessary to critique the formation of centers as well as peripheries as modernist productions. One way to begin to examine the production of cultural margins through formations such as Euro-American modernist exile is to look closely at the operation of nostalgia in the aftermath of modern imperialism.

Imperialist Nostalgia and Aesthetic Gain:
Exile's Reward

Various manifestations of nostalgia participate in Euro-American constructions of exile: nostalgia for the past; for home; for a "mother-tongue"; for the particulars that signify the experience of the familiar once it has been lost. Such nostalgia is rooted in the notion that it is "natural" to be at "home" and that separation from that location can never be assuaged by anything but return. Elsa Triolet, the spouse of surrealist artist Louis Aragon, expressed this exilic sentiment when she wrote: "It must be accepted that it is natural for a human being to be born and to die in the same place or, at least, in the same locality; that everyone should be an organic part of all he calls his native land, his country."[19] Triolet likens human beings to plants and animals, arguing that "certain species" can never achieve "successful acclimatisation." The exile, in this formulation, suffers from a "terrible malady: homesickness."

The malady of homesickness that can never be cured without a return home is akin to melancholia. Freud's distinction between mourning and melancholia, between a "normal" period of grieving and a continuing, debilitating fixation on loss, proposes a useful model for the study of modernist exile poetics and politics. This psychoanalytic model locates the source of melancholia in unresolved anger toward one who has died or been irrevocably removed; unable to resolve the conflict or express this anger openly without guilt, the melancholic subject remains in a state of acute loss.[20] When this particular kind of aggression is turned inward, against the self, melancholia becomes a preoccupying state that replaces or fills the space left by death or separation.

Euro-American modernist exile formations foster a culture of nostalgic melancholia. In Renato Rosaldo's investigation of representational violence in modern nostalgia, he argues that there are degrees of difference between the common forms of nostalgia linked to childhood experiences and the cultural expression of dominance he terms "imperialist nostalgia."[21] Coming into use in the late seventeenth century, nostalgia ("from the Greek *nostos,* a return home, and *algos,* a painful condition")[22] has become naturalized into a pseudopsychological truism. Yet Rosaldo demonstrates that the seemingly innocent sentiment masks aggressive impulses: "Imperialist nostalgia revolves around a paradox: A person kills somebody, and then mourns the victim. In more attenuated form, somebody deliberately alters a form of life, and then regrets that things have not remained as they were prior to the intervention. At one more remove, people destroy their environment, and then they worship nature. In any of its versions, imperialist nostalgia uses a pose of 'innocent yearning' both to capture people's imaginations and to conceal its complicity with often brutal domination."[23] The structural similarities between Euro-American childhood and imperialist nostalgias may contribute to the deployment of the latter version in modernity. Imperialist nostalgia erases collective and personal responsibility, replacing accountability with powerful discursive practices: the vanquished or vanished ones are eulogized (thereby represented) by the victor. When the loss concerns a nation, culture, or distinct territory, the representations articulate nostalgic versions of the past (the recent rash of "Raj" nostalgia or the colonial discourse of "big game" hunters in Africa are two of the most obvious examples of this phenomenon). Within the structure of imperialist nostalgia, then, the Euro-American past is most clearly perceived or narrativized as another country or culture.

Dean MacCannell has characterized this propensity of occidental "moderns" to look "elsewhere" for markers of reality and authenticity as a primary facet of Euro-American modernity. The quest for better models, new forms, fresh images, and relief from the ills of metropolitan centers compels the modernist to move further and further into what are perceived to be the margins of the world. As MacCannell writes: "For moderns, reality and authenticity are thought to be elsewhere: in other historical periods and other cultures, in purer, simpler lifestyles. In other words, the concern of moderns for 'naturalness,' their nostalgia and their search for authenticity are not merely casual and somewhat decadent, though harmless, attachments to the souvenirs of destroyed cultures and dead epochs. They are also components of the conquering spirit of modernity—the grounds of its unifying consciousness."[24] A distinctive aspect of this form of modernity lies in a complicated tension between space and time. When the past is displaced, often to another location, the modern subject must travel to it, as it were. History becomes something to be established and managed through tours, exhibitions, and representational practices in cinema, literature, and other forms of cultural production. Displacement, then, mediates the paradoxical relationship between time and space in modernity.

Part of the configuration of contradiction and ambivalence that marks these theories of modernity includes tensions between progress and tradition. That is, modernisms promote both innovation and convention, change and stability. In modernity, cultural change is a given. Social theorists such as Marshall Berman have argued that moderns oscillate between a wholehearted endorsement of change and a deep desire for stability. If, as Berman argues, people struggle to "get a grip on the modern world and make themselves a home in it," then they also struggle to disengage or displace themselves in very deliberate and particular ways.[25] In addition, these specific displacements are not simply universal and global but can be particularized in time and space. Berman's view of modernity as totally unified in its disunity must be modified, therefore, to yield to more micro or local studies of the productions of modernisms.

Thus when we notice a critical insistence upon exile as the trope that best signifies all modes of displacement in modernity, along with an accompanying ambivalence toward redemption and return as well as a celebration of distance and alienation, we have to ask more pointed questions: *Whose* distance from *what? What* perspective of *whom?* To begin to answer these questions brings us to consider the specifically Euro-American histories of imperialist nostalgia in the construction of modernist exile, constructions that require the conflation of exile, expatriation, and tourism in the representational practices of cultural production.[26]

It is, then, not accidental that twentieth-century Euro-American expatriation generates a discourse of authorship that has come to be expressed in literary criticism as an imperative of displacement. This conflation of exile and expatriation by modern writers and critics can be read in the way that distance has come to be privileged as the best perspective on a subject under scrutiny and in the related discourse of aesthetic gain through exile. When detachment is the precondition for creativity, then disaffection or alienation as states of mind becomes a rite of passage for the "serious" modern artist or writer. The modernist seeks to recreate the effect of statelessness—whether or not the writer is, literally, in exile. As a result, even those writers who do not find themselves actually exiled may easily extend the metaphor. Within this form of modernism, exilic displacement occupies a privileged position, legitimating points of view and constituting a point of entry into a professional domain.

Thus, Euro-American literary criticism throughout this century has proposed a model of aesthetic gain through exile. In one typical, midcentury version of exile as aesthetic gain, Polish writer Joseph Wittlin argued that isolation and unhappiness, while lamentable on many levels, nevertheless yield particular benefits for the writer. In a talk delivered in 1957 at a meeting of the International P.E.N. Association, Wittlin referred to both the "sorrow" and the "grandeur" of exile: "[O]nly poets are able to look at *la condition humaine* from the proper distance . . ." Wittlin wrote; "a perfect distance or perspective is created for them by their lost country." [27] Wittlin's link between exilic vision and the creation of "great art" refers to the experience of involuntary displacement—he even uses the term "real exile" to distinguish his own situation from the more lavish peregrinations of a figure such as the Aga Khan (living in ostentatious luxury on the French Riviera). But Wittlin's version of the political exile's solitude and alienation does not sound much different from the descriptions of the creative benefits of expatriation in critical writing from the post-WWII period.

For example, in his study published in 1951, *Exile's Return,* Malcolm Cowley described the lure of exile for the young Euro-American writers between the two World Wars as yielding immense cultural benefits ("They do things better in Europe: let's go there.") [28] I will discuss Cowley's representation of exile and literary production in greater detail in the next section of this chapter, but it is worth noting it here to underscore the flow of exile tropes throughout modernist literary criticism and history in this important period of decolonization, superpower realignment, and cold war tensions. Western economic prosperity and technological innovations promoted more leisure travel while war and famine created refugee populations.

The critical perspective on displacement during this period, however, focused for the most part on transhistorical, even mythic aspects of exile such as the "fall from Eden" or the benefits of the distanced view. Wittlin makes recourse to biblical images of redemption and reunification to pose a theory of narrative closure. Exilic perspective becomes a vocation and a virtue, a reminder that writers with "great vision" take us with them through the shoals of loss and, having paid a terrible price, will lead us back into the safe harbor of reunion. A return is always possible in the distant future. In modernist exile formations, assimilation is never represented as conducive to literary production.

Harry Levin's influential essay from the mid-1960s, "Literature and Exile," provides an instructive example of modernist critical promotion of exile as aesthetic gain. Levin begins his essay by linking classical banishment with the occupation of writing (he points to Plato's expulsion of the poets from the republic). A history of exile and writing is constructed that stretches back to Ovid and forward to the present moment, a moment that Levin identifies as quintessentially "modern." Exile and literature have come to symbolize both the legacy of the past and a break with that continuity. Exile, Levin writes, has a new meaning in the twentieth century, following the "rise of nationalism, with its ensuing confusion of tongues."[29] Levin views the modern era as a "deracinated culture," marked by "the metic condition, the polyglot misunderstanding of our time."[30]

Language functions as a key category in modernist considerations of style and culture. The condition of language—its pure and impure states, its loss or recovery, its rules and deviations—appears stressed in modernist conversations in particular ways. Levin endorses a metaphysics of presence where meaning is found in the spoken utterance. Language, in this formulation, is weighted with location, with the positioning of the writing subject. While Wittlin emphasizes "the return of words," stressing the recurrent return of the native tongue which resonates in the mind of the exiled writer—a fragmented but continuing connection with a "lost" world through language—Levin is more concerned with instances of language barriers. His displaced writer makes a home in a new language without feeling particularly comfortable in it. What is lost remains lost and what is new remains unreal. Writing functions as a sign of the impossibility of living in such a stateless condition. Here distance is desirable inasmuch as formal innovation and insight can be derived from the strain on the relationship between meaning and language.

Levin does not discount historical instances of exile in his examination of metaphoric links between displacement and modernist literature. The consolidation of new national identities in the latter part of the nineteenth century, he argues, went hand in hand with developments in theories of art and creativity. As Levin points out, "homesickness" takes on an entirely new dimension during this period as *le mal du pays* and *le mal du siècle* become linked as preoccupations of both artists and politicians. In fact, the artists and politicians were often one and the same, or closely related. Exiled for political infractions or vilified for revolutionary developments in aesthetics, the artist/statesman can be viewed as doubly estranged. The exile is homesick at home or away, and exilic displacement becomes the sign of the creative, contemplative life in the West.

Thus the activity of writing and the professional legitimation of authorship provide a form of recompense for the loss and uncertainty of the modern condition. "Making a virtue of dreary necessity," the writers examined in Levin's study assume that the negative aspects of exile will result in creative gain. After Gide and Joyce, Levin argues, the exilic aesthetic strategy struggles to come to terms with what has been left behind "by working at some distance from it, yet looking homeward, bearing it continually in mind . . ."[31] Finally, the writer remains estranged from the multitude, the nation, the collective group. "Detachment," Levin writes, "of the one from the many . . . is the necessary precondition of all original thought."[32] Exile becomes a vocational imperative, a singular practice at odds with collective identity and historical experience.

In such a formulation, collective identities such as nationality and political affiliation come to be subsumed by the unifying category of authorship. For example, Levin discusses Euro-American modernist writers as diverse as Nabokov, Pasternak, Conrad, and Beckett. In an expanded sense of "exile" as authorship, all these writers are prototypes of "deracination," examples of "the artist as displaced person."[33] Yet their various personal and national histories are far more complex than a "celebration of vagabondage" would allow us to consider. It is, finally, this dislocation of historical conditions in the effort to construct a modernist aesthetic that demonstrates what is at stake in literary studies such as Levin's. As exile becomes the paramount model for the production of modern literature, the conflation of exile and expatriation results in the erasure of historically specific conditions of literary production.

The modernist critical tradition of conceptualizing exile as aesthetic gain continues in more recent studies.[34] Michael Seidel, in *Exile and the Narrative Imagination* (1986), defines the exile as someone who has a "belated romance" with the past, through memory heightened by distance. What has been lost can be recaptured by the imagination. The writer "comes home" in the writing itself, transforming the "figure of rupture back into a 'figure of connection.'"[35] By weaving "here" and "there" together in the space of the imagination, the writer uses fiction to resolve the worst terrors of dislocation and anomie.

Seidel is careful to place his theory of displacement and authorship outside the parameters of the experience of exile, stating that he does not mean to suggest that "aesthetic recompense is sufficient for history's countless refugees, expellees, émigrés, and dispossessed . . ."[36] Yet, in order to construct a theory of exile as an "enabling fiction," Seidel creates an ahistorical space — aesthetics — which functions only in a very limited and specialized sense.[37] When Seidel delineates what elements of exile and displacement he will not include in his study, he outlines the margins of modernist literary criticism. Beyond the pale of his critical consideration, Seidel lists translation, exile as a form of modern alienation in either its Marxist or psychological variants, and "modern exilic politics and émigré conditions."[38] Taken together, these "repressed" elements constitute a principle of literary criticism.

Robert Newman's critical study of the operation of exile in narrative constructions of readers and writers follows the contours of this ahistorical, universalized treatment.[39] Exile, in Newman's psychoanalytic paradigm, is generalizable to all modern subjects and can be characterized as the ground of most narratives. Readers, then, always search for a way "home" as they make their way through a wilderness of narrative fragmentation. Newman is careful to suggest that those "homes" will change through the process of displacement, but his notion of exile and narrative plays upon transcendental categories that cannot, ultimately, be extended in as universal a way as the critic suggests.

The paradigms of exile constructed in these modernist critical practices assume that all ages and figures participate in the same concept in the same way and that the history of the concept of exile within and without the development of aesthetic categories in the West is unidimensional (if it exists at all)—in short, exile is completely dehistoricized. Normalizing exile, aestheticizing homelessness, the critical mythologization of the "artist in exile" moves from a commentary on cultural production based on historically grounded experiences of displacement to the production of a *style* that emulates exile's effects. This said, I would resist establishing a moral order of "true" exilic discourse over and against a "false" expatriate version. Rather, I am calling for a more historically specific examination of how modes of displacement generate cultural practices. In Euro-American modernism, what Williams has described as the "experience of visual and linguistic strangeness" in the process of emigration has led to the rise of a universal myth: "this intense, singular narrative of the unsettlement, homelessness, solitude, and impoverished independence: the lonely writer gazing down on the unknowable city from his shabby apartment."[40]

Once this historically generated subject becomes mystified and dehistoricized, it becomes impossible to ask why the concept of exile as aesthetic gain lends itself so well to expatriate and tourist alike (as well as to the exile). How is it that the tourist can participate in exilic aesthetics without experiencing the prolonged effects of material exile? Why does the expatriate literary experience become possible at particular historical junctures? Even to begin to answer these questions one would have to add a consideration of the very elements that the critics have elided, that is, the history and politics of displacement in modernity.

Exile's Return: *Modernist Constructions of Authorship Through Displacement*

We were launching or drifting into the sea of letters with
no fixed destination and without a pilot.
—Malcolm Cowley[41]

The concept of exile as aesthetic gain has been deployed throughout modernist discourses of authorship, and one of the most interesting instances of that deployment remains Malcolm Cowley's *Exile's Return.* Part autobiographical memoir, part critical evaluation, *Exile's Return* examines the years between the two World Wars. First published in 1951, Cowley's account of the Euro-American expatriates of the 1920s has been reprinted numerous times, testifying to its popularity and longevity as a primary text in the postwar period. Most interestingly, Cowley's literary history does not simply establish an aesthetic of displacement; published on the threshold of New Criticism and in the midst of a Euro-American "cold war," *Exile's Return* produces a critique of the mystique of expatriation through an emphasis on the commodification of travel and authorship. Yet, as an account of modernism, *Exile's Return* constructs a mystified vocation that reinforces the conflation of exile and expatriation in modernist discourses of displacement.

Such highly aestheticized accounts of modernist exile suppress most economic or historically material elements in constructing explanations and legitimations of authorship. Within this ideological construct, writing accrues power as a social practice if it can transmit authority and credibility. When art is seen as a transcendental category, the process of producing it must be hidden or masked in such a way as to signal value without highlighting its production process. Thus an emphasis on style or form is essential in distinguishing between "high" and "low" culture. Discourses of modern art offer the certainties of legitimated value even as they provide and depend upon representations of newness, uniqueness, and fragmentation.

The vocation of author is particularly charged within this system of modernist artistic production of product and value; avoiding crass commercialism (with its "low" art associations), facing imperatives of uniqueness, bearing in mind the "lifestyle" choices of predecessors as well as their products and achievements, the Euro-American modernist writer might very well embrace expatriation (of varying lengths of duration) as a way to find fresh subjects, affordable living, and a location of sufficient strangeness to encourage concentration through isolation. Just as importantly, the expatriate writer affirms a particular vision of reality for a community of readers. Serving as proof that the values and practices of modernity have meaning, the representation of literary "exile" fills a need in the home culture for a reified product. This inevitable process of commodification, as writing enters the literary marketplace, exists in extreme tension with most modernist aesthetics. *Exile's Return* portrays a group of writers and artists who seem to be simultaneously world-weary and naive; longing for the impossible—a total escape into art and liberation from commerce—they discovered economic necessity, historically specific conflicts, and the constraints of emigration.

In *Exile's Return,* Cowley is concerned with a primarily North American phenomenon: the large wave of expatriation that followed the end of the First World War. His history of the desire of young people to get away, their sense that liberty and inspiration could only be achieved elsewhere, depends upon a complicated relationship to tradition and the past. The Americans who longed to leave home may have rejected the commercialization of bourgeois existence and the conventions of puritanical communities and families, but the lure of Europe itself was based on a kind of tradition. Sounding for all the world like an advocate of the Grand Tour for nineteenth-century genteel youths, Cowley notes: "England and Germany have the wisdom of old cultures; the Latin people have admirably preserved their pagan heritage."[42]

The "lost generation," according to Cowley, consisted of a group of writers born around the turn of the century. While Gertrude Stein apparently coined the phrase, it has hovered about the heads of the writers it designates, surrounding them with a nostalgic halo. Dictionary definitions of "lost" include "no longer possessed or retained, no longer to be found, having gone astray or missed the way, not used to good purpose, not won or gained, destroyed or ruined, preoccupied or rapt."[43] Each nuance of "lost" signifies something slightly different, but the stress usually falls on waste, ruin, ecstasy, loss of control, or confusion. As Cowley is quick to point out, the typical "lost generation" author was a college graduate who achieved literary fame (and a comfortable income) at an early age. Unlike the writers of the 1890s, the "new" generation did not have to labor in uncongenial jobs or write for a public that was unready for their styles or subjects. The rubric "lost" has stuck with them, yet they were not particularly "unfortunate or thwarted."[44] Their disengagement, their qualities as "lost," therefore, must be ascribed to more psychological properties. This generation was "lost" because it was modern. Cowley writes:

> It was lost, first of all, because it was uprooted, schooled away and almost wrenched away from its attachment to any region or tradition. It was lost because its training had prepared it for another world than existed after the war (and because the war prepared it only for travel and excitement). It was lost because it tried to live in exile. It was lost because it accepted no older guides to conduct and because it had formed a false picture of society and the writer's place in it . . . They were seceding from the old and yet could adhere to nothing new; they groped their way toward another scheme of life, as yet undefined.[45]

In their steadfast rejection of their own cultural location as tradition and of cultural context as a limit to the powers of the imagination, the Euro-American writers in Cowley's study are thoroughly modern. In their search for the signifiers of history and culture in other people's countries (countries that may have been economically ravaged by the very war that brought about the conditions that led to modernist expatriation) they also reveal themselves as structurally modern, oscillating between myth and history, home and away, center and periphery.

The subtitle of Cowley's text, *A Literary Odyssey of the 1920's,* suggests that expatriates such as John dos Passos, Ernest Hemingway, F. Scott Fitzgerald, Ezra Pound, and Hart Crane were engaged in an epic voyage, a voyage that sent them far from home. The "odyssey" of expatriation was shared by people of varied ages and backgrounds, but this particular literary diaspora has come to be characterized by one generation and even one nationality. In the popular imagination, due in part to studies like *Exile's Return,* the "lost generation" consisted very much of the type of people Cowley writes about: young, rebellious men from the middle class. This male Caucasian pantheon may not reflect the entire demographic phenomenon of expatriation and displacement in the 1920s, but it certainly speaks to the literary success of this subgroup. Despite important feminist literary histories that have challenged the masculine dominance in modernist canons, the list of writers invoked in Cowley's study has become generalizable to an entire generation.[46]

Cowley's description of his generation's expatriation reveals the characteristic modernist anxiety about the relationship between the past and the present. He writes of the burden of influence and the search for inspiration: "Literature, our profession, was living in the shadow of its own great past. The symbols that moved us, the great themes of love and death and parting, had been used and exhausted. Where could we find new themes when everything, so it seemed, had already been said already? Having devoured the world, literature was dying for lack of nourishment. Nothing was left to ourselves — nothing except to deal with marginal experiences and abnormal cases, or else to say the same things over again with a clever and apologetic twist of our own."[47] Cowley and the writers in his study came from a world they felt was overly secure. They had, as Cowley describes it, "the illusion of belonging to a great classless society."[48] This rather privileged group, a group that did not ponder the situation of immigrants to America or the racial and class tensions that plagued their society, took refuge in flight. It is not uncharitable to point out that for this set of college-educated, solidly middle-class young men, their escape was from the tedious, uncreative careers of their fathers and from the unattractive, sensible marriages and alliances they were expected to embrace. A downwardly mobile life in foreign settings could provide adventure and, most importantly, something to say, a point of view. The poor might look exotic in foreign settings when the poor at home seem invisible, uninteresting, or threatening. Politics in Europe seemed vigorous and linked to art when politics at home seemed sunk either in the petty rituals of the middle class or in the lower-class milieu of immigrants engaged in union or anarchist activities.[49]

Expatriation negotiated fears of dependency and rationalized otherwise baldly ambitious or venal concerns. The expatriates felt their own cultures were exhausted and drained of significance; the cultures of other people might afford traditions and customs that would appear "new" to young North Americans. Dean MacCannell has described such quests for tradition as a hallmark of modernity: "Tradition is there to be recalled to satisfy nostalgic whims or to provide coloration or perhaps a sense of profundity for a modern theme. There is an urgent cultivation of new people, new groups, new things, new ideas, and a hostility to repetition: a built-in principle of escalation in every collective work from war to music. There is a desire for greatly expanded horizons, a search for the frontiers of even such familiar matters as domestic relations."[50]

Cowley represents his expatriates as alternating between a desire for tradition (European-style) and a loathing for tradition (U.S.-style). According to such an idealization of exile, expatriation would bring both personal liberation and professional development. Only expatriation could solve individual and aesthetic constraints. As Cowley writes, "by expatriating himself, by living in Paris, Capri or the South of France, the artist can break the puritan shackles, drink, live freely and be wholly creative."[51]

This fantasy of escape (often expressed in sexual metaphors) brought two powerful discourses into proximity: the exoticization of the past in another location or country and the exoticization of another gender, race, or culture. "We dreamed of escape," Cowley writes, "into European cities with crooked streets, into Eastern islands where the breasts of the women were small and firm as inverted teacups."[52] The masculinization of the modernist literary canon is reinforced by critical "histories" such as *Exile's Return* that universalize this fantasy. Thus the flight from home included leaving behind both egalitarian impulses and bourgeois sexual norms while reinforcing the social power and privilege of a gendered class. This belief in the sexually liberating or thrilling aspects of travel is deeply encoded in the discourses of desire and distance that form the core of Euro-American modernist theories of authorship as exile. Part of the compensation for "exile" or even the goal of such displacement may be expressed in sexual metaphors of conquest and seduction. The relentless gendering of expatriation as a masculine phenomenon in modernist literary histories participates in imperialist nostalgia—the melancholic quest for substance while erasing or violating the object of concern.

The modernist trope of exile utilizes the modes of displacement more characteristic of tourism but masks and submerges all references to commerce or popular culture by promoting artistic concerns. Modernity's commodifications are resisted or denied in the hypervaluation of the aesthetic and the celebration of "experience." Cowley's discussion of the commercial activities of the expatriates supports Dean MacCannell's contention that the value of tourist activities is not determined by the classic equation of labor and use value. The value of "such things as programs, trips, courses, reports, articles, shows, conferences, parades, opinions, events, sights, spectacles, scenes and situations of modernity" are determined by "the quality and quantity of *experience* they promise."[53] While the commodity is the end product of older forms of economic analysis, MacCannell identifies a completely different order at work in modernity: "The commodity has become a means to an end. The end is an immense accumulation of reflexive experiences which synthesize fiction and reality into a vast symbolism."[54]

Within this analytical framework we can view Cowley's expatriate writers of the 1920s as among the first generations to be caught up in this particular change in relations between value and labor. The works they produced did not just result in salable objects; they dispersed into a world that required the imaginative properties of the displaced writers to underscore and affirm the new world order in the aftermath of colonial expansion, decades of large-scale immigration, and World War I. Their ability to roam about the metropoles as well as the rural areas, to cross national boundaries, and to witness differences between those nations created a particular perspective of diversity, documented by Cowley's memoir: "Following the dollar, we saw a chaotic Europe that was feverishly seeking the future of art, finance and the state. We saw machine guns in the streets of Berlin, Black Shirts in Italy, were stopped by male prostitutes along the Kurfurstendam, sat in a cafe at Montpellier with an Egyptian revolutionist who said, 'Let's imagine this vermouth is the blood of an English baby,' drained the glass deep — 'Bravo!' we said, and drifted down to Pamplona for the bullfights."[55]

In the passage cited above, the relativist bravado of the wandering point of view approaches the touristic discourse of collecting experiences. An almost nihilistic distancing from any connection or commitment except to the project of experiencing "otherness" brings this group into cultural peripheries that provide "color" and excitement. The power of imagination creates fellowship with an anticolonial Egyptian for an evening's entertainment only to slip into a new "country" of experience — the bullfights. Here the "geography of modernism," which offered a theory of dwelling and repatriation through cultural production in the cosmopolitan metropolis, begins to disintegrate into bands of permanently displaced tourists. That is, they exist precisely through a form of voluntary homelessness, yet their lack of commitment or roots limits them to a role as witness to other people's revolutions, other people's tragedies and successes, and all the other "real" events that seem to swirl around them. More and more like voyeurs of the decadent and exotic, the expatriates *see* "others" or "otherness" but do not yet divine their own role as actors in the production of the world they believe they are simply observing.

In a demystifying move, Cowley's text suggests continually that these expatriates may have *wished* to feel like exiles (alone, estranged, radically displaced, melancholic), but they often behaved like tourists. All modes of displacement in modernity may share some characteristics (particularly in the realm of representation), but the differences between the discourses of exile and tourism are so strenuously asserted that any overlap or confusion is worthy of note. Most obviously, while exile's experience could be mined for creative insight, tourism's association with commerce and leisure (rather than art for art's sake and professionalism) would have forced it "underground," as it were, or marked it in particular ways. Reading tourism as a crucial component in the construction of transnational culture brings the role of artist expatriates into this complex network of commerce, experience, and representation not as passive witnesses but as vital actors and agents of modernity.

Thus Cowley argues that the restless wandering of the expatriates actually altered or played a part in the development of commercial exchange, including the development of modern tourism. Euro-American expatriation, therefore, brought increased exchange between the United States and other countries: "The exiles of art were also trade missionaries: involuntarily they increased the foreign demand for fountain pens, silk stockings, grapefruit and portable typewriters. They drew after them an invading army of tourists, thus swelling the profits of steamship lines and travel agencies. Everything fitted into the business picture."[56]

As a simultaneous critique and celebration of Euro-American

modernist expatriation, Cowley's text stands somewhat alone. Because the "business picture" does not usually fit into the modernist trope of exile as a mode of cultural production, *Exile's Return* remains, perhaps, more "popular" than "literary." Perhaps a clue to this memoir's method can be discerned in the title, which offers us the metaphor of "exile" but also stresses "return." In focusing a significant section of the text on the return to the United States of his literary cohort, Cowley clearly ironizes the term "exile"—the "literary odyssey" of his expatriates leads them to repatriation rather than eternal wandering and melancholia. As nationalisms intensify between the two World Wars and the global economy struggles with the effects of the depression of the 1930s, Cowley's expatriates find that they must choose sides, as it were. Interestingly, Cowley represents the return home in ecumenical terms: "These young Americans had begun by discovering a crazy Europe in which the intellectuals of their own middle class were more defeated and demoralized than those at home. Later, after discounting the effects of the war, they decided that all nations were fairly equal, some excelling in one quality, some in another . . . Having registered this impression, the exiles were ready to find their own nation had every attribute they had been taught to admire in those of Europe."[57]

MacCannell identifies the imperative of this dialectic as a "repressive encircling urge": the "movement or idea that everyone ought to be coming together in a modern moral consensus."[58] Thus the search for inspiration and the desire to break with the past inevitably lead to a greater closure and a narrower vision; ergo return. Yet were all nations "fairly equal" in the late 1920s? The world between the wars was in a state of flux; burgeoning fascism, varying degrees of colonial and imperialist expansion and retrenchment, legally codified racism, and labor movements in struggle with national and transnational capital coexisted among many other conflicts and conditions. How do we read international conditions such as these? Do these conditions link nations or distinguish between them? If the language of "difference" and "similarity" is always coded, always a narrative of the power of representation, then the question of how the world is *described* becomes particularly important. When the discourse of "difference" is utilized (as in "they do things better in Europe"), similarity is subsumed. When the discourse of "similarity" is adopted (as in "all nations are fairly equal"), differences disappear or become "naturalized" in historically specific ways. When these two aspects, two arms of a binary opposition, occur within the same text, we may inquire into the product of the opposition; that is, what is produced by the oscillation between difference and similarity in a text such as *Exile's Return?* Specifically, what rhetoric of international relations or global unity is constructed by this representational practice?

I have argued that Cowley's discourse of return constitutes a critique of expatriation as exile: conducting a partial deconstruction of the conflation of expatriation and exile, undermining the myth of exile by focusing on tropes of tourism and devoting a significant section of the text to a discussion of repatriation. Nonetheless, the text remains caught up in the binary model of modernity, oscillating between past and present, home and away, center and periphery. Euro-American expatriate displacement in Cowley's text has been, then, less an experience of expansion and a new appreciation of differences than an act in consonance with imperialist nostalgia; the deliberate courting of melancholia as repression of difference eradicates the object of desire. The displacements of "exile" have brought the modernists of Cowley's group not to a fuller understanding of the histories and particularities of the places they have traveled through but to a will to power that consolidates nationalist identities and confirms a repressive hierarchy of values. In this narrative of modernity, the "international aesthetic" is no match for the "business picture" and its allied nationalist agendas.

Touts, Tourists, and Travelers:
Mapping Literary Modernism

Another critical variation on the Euro-American modernist trope of exile as authorship revolves around a second group of male travelers between the two World Wars. In *Abroad,* first published in 1980, Paul Fussell writes that his aim is "to imply what it felt to be young and clever and literate in the final age of travel."[59] Fussell's study of British writers eschews the term "exile" in favor of "travel," yet many of the characteristics of literary production in *Abroad* share attributes with those associated with "exile" in *Exile's Return. Abroad* rails against modernity, certainly in its elegiac notion of "travel" as a lost art in and of itself, but it participates in the critical construction of Euro-American modernisms through its valuation of distance and cultural difference. More particularly, *Abroad* demonstrates the critical conflation of exile, expatriation, and tourism in the representation of Euro-American literary history in modernity.

Abroad illustrates how heavily the Euro-American modernist exile trope depends upon discourses of upper- and middle-class travel from the nineteenth century. Thus the leisure pursuits of the Grand Tour, which were pursued by Euro-Americans of means (sketching, keeping a diary, collecting souvenirs, observing customs and manners), combined with the material displacement of professional populations (and their dependents) in the economic and military procedures of high imperialism. The entire world appeared to belong to the "West" as travel became supported by technological innovations and financed by industrialization. Earlier in the nineteenth century, as Mary Louise Pratt's work has shown us, diversified discourses of travel produced writing that influenced occidental science and literature as well as foreign policy for several generations to come.[60] By the turn of the century, then, travel had become a crucial part of the imaginative capacities of the middle and upper classes in Europe and the United States.

The "traveler" who occupies primary place in this formation can be characterized as a Western individual, usually male, "white," of independent means, an introspective observer, literate, acquainted with ideas of the arts and culture, and, above all, a humanist.[61] Certainly, this "position" has been inhabited partially or fully by women and men of all races, classes, and nationalities. In characterizing the "traveler" in such a way, I am referring to a mythic figure produced through myriad contradictory practices and discourses. In modernity, this "traveler," I will argue, is produced in popular culture as well as in high art. An ideal figure, the "gentleman traveler" populated the imaginative faculties of the era that produced him, and provided the model for Indiana Jones and the inspiration for Paul Theroux.

Paul Fussell's *Abroad* resurrects this tradition within modernity, claiming for "travel writing" the prestige of "literature" and for its authors a place in a cultural pantheon. The "blurbs" on the back of the paperback edition, for example, hail the value of a history of an underrecognized genre: "It admits a whole area of writing—at last!—

to its proper place in literary history," wrote Jonathan Raban in *The New York Times Book Review;* it reclaims for travel writing "a large measure of respectability," asserted Peter S. Prescott in *Newsweek.* Even more interesting, two reviewers focus on the metaphor of travel to describe their reception of Fussell's text. Christopher Lehmann-Haupt refers us to the modernist geography of international aesthetics, writing: "An absolutely dazzling continent of sociology, literary criticism, cultural history, biography and amusing anecdote, so borderlessly fused that we hardly realize what great intellectual distances we are covering." Paul Gray, writing in *Time* magazine, opines that *Abroad* is a "fitting substitute for the real thing; it is a journey in space and time, offering the serendipitous pleasures of the open road."[62] As a text, then, that constitutes a "continent," a substitution for "the real thing," and a "borderless fusing" of disparate elements that brings the reader across "great intellectual distances," *Abroad* (along with its mainstream critical reception) produces and participates in the primary tropes of Euro-American modernisms.

Fussell's study begins at the end of the First World War. Arguing that the war transformed social relations, Fussell links shifts in modes of travel to the Defense of the Realm Acts of 1914 and 1915, which severely limited private travel for British citizens both abroad and at home. The restlessness and claustrophobia engendered by these restrictions, Fussell suggests, resulted in the "British Literary Diaspora"—the surge of young writers in the '20s and '30s who expatriated to other climes. Much like Cowley's *Exile's Return,* then, Fussell's literary history probes the expatriation of the postwar generation, linking displacement to the production of literary modernism: "This diaspora seems one of the signals of literary modernism, as we can infer from virtually no modern writer's remaining where he's 'supposed' to be except perhaps Proust—we think of Pound in London, Paris, and Italy; Eliot in London; Joyce in Trieste and Paris; Mann ultimately in the United States. The post-war flight from the Middle West of Hemingway, Fitzgerald, and Sinclair Lewis is the American counterpart of these European flights from a real or fancied narrowing of horizons."[63]

There are two world maps in operation here: before the First World War and after. Before the war, Fussell's favored group of British writers roamed a wide-open space (the sun never set on the imagination and resources of the empire's writers in this halcyon view). There were no passports, no legal restrictions, and the world drew no impassable borders for writers who wished to travel. Fussell quotes C. E. Montague, who exemplified this early twentieth-century attitude: "Europe lay open to roaming feet . . . All frontiers were unlocked. You wandered freely about the Continent as if it were your own country."[64] This appropriative view of the countries of Europe was certainly extended to the dominions of the empire. Robert Byron, J. R. Ackerly, and E. M. Forster are just a few of the writers who are cited in Fussell's study as examples of British avatars of modernism whose status as travelers abroad (often in the colonies) is almost inseparable from their personae as artists.[65]

Fussell asserts that the First World War affected the attitudes of a generation of writers not just because they were the survivors of a particularly brutal and large-scale war and not only because those left at home had been denied the pleasures associated with prewar travel. World War I literally changed the maps of the world: there were new borders and new legal restrictions. Passports and identity cards remained in place long after the war that had initiated their use had receded into memory. All these changes, losses, and rearrangements constituted a new "modern sensibility." And this modern sensibility, Fussell argues, changed writing itself: "Fragmenting and dividing anew and parcelling out and shifting around and repositioning — All these actions betray a concern with current space instead of time or tradition. All imply an awareness of reality as disjointed, dissociated, fractured. These actions of dividing anew and shifting around provide the method we recognize as conspicuously 'modern,' the method of anomalous juxtaposition."[66]

Fussell is relatively ambivalent about the possibilities of "modern" literature and the "modern" sensibility in general. *Abroad* narrates a teleological history of travel writing that stretches back to the European Renaissance and forward to the present moment in modernity. This continuum is divided into three categories that are representative of their "ages": exploration, travel, and tourism. Exploration, associated with the European Renaissance, participates in a discourse of adventure. Fussell not only endorses early entrepreneurial capitalism as a justification for imperialism, he fashions an account that celebrates the European expansionism that gave rise to the flowering of travel writing. But it is the rise of bourgeois culture in the nineteenth century that yields Fussell's "golden age" of travel writing: travel as study and vocation. Fussell reserves his most scathing comments for twentieth-century tourism.

In *Abroad,* tourism causes the destruction of "real" travel and (implicitly) the end of "good" writing. Fussell's study concerns a group that falls between the extreme heroism of exploration and the crass vulgarisms of tourism—the "genuine traveler": "If the explorer moves towards the risks of the formless and the unknown, the tourist moves toward the security of pure cliché. It is between these two poles that the traveler mediates, retaining all he can of the excitement of the unpredictable attaching to exploration, and fusing that with the pleasure of 'knowing where one is' belonging to tourism."[67] The myth of "discovery" has been deconstructed by critics ranging from Tzvetan Todorov to Martin Green, and the cultural impact of Euro-American representational erasures of indigenous populations in the lands so "discovered" has been carefully documented by several generations of critics.[68] As powerful masculinist discourses, adventure and exploration writing proved to be instrumental in the construction of rationales for imperialism. Martin Green has argued that adventure stories, the fiction that "England told itself as it went to sleep at night," influenced and even determined national identity and colonial policy.[69] As an "energizing myth of empire," the tradition of heroic travel and exploration literature "charged England's will with the energy to go out into the world and explore, conquer, and rule."[70] Fussell's acceptance, even his endorsement, of this strong mythic construction circulates throughout his text as a form of imperialist nostalgia, identifying the critic as an apologist for empire.

Fussell's evocation of an edenic period preceding vulgar tourism is just as reductionist as his ethnocentric view of Renaissance travel. Since Fussell's concerns are with the development of a particular literary genre, his fusion of genre and class-bound activity is particularly cogent. "One by-product of real travel," he writes, "was something that has virtually disappeared, the travel book as a record of an inquiry and a report of the effect of the inquiry on the mind and imagination of the traveler."[71] Here Fussell only emphasizes his primary objective: to establish a canon of valued texts and authors. "Real" travel produces "real" travel books. Any other form of writing associated with any other form of travel is not truly valuable. Fussell assumes that the Euro-American, middle-class traveler of the late nineteenth and early twentieth centuries held a normative view of the world that rendered all accounts virtually factual. The "truth-effect" of the travel memoir is, of course, a very strong influence on readers who learn to expect that the traveler's *experience* can only render the text *more* truthful.[72] Arguing that the Victorians read the Renaissance exploration texts as historical truth, Fussell suggests that late-twentieth-century readers derive an accurate sense of the recent past from the records of travel made by *his* canonical authors: Graham Greene, Robert Byron, Evelyn Waugh, D. H. Lawrence, Norman Douglas, Christopher Isherwood, and W. H. Auden.

The absence of any Euro-American women writers from Fussell's canon suggests that "real" travel books (and "history" and "truth") are the creation of an elite group of British, male writers between the two World Wars.[73] This characterization is, in fact, Fussell's main contention: that *this* particular class, gender, race, and nation by virtue of those very identities held a certain standard of literary achievement and cultural vanguardism against a rising storm of changing norms and practices. Fussell's aim is to assert the value of his canon and the aesthetic discourses that attach themselves to his conception of the genre of travel writing.

Thus tourism marks the demise not only of genuine travel (the leisurely journey taken in the company of people of your own class amongst others who recognize and respect your status) but of the "best" travel writing. Tourists, Fussell claims, are not honest about their aims and activities; they travel in conspicuous crowds, only in certain seasons, and so on: "What distinguishes the tourist is the motives, few of which are ever openly revealed: to raise social status at home and to allay social anxiety; to realize fantasies of erotic freedom; and most important, to derive secret pleasure from posing momentarily as a member of a social class superior to one's own, to play the role of a 'shopper' and spender whose life becomes significant and exciting only when one is exercising power by choosing what to buy."[74] Certainly the realization of erotic freedom has not been limited to tourists alone in the history of Western travel experience and writing! As Griselda Pollock has argued in "Modernity and the Spaces of Femininity," the late-nineteenth-century European male flaneur constituted the spaces of metropolitan modernity through circuits of movement through the bourgeois drawing room, the arcades and boulevards of the city, and the brothel. A precisely gendered and eroticized set of practices characterizes the production of modern spaces and modernist art, destabilizing and contextualizing the limits of such "freedom" and "eroticism."[75] At the very least, the attribution of sexual exploitation to tourists alone is inaccurate. Is it the democratization of such elite masculinist privileges that arouses the critic's ire?

In Fussell's hostility toward the class that he believes has literally ruined contemporary travel, one primary salvo recurs. His greatest fear is that the tourist predilection for one-shot "pseudo-places" will contaminate the "real" places. Only these "real" places inspire literature; "places are odd and call for interpretation."[76] Nostalgia saturates Fussell's sense that the world is shrinking and that there may not be any places far distant enough or different enough to generate interpretations. Yet nostalgia signals the functioning of a great myth; the world that Fussell laments is a world his travelers helped bring about. Blaming the tourists results in a querulous evasion of any complex evaluation of transnational culture and the role of displacement in literary production.

Not surprisingly, Fussell never inquires into the point of view of those who have been "visited" by his literary cohort. Just as he constructs an ideal traveler, he constructs an ideal native. His attack on tourists pauses just long enough for a particularly vicious diatribe on "touts," those seemingly pesky beggars or persistent entrepreneurial types who frequent resorts and ports in hopes of gaining some money from travelers. "Touts," Fussell writes, "make contemporary tourism a hell of importunity, and many of my memories of tourist trips reduce to memories of particular touts."[77] For example, touts keep Fussell, the would-be "true" traveler, from leaving the hotel. They are contrasted with a few pleasant waiters and students eager to learn English. In general, for Fussell, the persistent, aggressive "native" serves as a painful reminder not of how the indigenous economies have been disrupted by European imperialism but of how much better it was when a traveler could assume that native people accepted class and nation hierarchies without audible complaint.[78]

Just as Fussell's reader might be tempted to categorize the critic as "antitourist," Fussell differentiates between the true "antitourist" and the true "traveler:" the former is not to be confused with the latter, as the traveler's "motive is not inquiry but self-protection and vanity."[79] According to Fussell, the middle-class traveler who snobbishly squirms at the sight of masses of fellow countrypeople on holiday, who refuses to carry a camera, who eschews the comfortable hotels for the "authentic" or out-of-the-way spot, this kind of traveler is reserved special scorn. This sort of "tourist angst" is, apparently, a signal of middle-class discomfort with any blurring of boundaries between middle and working classes. In Fussell's schema, it is the upper class who cheerfully emulate the common folk: "the upper class, unruffled by contempt from any source, happily enrolls in Linblad Tours or makes its way up the Nile in tight groups being lectured at by a tour guide artfully disguised as an Oxbridge archaeologist."[80]

In the hierarchy of travel in *Abroad* there are levels of virtue, all linked to a lineage of worthy origin: the true traveler follows a tradition stemming back to the golden age of exploration narrative (and landed gentry). The true traveler represents a knighthood of the upper middle class or a democratization of the British aristocracy. The discourse of the "true" traveler signals, in its idiosyncratic way, the birth of a modern figure who is created out of the best of the lineage of travel and exploration, who travels in a discrete but not self-consciously self-effacing manner, who admits to privilege and observes the correct rank of others as a form of homage, and who, most importantly, believes in the sanctity of objectivity and the universalization of interpretation.

Once Fussell has brought his account of the distinctions between kinds of travel and types of travelers to a conclusion, he admits that all travel is now structured *as* tourism: "We are all tourists now, and there is no escape."[81] Fussell's account of a golden age of travel writing neccesarily looks backwards, then, and strikes an elegiac tone. The once-young writers he strives to canonize are sketched in nostalgic terms as the avatars of a new group that was fading even as it was being created. It is almost as if what the First World War did not do, the effects of modernization accomplished. In Fussell's literary history, one bright, brief moment in the twentieth century produced a brilliant constellation of writers who blazed, then flickered and died out. While the writers in Cowley's *Exile's Return* changed the entire paradigm of displacement by returning home, Fussell's group is more dramatically figured as victims of modernity which displaces too many, too indiscriminately, making meaningless the particular travels of his elite group.

Literary histories such as *Abroad* construct distinctions between high and low culture, between "popular" and "elite" literary production. As Andreas Huyssen has argued, modernism constitutes itself "through a conscious strategy of exclusion, an anxiety of contamination by its other: an increasingly consuming and engulfing mass culture."[82] But Euro-American modernism has always undermined its own exclusivity by privileging innovation and new points of view. The tensions between tourist and true traveler/writer, for example, in Fussell's typologies, suggest that the structure of modernism is always strained by its own internal tendencies. Following the fault lines, as it were, between elite and popular configurations of travel and authorship provides a critical reading of transitions from modern to postmodern, that is, the production of specific modernisms in cultures of modernity.

Touring Modernity: Displacing the Subject

Most Euro-American modernist theories of authorship that utilize metaphors of displacement have worked to differentiate themselves from notions of tourism, but a set of Euro-American critics has argued that it is tourism that defines the vantage point of modernity. Drawing upon structuralist methodologies and focusing more specifically on economic exchange and cultures of consumerism than aesthetic concerns, the theorists who privilege tourism seek to account for the rootlessness and anomie of modern, urban life through recourse to a powerful metaphor of travel. In many ways, posing the modern subject as a tourist destabilizes the elitist formations of some forms of cultural modernisms and demands a more historically specific, economically grounded theory of cultural production.[83] Reading Dean MacCannell's study *The Tourist: A New Theory of the Leisure Class* (1976) and Donald Horne's *The Great Museum: The Re-Presentation of History* (1984) as modernist texts, however, I will also argue that the tourist cannot be universalized to stand for every subject position in modernity.[84]

For both MacCannell and Horne, the notion of the tourist functions as a lens for viewing the structure of modernity. According to MacCannell, the production of "tourist experiences" depends upon a specifically modern world that is marked by an ambivalent relationship to the past, by technologies of simultaneity, and by the displacement of populations during a century of economic and social change. This modern world system, where all parts of the globe are connected through economic ties, enables what Horne calls the "tourism of the modern."[85] According to MacCannell and Horne, travel affirms modernity, creating a dialectical relationship between travel and modern imaginary communities. Modernity displaces its populations in both metaphysical and concrete modes while moderns travel to organize their perception of and verify the structure of relations of location. MacCannell expands the term "tourist" from actual sightseer to a metasociological term to designate "modern-man-in-general."[86] While modernity may be comprehended through various subject positions, MacCannell argues that the tourist provides a particularly complex vantage point. Modernity cannot be accounted for by examining discrete categories such as religion, language, or nation, MacCannell argues, because of the uneven nature of "development" that leaves parts of the world in varying degrees of relation to the modern. "Modernity cannot be defined from without," he writes; rather, "it must be defined from within via documentation of the particular values it assigns to qualities and relations."[87] The tourist literally and figuratively traverses these boundaries.

The tourist is not, however, free to move about willy-nilly in a libertarian world. If the tourist traverses boundaries, they are boundaries that the tourist participates in creating; that is, an economic and social order that requires "margins" and "centers" will also require representation of those structural distinctions. The tourist confirms and legitimates the social reality of constructions such as "First" and "Third" Worlds, "development" and "underdevelopment," or "metropolitan" and "rural." Created out of increasing leisure time in industrialized nations and driven by a need to ascertain identity and location in a world that undermines the certainty of those categories, the tourist acts as an agent of modernity.

The relationship of modernity to the past is of central concern to MacCannell's formulation of the modern in which modernity itself comes to be legitimated by and defined against that which is perceived to be nonmodern or premodern. Rather than marking the contradictory eruptions of the traditional in modernity and the modern in traditional societies, modernism always posits a progressive development that erases the past. The "vanishing" native, the "lost" ideal culture, the end of "pristine" experiences: all these tropes of the modern era reflect the conviction that modernity destroys or cannot salvage the traditional or nonmodern aspects of the past. MacCannell argues that the assumption of the erasure of the premodern is as complicated as the assumption of the erasure of the past. Modernity, he writes, is set in "opposition both to its own past and to those societies of the present that are premodern or un(der)developed."[88] Thus in modernity the nonmodern must be construed as pre-, as historically past to modernity's present. The construction of nonmodern as past is reinforced by efforts to "museumize the premodern," to preserve the premodern in ritualized or static forms. Once the destabilizing or resisting elements of culture are fixed as "vanishing," "endangered," and "local," they may be visited. Tourist travel to other locations to view conditions or practices that might just as well be viewed at "home" has been insufficiently ironized. What do tourists, that is, affluent moderns, really want?

According to MacCannell, all tourists share a "deep involvement" with culture and society; that is, every tourist hopes to surpass the superficialities of tourism to achieve "a more profound appreciation of society and culture."[89] Thus the expatriate modernist writer and the vacationer may share the same desire for new experiences or places in order to "see" or "feel" differently. They may share a need to escape for longer or shorter periods from a routine or a mode of life that may be less than inspiring. They may both look to whatever trace of the past or of the alternatives to the modern they may be directed to find. As I will discuss shortly, however, this "experience" is not evenly or unproblematically shared by every human being on earth. MacCannell's "moderns" may be ubiquitous but they are not universalizable on a global scale. Nevertheless, if we read *The Tourist* as specific to certain historical formations then the generalization of experience as a "modern" phenomenon tells us a great deal about Euro-American discourses of displacement.

The paradox of modernity for the Euro-American tourist lies in the contradictory dynamics of totalities of meaning. Though the production of tourist experiences strives to bring the disparate fragments of modernity together, this unity is ephemeral: even as modernity tries to construct totalities, MacCannell writes, "it celebrates differentiation."[90] The figure of the tourist embodies this contradiction to perfection. As Donald Horne argues in his study, tourists look for new meanings in other locations, in other landscapes, cities, and social customs, "even if they go home confirmed in their old meanings."[91] Going home with the "old" meanings confirmed resolves the crisis in determining reality.

Horne and MacCannell argue that, as part of this process of mediating reality, all tourists search for verifiable markers of "authenticity." For the tourist, a souvenir or photograph, developing relationships with indigenous people, documenting customs, manners, and landscapes, or learning a language will serve to mark the portals of "entrance" into the "authentic." MacCannell describes the search for authenticity as a response to the generalized anxiety of modernity; that is, the certainty of tourist sights (and sites) helps assuage the feeling of drifting or fragmentation that afflicts the modern subject in the West.[92]

MacCannell borrows Erving Goffman's concept of "front" and "back" regions to illustrate the importance of "staged authenticity" in travel discourse: stage 1 is the front region, the "kind of social space tourists attempt to overcome or get behind"; stage 2 is a touristic front region that appears to resemble a back region, even deliberately decorated as a back region for "atmosphere"; stage 3 is a front region that openly simulates a back region (this is the most ambiguous stage); stage 4 refers to a back region that is "open to outsiders"; stage 5 is a back region that is organized in recognition of visits from tourists; and stage 6 is the ultimate social space that motivates the traveler's imaginary, the ideal, uncontaminated back region.[93] Tourists, MacCannell argues, long to enter this sixth space, the ideal location of "authenticity." They are more on guard against "false" back regions than anything else, since the object of the trip is to experience the sixth, ultimate version of unique, essential authenticity. That it is difficult to know what is "front" or "back" in new settings only adds to the intensity of the quest.

In *The Great Museum,* Donald Horne argues that valid expressions of modernity are nervously acquired by moderns through travel, thus the need for documentation of the modern.[94] Tourism, as a manifestation of a crisis in reality, insists upon proof of the authentic. The photographic component of documenting a trip, the collection of souvenirs, the writing of postcards, the travel diary: these activities become part of a technology of documenting the "real." When tourists believe that they have found the ultimate "real," that they have attained the "back" region, the need for proof is especially pressing. Horne points out that taking a photograph puts the tourist into a relationship with the world that "feels like knowledge—and, therefore, power."[95] If we gain possession of something by taking its photograph, what do we gain through writing about it?

Critics of ethnographic practices have maintained that writing is a kind of technology of power that exercises dominant relations through representation.[96] Representational practices of all kinds, from ethnographies to popular films to postcards, produce views of the world that participate in discourses of displacement in powerful ways. Whether we see representation as "gaining possession of an experience," "getting a grip on reality," or expressing a partial viewpoint, the process is never free of power relations. The questions become: What kind of power? exercised in what ways? to whose benefit? and to whose loss? The writing that is generated by the generalized tourist/subject described by MacCannell and Horne in their studies is deeply implicated in the power relations of modernity. The writing of criticism participates in these discourses of displacement as well, producing modernisms as complex and as pervasive as those created by the "artist in exile," the expatriate, or the tourist. What links these discursive articulations is the mediation of reality that Euro-American modernity requires and the universalization of those mediations on a global scale.

Both MacCannell and Horne would assert that tourists want confirmation of reality without acknowledging their role as agents in the construction of reality effects. The quest for "authenticity" as relief from a culture that is perceived to be false and empty shifts the responsibility from the individual to an amorphous expression of anxiety. Exploration and discovery, those exhausted terms from an era when Euro-American travel was physically and conceptually more difficult, can be rationalized by general notions of cultural "difference," notions that can be deployed in the discourse of tourism today. To explore what we already know, to discover what other people have always known, requires a kind of collective delusion. The crux of the discourse of the tourist as a model of modernity constitutes the transformation of middle-class, Euro-American perspectives into universals. Only a group that has the privilege to ignore alternative points of view can entertain the cultural myopia demonstrated in the cultural production of this kind of travel discourse.

The limitations of such cultural myopia power the critique of tourism in *A Small Place,* Jamaica Kincaid's memoir of growing up in Antigua. "If *you* go to Antigua as a tourist, this is what *you* will see" (my emphasis).[97] This text is addressed not to "moderns" everywhere but distinguishes between "tourists" and "Antiguans": "An ugly thing, that is what you are when you become a tourist, an ugly, empty thing, a stupid thing, a piece of rubbish pausing here and there to gaze at this and taste that, and it will never occur to you that the people who inhabit the place in which you have just paused cannot stand you . . ."[98] Yet, as the passage just quoted indicates, tourists are formed through their actions, they are as commodified as the people and places they visit but only insofar as they practice tourism. Kincaid's binary oppositions strategically operate to denounce the universalization of "tourism" without staging authentic essentialisms between "native" and "visitor": "That the native does not like the tourist is not hard to explain. For every native of every place is a potential tourist, and every tourist is a native of somewhere . . . But some natives—most natives in the world—cannot go anywhere . . . They are too poor to escape the reality of their lives; and they are too poor to live properly in the place where they live, which is the very place you, the tourist, want to go . . ."[99]

Yet despite counterdiscourses of tourism such as Kincaid's that stress political and economic asymmetries, the notion of the tourist as modern subject position par excellence persists. This tourist travels, crosses boundaries, is freely mobile, consumes commodities, produces economies, and is, in turn, commodified to a lesser or greater extent. Rather than simply inventing modernity through a process of recognition and documentation, the tourist acts as a witness to the breakup of modernity. The tourist, in this formulation, straddles eras, modes of production, and systems of thought—this tourist has a passport, but what that passport signifies may have changed as we move from national to transnational eras.

The tourist in MacCannell and Horne's formulation enables a critique of modernity but cannot subvert modernity's Eurocentrisms. The tourist, then, is not a postmodern cosmopolitan subject who articulates hybridity for anxious moderns but a specifically Euro-American construct who marks shifting peripheries through travel in a world of structured economic asymmetries. Thus we cannot transform the tourist into the primary figure of our era because the tourist is as time bound and historically constructed as any other trope and cannot be made to stand for what it does not signify. Tourism must not be separated from its colonial legacy, just as any mode of displacement should not be dehistoricized or romanticized. Writing about tourism in Europe, Donald Horne has described touring as walking among the "monuments to the wreckage of Europe's greatest ambition—to rule the world."[100] Imperialism has left edifices and markers of itself the world over, and tourism seeks these markers out, whether they consist of actual monuments to field marshals or the altered economies of former colonies. Tourism, then, arises out of the economic disasters of other countries that make them "affordable" or subject to "development," trading upon long-established traditions of cultural and economic hegemony, and, in turn, participating in new versions of hegemonic relations.

Finally, MacCannell's formulation of the tourist participates in the hegemonic dynamics of Euro-American critical production in modernity. In this specific sense, his text maps the relentless quest for knowledge and structural totality that marks so many critical enterprises. In his insightful reading of MacCannell's text, George Van Den Abbeele argues that the tourist and the theorist are *both* sightseers, desiring immediate access to an authentic substance or object of study: "The theorist's pretension is even greater though than that of seeing a sight, for he wants to be a seer in another sense of the words as well, someone who knows. He not only wants to see the sights, he wants to possess them and his fellow sightseers through his superior knowledge."[101]

Yet such possession is more the province of Euro-American masculine travelers than of their female counterparts—or such acts of power may structure the imagination and desire for travel in specifically gendered, classed, and raced ways. Meaghan Morris reads Mac-Cannell's and Van Den Abbeele's intertextual theories of tourism as masculinist valorizations of a binary division of labor that constructs displacement as a space of intellectual work and erases the engagement of culture and politics that occurs at "home." [102] The notions of exile and tourism that I have examined in this chapter are established through their difference from a point of origin or from a condition of placement. Morris's feminist critique of the binary opposition between "home" and "displacement" underscores the limits of modernist celebrations of "transcendental homelessness" at the expense of a fully articulated cultural studies of those spaces that are more conventionally designated as points of arrival and departure.

Despite their different effects, then, exile and tourism are linked through their structural opposition as well as through their structured similarities. For example, both exile and tourism construct authenticities. For the exile, the site of the authentic is continually displaced, located in another country. For the tourist, authenticity is elsewhere as well, and the present is inauthentic. The figure of exile represents a single break with the past, while the tourist negotiates numerous rifts and fragmentations of experience. But the belief in a truer, more meaningful existence somewhere else is shared by exile and tourist alike. Both figures, when mystified into primary subject positions, represent melancholic seekers after a lost substance or unity that can never be attained.

In this chapter I have linked a range of discourses of displacement that generate similar modernisms within modernity in order to understand the hegemonic effects of Euro-American cultural production. The chapters that follow identify the continuities and discontinuities of these specific modernisms in critical practices that are more obviously connected to poststructuralist methodologies and cultural articulations of postmodernisms. Tracing the operation of modernisms in these critical practices illuminates the way that postmodernity generates modes of representation and critical practices through erasures of the secondary terms in binary configurations, producing Eurocentrisms and other forms of cultural domination.

2 BECOMING NOMAD

Poststructuralist Deterritorializations

We came like bedouins . . .
—Sergei Eisenstein[1]

California is not what it was
Rome too is not what it was
No more imperial cities
No more crazy societies
Where is one to go?
Berlin   Vancouver   Samarkand?
—Jean Baudrillard[2]

Describing the heady days of the early 1920s, when Russians "discovered" a revolutionary Soviet cinema, Sergei Eisenstein likened the
construction of this cultural form to a "place with unimaginably great
possibilities," "something not yet existent." "We came like bedouins,"
he wrote, and "pitched our tents."[3] In distinguishing the new field
of cinema from theater (with its written traditions, stylistic require-
ments, and canonical masters), Eisenstein chose to use the metaphors
of desert and bedouin to emphasize the values of freedom, hybridity,
and modernity. Eisenstein's rather charming autobiographical pro-
logue to "Through Theater to Cinema" underscores the powerful
hold of a set of metaphors and tropes from an earlier era, metaphors
and tropes that continue to construct colonial spaces in postmodern,
poststructuralist theories.

  As Ella Shohat has persuasively argued, the colonialist imaginary has long relied upon the positioning of different regions to

"define the 'West' itself."[4] Mapping "terra incognita" requires the open spaces and depopulated zones constructed by colonial discourse. While the "dark continent" signals Africa's imbrication in imperial modern culture's self-construction, the blinding white spaces of the desert present another opportunity for Euro-American inventions of the Self.[5] From Isabelle Eberhardt to Jean Baudrillard, from T. E. Lawrence to David Lean, the philosophical/literary trek across the desert leads to a celebration of the figure of the nomad—the one who can track a path through a seemingly illogical space without succumbing to nation-state and/or bourgeois organization and mastery. The desert symbolizes the site of critical and individual emancipation in Euro-American modernity; the nomad represents a subject position that offers an idealized model of movement based on perpetual displacement.[6]

Euro-American recourse to the metaphors of desert and nomad can never be innocent or separable from the dominant orientalist tropes in circulation throughout modernity. Yet in marking a tradition of romanticizing the desert nomad throughout Euro-American culture I do not intend to argue that the exact same figure is at work in each instance. Rather, enthusiastic adoption of Gilles Deleuze and Félix Guattari's notion of "nomad thought" in poststructuralist theory (particularly Euro-American literary criticism) suggests that further historicization of terms is required.[7] For mystified versions of the "romance of the desert" remain with us in postmodernity, often in the supposed service of a "postcolonial" critical practice. In querying the deployment of the "nomadic" through the affiliated concept of "deterritorialization" in Euro-American poststructuralism, I intend to caution against critical practices that romanticize or mystify regions or figures that can only be represented through the lens of colonial discourse. More specifically, the desire to become like or merge with the periphery or margin that one's own power has established demonstrates the pitfalls of theoretical "tourism." When poststructuralist theory constructs a "no-man's land" that permits the erasure of the subject positions of the critic in the formation of theory, historically diverse forms of colonial discourse combine to create a postcolonial, postmodern practice of cultural hegemony.

In this chapter I will examine two primary instances of the construction of Eurocentric modernisms through poststructuralist theories. Jean Baudrillard's *America*[8] participates in the discourse of the modernist travel memoir; it is episodic, poetic, fragmentary, and nostalgic. As theory, *America* is characteristic of Baudrillard's work in the '80s, produced during a decade that saw his reputation as a "postmodern theorist" expand in international reception. Particularly in North America and Europe, Baudrillard's work signifies the nth degree of postmodernism—for example, celebrated by British critic Mike Gane, rigorously engaged by Fredric Jameson, and subject to intense critique by critics as diverse as Douglas Kellner and Christopher Norris.[9] Yet texts such as *America* or *Cool Memories* from the mid-'80s generate theory through binary oppositions and essentialisms, deploying modernisms throughout the supposedly "postmodern." Such a contradictory practice at the outer limit of poststructuralist theorization poses a number of critical questions. If modernisms permeate Euro-American postmodern theories, what is the relationship of the modern to the postmodern? Certainly such contradictory and uneven productions point toward linkages and continuities rather than a strict rupture. If Baudrillard, as postmodern theorist, recuperates such modernist tropes as the "artist in exile" and the aesthetic benefits of distance, is this form of critical practice only capable of reproducing Euro-American colonial discourses?

To begin to answer the last question, I will turn in the latter section of the chapter to Deleuze and Guattari's theories of nomad thought and deterritorialization.[10] While Baudrillard represents a version of postmodernism that rejects politics in an effort to make a break with the Western liberal tradition, Deleuze and Guattari's representations of displacement enact a different strategy. In *Anti-Oedipus* and *A Thousand Plateaus,* among other important collaborative texts, Deleuze and Guattari recast liberation struggles within the practices of radical psychoanalysis. Rejecting the humanism of mainstream psychoanalysis and the liberal philosophical tradition, Deleuze and Guattari theorize postmodern subjectivities and alternative political practices. Yet a deeply modernist strain runs through Deleuze and Guattari's texts at the very instances when they claim the most extreme break with modernity.[11] I will argue that we can read these contradictory occasions as opportunities to examine the way that postmodern discourses of displacement link modernity and postmodernity.

Baudrillard: Deconstructing Euro-American Reception

Is Jean Baudrillard our Jerry Lewis, or we his?
—J. Hoberman [12]

Reading Baudrillard as a Eurocentric modernist runs counter to the most prevalent reception of his work. European and North American critics and social theorists of consumer culture hold Baudrillard in very high regard. Indeed, Baudrillard's critiques of Marxist orthodoxies have spurred some of the more inspired reworkings of contemporary Euro-American theorization of commodification, media, and culture.[13] Baudrillard's work over the last two decades has evoked extreme reactions from the political Left as well as the Right. His stance as a loner in the crowded pantheon of "French" poststructuralist theorists of the contemporary period has, perhaps, left him more open to both adulatory defense and vituperative attack. Throughout the 1980s in the United States, critical reception of Baudrillard constructed a theorist provocateur. Although Baudrillard rejects Marxism per se, his work has been rigorously engaged by such U.S. Marxist literary critics as Fredric Jameson.[14] The production of a critical literature on cyberpunk and the proliferation of cultural studies of television and consumer culture have also contributed to Baudrillard's growing international readership.[15]

Within this context of reception, it is noteworthy that very few Euro-American feminist critics have engaged Baudrillard's work to the extent that the work of Derrida or Deleuze and Guattari has been strenuously interrogated, revised, and adopted.[16] Nor have theorists interested in formulating antiracist poststructuralist strategies or reworking nationalist theories of identity been much interested in Baudrillard's work. This less discussed aspect of Baudrillard's critical reception matters to this study because a more nuanced understanding of the contradictory and uneven nature of Baudrillard's theoretical articulations leads us to a much clearer acknowledgment of Euro-American poststructuralism's complicities with Eurocentric social formations.

The key to Baudrillard's "metaphysical turn" lies in his reliance on modernist poetics and his attachment to European notions of national identity and character. Other commentators have more than adequately established that Baudrillard's critique of humanist Marxist theory leads to a position where no production, revolution, or rational social change is possible.[17] This form of postmodern break with modernity, then, can be seen in the random, apocalyptic events that destabilize all meaning on a global scale. No authenticity is possible, only simulation. While these theoretical proclamations send critics such as Christopher Norris into paroxysms of counterproclamations, I think it is more useful to bracket any effort to prove that Baudrillard is *wrong* or immoral (as Norris's book on the Gulf war and Euro-American contemporary theory attempts to do) in favor of a deconstruction of his terms.[18] That is, Baudrillard's most excessive and seemingly offensive textual articulations can be usefully employed as maps of the relationship between modernity and postmodernity. In addition, reading Baudrillard against the grain demonstrates the hegemony of Euro-American modernisms in so-called radical, postmodern discourses of displacement. Most importantly, such a reading of *America* deconstructs the apparent unity of the Euro-American formation, revealing the contests for representational power between former colonizing and colonized nation-states. Employing travel as a mode of theorizing, Baudrillard constructs a specular relationship between "Europe" (that is, France) and "America," a relationship that produces colossal stereotypes of both subject and object but leaves no question as to which has the power to represent, judge, and interpret.[19]

Baudrillard's America: A Busman's Holiday

Why should I go and decentralize myself in France, in the ethnic and the local, which are merely the shreds and vestiges of centrality? I want to ex-centre myself, to become eccentric, but I want to do so in a place that is the centre of the world. (*A* 28)

In *America,* Jean Baudrillard produces a postmodern discourse of displacement that relies upon a host of Euro-American modernist tropes: exile, solitude, distance, emptiness, nostalgia, and loss. Following the parameters of Euro-American modernist articulations of displacement, Baudrillard romanticizes travel and, through a deeply mystical metaphysics, constructs essentialist entities that function in binary opposition to one another. Eschewing tourism, Baudrillard espouses a "pure travel" in which a "trip without objective" speeds up the "evaporation of meaning" (*A* 9). Thus the wide open space of the desert offers the theorist/traveler only surface rather than a deep structure. "I went in search of *astral* America," he writes, "not social or cultural America, but the America of the empty, absolute freedom of the freeways, not the deep America of mores and mentalities, but the America of desert speed, of motels and mineral surfaces" (*A* 5). Yet, despite Baudrillard's quest for "deliverance from the social," *America* can never be read in a vacuum. In refusing *any* history, culture, context, or meaning, Baudrillard proposes value-laden assertions with no possibility of critique. As J. Hoberman points out in his review of *America,* everything in the United States is simulation *except* the point of view of Baudrillard himself: "Baudrillard is the last nonsimulacrum in *America.*"[20] There is no vacation from modernity when the terms of travel are modernist.

Thus, although Baudrillard's *America* insists upon a radical deterritorialization from culture, politics, and the social, its reliance upon a version of modernist exile poetics produces a text that is laced with Eurocentric stereotypes and other hegemonic representational practices. I am not suggesting that there is a truer or purer "picture" of America to be substituted for a flawed representation. Rather, I am arguing that a continuum of Euro-American representational and epistemic violence reproduces itself in the practice of some versions of postmodern poststructuralism. *America*'s discourses of displacement stress ahistorical and mythic figures of exile and travel that deploy Euro-American modernist notions of subjectivity, legitimating and authorizing "theory."

In the previous chapter, I drew upon Renato Rosaldo's notion of "imperialist nostalgia" to delineate the operation of representational aggression in "Western" culture. I argued that this mode of expression is often at work in Euro-American modernist discourses of displacement; that is, as displacement is represented as exile or as an elite activity of "true" traveling or as tourism, articulations of nostalgia lament the end of always already vanished spaces or kinds of subjects (paradise, home, the native). These melancholic lamentations can be read as constructions; that is, while distance and difference are desired and achieved, similarity and connection are subsumed. In modernity, it is often a notion of the "past" that is believed to be lost, as well as notions of territorial blankness and ownership. Thus imperialist nostalgia addresses the ambivalent relationship between concepts of space and time, location and history that mark most Euro-American articulations of modernity.

America raises nostalgia as a key issue in the first line of the text:

> Nostalgia born of the immensity of the Texan hills and the sierras of New Mexico: gliding down the freeway, smash hits on the Chrysler stereo, heat wave. Snapshots aren't enough. We'd need the whole film of the trip in real time, including the unbearable heat and the music. We'd have to replay it all from end to end at home in a darkened room, rediscover the magic of freeways and the distance and the ice-cold alcohol in the desert and the speed and live it all again on the video at home in real time, not simply for the pleasure of remembering it but because the fascination of senseless repetition is already present in the abstraction of the journey. The unfolding of the desert is infinitely close to the timelessness of film . . . (*A* 1)

This passage rehearses many of the themes and issues to be found in the text that follows: the romance of travel in tension with the monotony of "real time," the postmodern construction of "reality" through simulation, emblems of North American popular culture, and the unique configuration of the desert that instigates nostalgia. The first passage in *Cool Memories*,[21] a text that functions as a kind of companion piece to *America*, elaborates on the link between landscape and nostalgia: "The initial stunning impact of the deserts and California is gone, and yet, to be fair, is there anything more beautiful in the world? It seems unlikely. I have to assume, then, that I have come across—*once in my life*—the most beautiful place I shall ever see. It is just as reasonable to suppose that I have also met the woman whose beauty stunned me most and whose loss wounded me most" (*CM* 3). Throughout both texts, the theorizing subject appears to be struggling with a traumatic sense of irrecoverable loss— a free-floating loss that attaches itself to numerous figures (women, particular landscapes, "foreign" cultures, etc.). As a system of signification, then, these texts deploy exilic melancholy to establish a world of vanishing substance and lost directions. Rather than the carnivalesque hybridity that some Euro-American postmodernists articulate on a global scale, promoting a kind of prototourism of transnational technoculture, Baudrillard's texts appear mired in the sublime realm of romanticized, unified intensities. Tortured, ambivalent, contradictory: the theorist of *America* and *Cool Memories* hails Hegelian idealism as well as Nietzschean nihilism. In these texts, the owl of Minerva has not only flown, as it were, she is circling over Baudrillard's Chrysler as it barrels through the desert on the road to nowhere, the ultimate vanishing point.

Although Baudrillard's text is profoundly melancholic, marked as it is by exile poetics and modernist discourses of displacement, it is not simplistically available to a Freudian reading. Baudrillard distinguishes between dying and disappearance, for instance, resisting any suggestion that the theorist might be anxious about or uncomfortable with death: "Dying comes down to biological chance and that is of no consequence. Disappearing is of a far higher order of necessity. You must not leave it to biology to decide when you will disappear. To disappear is to pass into an enigmatic state which is neither life nor death. Some animals know how to do this, as do the savages, who withdraw, while still alive, from the sight of their own people" (*CM* 24).

Regardless of Baudrillard's clear assertion to the contrary, his texts' obsession with disappearance resounds with melancholic anxiety. They represent a subject who would rather will his own disappearance than grapple with change. Such melancholic despair is expressed in *Cool Memories* in several key passages on exile, for example, "One thing protects us from change: exile" (*CM* 83). Here Baudrillard lifts the modernist trope of exile and places it into his own postmodern paradigm. His exiles are simulators; they do not mourn the loss of a specific, historical nation or home. Rather, they are the negotiators of imaginary identities and simulated locations: "Only the exiled have a land. I know some people who are only close to their country when they are 10,000 kilometers away, driven out by their own brothers" (*CM* 83). Within this context, Baudrillard finds exile a "marvelous and comfortable structure":

> All things considered, what we look for in other people is perhaps the same gentle deterritorialization we look for in travel. The temptation of exile in the desire of another and of journey across that desire come to be substituted for one's own desire and for discovery. Often looks and amorous gestures already

have the distance of exile, language expatriates itself into words which are afraid to mean, the body is like a hologram, gentle on the eyes and soft to the touch, and can thus easily be striated in all directions by desire like an aerial space. We move circumspectly within our emotions, passing from one to another, on a mental planet made up of convolutions. And we bring back the same transparent memories from our excesses and passions as we do from our travels. (*CM* 120)

This passage participates directly in Euro-American modernist exile poetics; thus language "expatriates itself," the passion of an individual's life is metaphorically expressed through travel, the "distance" of exile emulates the limits of intimacy between human beings, and so on. If this discourse is so closely linked to modernism, how does this affect designations of postmodernism within Euro-American cultures of criticism and theory? I would agree with Douglas Kellner's assertion that Baudrillard's emphasis on aesthetic display stages a "new metaphysics" that cannot provide a "social theory of postmodernity."[22] An exilic, melancholic romance with "distance" belies a strong attachment to its opposite—a metaphysics of presence—no matter how speedily the theorist moves through the "astral" landscape of the imagined space of "America."

A fear of the conditions of postmodernity haunts these texts. *America* and *Cool Memories* struggle with intense anxieties about changing or mixing categories. Any social forces that deconstruct the particular binaries that maintain divisions between national cultures, genders, and races are suspect. Social change in North America cannot be accounted for in a text that stresses only the simulations and ironies of late capitalism as modernity interacts with postmodernity. The transnational cultures of similarity that provide new possibilities for resistance as well as for hegemony are utterly absent from these texts. Instead, we read passages of xenophobic distinctions, misogynist differentiations, and, always, a romanticization of speed and distance. This inability to accept and participate in change produces a subject embedded in a state of limbo—a state that generates more efforts to disengage, to deterritorialize in an ever purer and more unobtainable manner.

If *America* and *Cool Memories* were simply travel pieces, we might overlook or excuse these texts as formulaic media events or self-indulgent memoir. But when travel writing is represented as "theory," something interesting is taking place. Gathering speed, skimming across surfaces, courting "amnesia," Baudrillard's texts deploy metaphors of exploration and heroism that position the theorist as nomad par excellence. Yet such versions of imperialist nostalgia produce specific forms of modernist metaphysics; in particular, the theorist as nomadic subject in the poetics of space is situated through and against Others—the other gender, other races, and other nations and cultures. Moving west, the theorist defines the West as a mystified reflection of Europe in the mirroring space of the desert. And the philosophical pleasures of the desert are available only to the subject who can emulate nomadism, who appears to be unattached, and who has an unquestioned power and ability to deterritorialize.

Gender Mysterioso: Postmodern Metaphysics

Death Valley is as big and mysterious as ever. Fire, heat, light: all the elements of sacrifice are here. You always have to bring something into the desert to sacrifice, and offer it to the desert as a victim. A woman. If something has to disappear, something matching the desert for beauty, why not a woman? (*A* 66)

Gender relations in Baudrillard's texts observe conventional Euro-American masculinist terms of difference. His objectification of women operates in a similar manner to his essentialist constructions of race, ethnicity, and nation. Rather than simply charge these texts with overt and provocative sexism and racism, I would argue that it is precisely these metaphysical constructs that link imperialist nostalgia, Euro-American modernist exile poetics, and epistemic violence. The most masculinist and racist rhetoric in Baudrillard's texts has to be rigorously read through a deconstructive lens in order to recognize how Euro-American modernity reproduces its aggression against the less powerful through theory and philosophy, even through postmodern poststructuralist textual strategies.

In *America* and *Cool Memories,* women are summoned to signal loss, conquest, and vengeance, constructs that symbolize the subject's relationship to power. Any difference between women that might contextualize the construction of social categories and the hierarchical nature of theoretical representational practices is subsumed by

alternate objectifications and stereotypical identities. Thus, a generalized "woman" appears in discussions of the desert in relation to articulations of desire, loss, and seduction. Specific women are marked
by status (student) or race or ethnicity (black, Puerto Rican, etc.),
and their anecdotes occur more often in metropolitan contexts: "The
beauty of the Black and Puerto Rican women of New York. Apart
from the sexual stimulation produced by the crowding together of
so many races, it must be said that black, the pigmentation of the
black races, is like a natural make-up that is set off by the artifical
kind to produce a beauty which is not sexual, but sublime and ani-
mal—a beauty which the pale faces so desperately lack" (*A* 15–16).
Baudrillard's terms in this passage establish an alternative aesthetics to his *sidéreal* desert epiphanies.[23] Here the sublime is not constituted through emptiness, space, and monumentality but through
crowding, animality, and ethnic specificity.[24] Such textual inconsisten-
cies are sutured by their structural dependence upon binary oppositions: city/desert, natural/artificial, woman/man, Europe/America,
black/white, and so on.

These objectifications express the logic of Baudrillard's theoretical approach. That is, the "fatal strategies" of objects reverse the
classical power dynamic between a mastering subject and an enslaved
object. Privileging the object, viewed by Baudrillard as an active agent
of resistance rather than an inert "thing," challenges conventional
Euro-American Enlightenment theories of power. The supremacy of
objects is also linked to Baudrillard's emphasis on speed: the greater
the speed, the more superficial and objectified surroundings may appear. In haste to escape from the effect of "reference points," in a
hurry to simulate more and more objects, the theorist produces stereotypes and generalizations. It is on these theoretical grounds that a
primary commentator on Baudrillard such as Mike Gane insists that
the theorist's work cannot be labeled "racist" or "sexist." Baudrillard's
"cultural criticism," Gane writes, does not "aim at depth or at dialectical analysis . . . The problem for the reader is to find, therefore, an
appropriate superficial form of reading."[25]

Gane's ideal reader would participate in the project of evacuat-
ing meaning and pushing the envelope, as it were, of communication.
Yet *this* reader cannot disassociate her own various subject positions
enough to comply with this textual demand. When I read "I call that

woman a slut who is capable of shying away from you out of sheer perversity" (*CM* 29), I am unable to identify myself with the theorist's subject position. His "you" is meant to be universal, yet my "I" cannot be he. Is this deterritorialization of meaning or is this aggression taking the form of institutionalized "theory"? Pronouns as well as metaphors have been proven to be weapons in the Euro-American arsenal of cultural production.[26] Most importantly, absolving Baudrillard's texts of "depth" leaves the subjective responses of diverse readers outside the pale of "theory"—no one can participate in Baudrillardian theory, then, unless they can loosen their grip on historical and personal context enough to "identify" with the powerful yet unacknowledged privilege of the theorist. While this exclusionary rhetoric structures most Euro-American theory, leaving so many white women and nonwhite people convinced that "theory" is a province that does not engage them in any empowering way, in Baudrillard's "travel" texts we see the power dynamics in the construction of masculinist, Eurocentric theory revealed with startling clarity—the humanist "gloves," as it were, are off.

Perhaps in Baudrillard's valorization of the object over the subject he could be seen to "honor" women through objectification. Clearly, Baudrillard's theoretical project is not friendly to any version of modern feminism, rejecting a rather narrowly defined version of feminism as part and parcel of liberal humanist agendas in modernity. "French feminism," the only variant of feminist practice with which he appears to be familiar, is critiqued as essentialist. Yet his attack on Luce Irigaray's biologism is undermined by his own universalizing statements about "women": "Women constitute a secret society. They are all involved together in secret discussions" (*CM* 101–102), or "Thai women seem spontaneously to embody the sexuality of the Arabian Nights" (*CM* 168).[27] Comments such as these signal still another deeply embedded modern discourse in the field of postmodern critical practices. Baudrillard's overwhelming animosity toward all women and other cultures can be read as merely another recent chapter in Enlightenment philosophy—no radical break with modernity here, just the conventional construction of "others" found in any "Western" theory.

Baudrillard's most infamous discussions of "femininity" occur in his work on the concept of seduction.[28] Part of his critique of Marxist theories of production and poststructuralist "micro-politics of desire," Baudrillard's theory of seduction refuses the logic of pro-ductivist sexuality, replacing symbolic exchange with the subversive power of seduction. In this scenario, the representatives of an ab-stract category, "women," supposedly have the upper hand in culture (having been dependent upon seduction to manipulate their way into power). Presumably, this psychological or cultural dominance com-pensates "women" for their less-than-equal legal and social existence in Euro-American modernity. Once again, Baudrillard critiques an essentialist position by constructing a counteressentialism. "Women" in his text are always homogeneous, undifferentiated by any histori-cal or social categories, an impossible amalgam of film noir femme fatale and radical feminist—always loving him and rejecting him at the same time, always seducing him only to leave him alone. Bau-drillard's fascination with such monumentalized gender differences generates a theoretical smoke screen. As Jane Gallop astutely com-ments: "Baudrillard cannot seduce feminism with his truth, because he protects his truth from being seduced by feminism."[29] Thus femi-nist critical practices that might inform and transform Baudrillard's theories of postmodern culture cannot be admitted or recognized.

In *America,* the generalized term "woman" is most often linked to landscape, in particular the "desert." When Baudrillard describes the desert as "radical indifference," it is not far from that gesture to his rhetorical construction of a woman who always signifies seduction yet can never be fully seduced. Similarly, if the desert is also represented as "an ecstatic critique of culture," then we can see that woman is, as usual in Euro-American modernity, positioned outside culture in those seemingly fascinating margins constructed by the occupants of the so-called center. Within this generic representational practice, a curious twist in Baudrillard's metaphysical logic occurs. If the desert *is* a woman who must be seduced out of radical indifference (by speeding through her?) in an admittedly endless quest, then what do we make of Baudrillard's argument that woman has to be "sacrificed," that is, that she must be brought *to* the desert in order to make her disappear?

This move is itself not unusual in the metaphysics of modernity, as the figure of "woman" is required to signify the terrain or space of theorization as well as the enigmatic object of desire who can be con-trolled only through elimination. In this scenario, narrative consists of the "story" of this effort to construct, control, and then eliminate or subsume the "beloved." The poetics of the sublime articulate this process of worship and contempt in Euro-American masculinist aggression and will to power. In *America* and *Cool Memories,* the term "woman" functions as a kind of free-floating signifier that works overtime, used to such an extent as to defy signification (no term can mean everything and anything—or, rather, when a term is strained in such a way, it confounds logocentric systems of meaning). Thus "woman" becomes an almost hysterical "effect" of the text's obsessive quest for the sublime: "Every woman is a timezone. She is a nocturnal fragment of your journey. She brings you unflaggingly closer to the next night . . . Some women have disguised themselves as Congolese dugouts or Aleutian pearls. Why shouldn't they disguise themselves as a timezone, or even as the ecstasy of the journey? Everywhere there is pleasure you will find a woman in disguise, her features lost or metamorphosed into the ecstasy of things. Everywhere there is a woman dying" (*CM* 196). Woman is a "timezone," a "Congolese dugout," and "Aleutian pearls." What, we might ask this theorist, is "man"? Apparently this question requires no answer, because none is forthcoming in these texts in as direct a mode of address. "Man" can only be inferred as the one who has the right to the point of view, to the acts of theorizing and writing, and, of course, to the seeking of ecstasy through travel. This "man" could also be seen as a construction of Euro-American prerogatives: "central," he visits the margins; "empty," he recreates emptiness in the world around him; "modern," he looks for an escape from modernity.

Too Many Westerns: The Revenge of the Object

The local is a shabby thing. There's nothing worse than bringing us back down to our own little corner, our own territory, the radiant promiscuity of the face to face. (*CM* 110)

Baudrillard's modernist quest is a trip without end, a metaphysical journey of discovery that is fueled by distance itself, a heroic maneuver of estrangement and alienation that produces "theory." Reinvesting travel with modernist exilic qualities, Baudrillard's flight from humanist contexts reinscribes Euro-American modernist aesthetic values. Thus, in *America,* Baudrillard poses the realm of "pure travel" over and against the impure travel of tourism:

In fact, the conception of a trip without any objective and which is, as a result, endless, only develops gradually for me. I reject the picturesque tourist round, the sights, even the landscapes (only their abstraction remains in the prism of the scorching heat). Nothing is further from pure travelling than tourism or holiday travel. That is why it is best done in the banality of deserts, or in the equally desert-like banality of a metropolis—not at any stage regarded as places of pleasure or culture, but seen televisually as scenery, as scenarios. (*A* 9)

I have already argued that the rejection of tourism in favor of "pure traveling" signals powerful anxieties about hierarchical values and the boundaries between sociopolitical and aesthetic distinctions in modernity. The more the point of view of the tourist is rejected by the modernist, the more it reasserts itself as a structuring gaze. Baudrillard's theory seeks "deliverance from the social," rejecting the illusory "discovery of local customs" in favor of synchronic "scenery," and *America*'s hackneyed metaphors and overblown clichés emulate tourist discourses. "Pure traveling" and tourism, two ends of a binary configuration, produce the usual truisms about a difference that exists only through its assertion. In reinforcing rather than deconstructing this binary opposition, *America* eschews critique in a radical antihumanism that nevertheless overtly reproduces Euro-American modernist aesthetics.

More specifically, as Jean-Phillipe Mathy argues, Baudrillard's notion of the voyage without end deploys a paradigm of displacement that has a long-standing tradition in modern French intellectual discourse on the United States. Linked to both an anti-American sentiment based on ambivalence toward the scale and speed of production and consumption in the United States and a fascination with the utopian landscapes of the Southwest and West Coast, Baudrillard's nostalgic yet apocalyptic tone follows a long line of French commentators ranging from Tocqueville to Beauvoir.[30] Mathy points out how cohesive and continuous the "French intertext of America" has been and how such texts have played a crucial role in formulating a French national culture, rooted as they are in a specific humanist and aristocratic ethos: "Judgements passed on the United States *from* France must be read as discourses *about* France; they tell us more about an author's position in French intellectual and ideological fields than about social and cultural processes within American society."[31]

In Mathy's study of French intellectual representation of the United States, the desert holds a primary place as a site of philosophical epiphany, a location where the loss of history and tradition presses the intellectual traveler and theorist to a confrontation with humanism and modernity. Mathy notes that the desert is used to symbolize both prehistory and posthistory (depending upon the philosophical proclivities of the writers), yet the constant factor remains the loss of bearings, the absence of any permanent marks of modern civilization, and the experience of literal dis-orientation.

Privileging nomadic rootlessness and an evacuation of signification, Baudrillard's *America* imagines a national landscape that emphasizes the disappearance of history. Rather predictably, then, the North American Southwest best provides an apocalyptic backdrop for the theorist's "pure" travel: desert spaces, kitschy motels, and monumental geological formations. In Baudrillard's representation, the "ravishing hyperrealism" of North America brings the traveler/theorist to the opposite of Europe: "The microwave, the waste disposal, the orgasmic elasticity of the carpets: this soft, resort-style civilization irresistibly evokes the end of the world" (*A* 31).

While it can be said that both the '50s and '60s inform the cliché-ridden text, it is not the McCarthy hearings or the civil rights struggles or the war in Indochina that inform *America* but the two decades of rock 'n' roll and pop culture. The text's selective deployment of stereotypes is generalized through universalizing statements and "travelogue" superficialities. Not just any stereotypes, the emblems of Americana that fill the text remain those culled from the kinds of cultural productions that reached Europe during the '50s and '60s: movies, music, magazines, best-selling novels in translation, and so on. Thus, as Jody Norton argues, *America* reads anachronistically, "more credible as a representation of the America of beehive hairdos and hula hoops, Bobby Rydell and Lesley Gore than the America of Black Flag and the Dead Kennedys, or now, Queen Latifah and the Jungle Brothers."[32] *America* appears anchored to the geopolitics and cultural conventions of the cold war era and thus tethered to French reception of U.S. pop culture in the aftermath of World War II.

In focusing upon the surface and the strictly cultural manifestations of life in the United States, *America* articulates an antihumanist postmodernism. The theorist/traveler assumes that he can escape cultural formulations by displacing himself from the familiar. As I argued in the previous chapter, such a move conjoins romanticist and modernist imperialist imaginations, creating a world of opportunity for privileged subjects:

> You have to travel, keep on the move. You have to cross oceans, cities, continents, latitudes. Not to acquire a more informed vision of the world — there is no universality any more, no possible synthesis of experience, nor even, strictly speaking, is there any pleasure of an "aesthetic" or "picturesque" variety to be had from travel — but in order to get as near as possible to the worldwide sphere of exchange, to enjoy ubiquity, cosmopolitan extraversion, to escape the illusion of intimacy. Travel as a line of flight, the orbital voyaging of the age of Aquarius. (*CM* 168–169)

In *America* the desert epitomizes the possibilities of travel as a "line of flight." The geological pecularities of the desert prompt searches for the *ur*text of disappearance by suggesting a certain emptiness. Such a perception is only enhanced by speed. Yet, another aesthetics of the desert could be imagined: a countermetaphor of life, of infinitesimal diversity rather than the sterile, mineral, alien forms that *America* invokes. In fact, like any location, the desert could be subject to any number of interpretations. Finally, after textual celebrations of nothingness, pure objects, no traces, disappearance, and so on, we are left with the suspicion that, for Baudrillard, the quest still leads to something, still brings him to the brink of a substance he desires, refers to that which he mourns as lost. The shattering of culture, of humanism, of subjectivity that motivates the journey in *America* leads not to an affirmation of antihumanist simulation but to a mystical metaphysics of presence — something is out there, lost, irreplaceable, overwhelming, generating an intense melancholia. The revenge of the object seems to be a truly crushing depression, a fatal melancholy.[33]

Increasingly, the world Baudrillard represents is marked by xenophobia and paranoia. *America* and *Cool Memories* articulate a desire for binary oppositions and radical difference at almost every opportunity while expressing an apprehension toward "mixture and change." In Douglas Kellner's view, such neo-Nietzschean metaphysics produce racist thinking by exaggerating differences to the point of stereotype "while covering over or erasing similarities."[34] What are the particular similarities that threaten Baudrillard's metaphysics and what really is at stake in the energetic textual articulation of these exhausted binaries?

The Specular Gaze: "Europe" and Its "Others"

Like it or not, "vulgar" American products—streamlined, plastic and glamorous—have been attractive to European audiences. Perhaps the problem is not really about a brash and material American culture, but rather about a fake antique Europe? American culture repositions frontiers—social, cultural, psychic, linguistic, geographical. America is now within. America is now part of a European cultural repertoire, part of European identity.
—David Morley and Kevin Robins[35]

America and *Cool Memories* produce the parameters of an exhausted paradigm that continues to reproduce itself in supposedly "postcolonial" times. In valorizing a cultural difference of imagined opposition to a European "center," Baudrillard's "travel" texts mirror the concerns of that center back "home." Yet that very "home" can be seen to be uncomfortable, increasingly unfamiliar, transformed. Travel, then, is not simply a luxury or a leisurely philosophical activity but operates as a metaphor for the cultural displacement and sense of unfamiliarity engendered by social change. Baudrillard's theoretical peregrinations adopt the codes and terms of colonial discourse, producing Euro-American modernist aesthetics in the face of postmodernity's transnational challenges to those values and forms of culture. Baudrillard's globalizing representational strategies construct a world system of culture where the peripheries offer the European subject (the stereotyped version: white, masculine, bourgeois) relief from the anomie and anxiety of modernity. Any shift in the paradigm of center-periphery threatens to undermine the power relations that produce Baudrillard's postwar, postcolonial Europe.

"America" may be a convenient former colony to appropriate through postmodern/modern travel discourse. Posing "America" as "other" provides a setting for theoretical "cruising"; always already "free" of Europe, "America" hails the powerful gaze of its progenitor. In this Hegelian dynamic, the two entities cannot survive without each other, and who, truly, is more dependent than the other? This long-standing binary configuration suppresses other U.S.-European or international relations. If Baudrillard's traveling theory constructs a mirror scene in which "America" and "Europe" constitute themselves through specular effects, who or what is left out and to what end do these elisions or erasures operate? If difference, distance, and estrangement mark Baudrillard's critical strategies, what critical practices challenge such Euro-American modernist hegemonies?

In *America,* one of the primary, unacknowledged "disappearances" is the complex field of relations between nations of the landmass that could be characterized as the "Americas." America includes, after all, Canada as well as Central and South America. In utilizing the term "America" to refer only to the United States, a persistent contextual "ghost"—the history of the power relations that give rise to names, nations, and borders—is eliminated. In a postmodern moment of cultural crisis that finds the economic and social primacy of the United States in considerable decline, Baudrillard resituates this country firmly in the "center"—there is no "North" or "South" or "Central," nor is there any destabilization of the meaning of this acquired term that refers us back to European economic expansion. There is only "America" to signify an imaginary place that operates through its asserted difference from "Europe."

Although, like the more clearly modernist writers, Baudrillard eschews the globalizing appropriations of modern Euro-American travel discourse, his travel/theory results in a circular return to the safety of his comfortable assumptions, to the reaffirmation of his point of view. Thus he can write without a trace of irony: "We in Europe possess the art of thinking, of analysing things and reflecting on them" (*A* 23). The very definition of Europe is now so destabilized as to render such a statement, if it was ever accurate, preposterous. In *America,* "Europe" is not reconfigured by immigrant populations in tension with nationalist ideologies of race and ethnicity or by changing monetary and trade agreements, nor is it transformed by telecommunications technologies. In short, none of the complex, transnational, contradictory elements that produce such uneven and diverse discourses of "Europe" today are critically examined or deconstructed.[36]

In the stereotyped schema presented in the text, Europe is old, crowded, and burdened with history while America is new, open, and ahistorical. The idealism of *America* is not simplistic or vapid, however. *America* presents a country that is as reviled as it is loved and admired: "It is a world completely rotten with wealth, power, senility, indifference, puritanism and mental hygiene, poverty and waste, technological futility and aimless violence, and yet I cannot help but feel it has about it something of the dawning of the universe" (*A* 23). I read this passage (and perhaps the entire text) as a deeply nostalgic effort to reinvigorate the dream of a powerful, transcendant Western culture—the superpower Allies of World War II. Rather than address the complex, transnational effects of postmodern cultures on a global scale, Baudrillard steadfastly tries to breathe life into an exhausted stereotype: the United States as the center of the entertainment industry (since heavy industry has been displaced "offshore") leaves France (and Europe) the center of civilized culture. Since Europe is "blasted" and no longer powerful, *America* narrativizes the dream of a common future: redemption of Europe in America's objectification.

Not unlike V. S. Naipaul or Redmond O'Hanlon, in *America* and *Cool Memories* the theorist travels through a postcolonial construct of oppositional binaries. In these texts the "Third World" is always located in a clearly defined periphery, the colonial relations have shifted from military/economic to cultural/economic, and stereotypes serve as explanatory legitimations of foreign policy. Thus the Japanese are "seductive" and Brazil is a "cannibalistic, amorous, seductive culture": the home of "evil fruits, whose flesh is like the product of a noxious imagination, dull and hairy, obscenely turgescent, having a melancholy freshness" (*CM* 61). A querulous Baudrillard finds that all is not well, even in the "seductive" atmospheres of other cultures and countries. He "detests" everyone in this mood; the former subjects of colonialism, for example, could be detested "for their feeble-mindedness, their suicidal rhetorics, if I did not already detest even more the little hardline Whites, who are so sure they will always have the upper hand" (*CM* 71).

In moments of cantankerous expostulation, Baudrillard's writing in *America* and *Cool Memories* lapses in its quest for difference. Inevitably, everyone, "Whites" and "non-Whites," are detestable, all the cities of the world are really the same thing, hotel rooms and planes are interchangeable. In postmodernity, Baudrillard's requirement for cultural, sexual, and ethnic difference is continually stymied. He finds that the world "is getting denser . . . You can't disappear any more" (*CM* 110). Literally world-weary, he is exhausted and depressed by the world: "These books, did they ever interest me? These women, did I ever feel any emotion for them? All these different countries, did I ever want to discover them?" (*CM* 97). If there are no empty places left to discover, what methods of evacuation and depopulation will the poststructuralist critic employ to make room for the logic of discovery? What does it mean to such a Western philosopher to lose the promise of geographical solace?

In poststructuralist thought the Euro-American modernist emphasis on displacement as an aesthetic benefit can be seen to operate in postmodern instances. Articulated as a binary between pure travel and tourism, such modernisms reproduce metaphors of space and place that signal the vibrant hold of Eurocentric conceptions of national, cultural, and racial differences on supposedly progressive theories of culture and politics. In particular, the conjoined figures of desert and nomad engage a poetics of space that privileges perpetual displacement and resistance to classical humanist valuations of communication, settlement, and rational economies. While Baudrillard's *America* fosters a neocolonial metaphysics of space through a reproduction of modernist exilic aesthetics, Deleuze and Guattari's emphasis on deterritorialization produces a distinct poststructuralist discourse of displacement. In their collaborative texts, Deleuze and Guattari construct a nomadic theory that travels through a process of "becoming minor"; that is, their notion of "lines of flight" brings their work to the desert as a site of alterity, but their methodology refuses the neo-Hegelian metaphysics of Baudrillard's *America*.

Becoming Minor: Rhizomes and Nomads

To bring language slowly and progressively to
the desert.
—Gilles Deleuze and Félix Guattari [37]

While poststructuralism potentially deconstructs the power relations inherent in Euro-American humanism, the metaphors of explanation utilized by many poststructuralist critics reinforce and depend upon specifically modernist versions of colonial discourse. While Deleuze and Guattari do not construct the sort of metaphysical binaries that we have seen in Baudrillard's later work, their metaphorical mapping of space can be read within the context of Euro-American discourses of modernism, emphasizing the benefits of distance and the valorization of displacement. Indeed, I would argue that their privileging of "nomadic" modes relies upon an opposition between a central site of subjectivity and zones of marginality. Thus their advocacy of a process of "becoming minor" depends upon the erasure of the site of their own subject positions. What links these European poststructuralist theorists of displacement, then, is the specificity of their modernist critical traditions along with an inability to account for the transnational power relations that construct postmodern subjectivities.

This said, Deleuze and Guattari's theories of territory mark significant departures in poststructuralist paradigms. The relative popularity of many of Deleuze and Guattari's concepts and terms in Euro-American literary criticism and philosophical studies prompts a rigorous reading of their collaborative texts. Associated with radical reworkings of philosophy, critiques of psychoanalytic practices, support for the Italian *autonomia* political movements and the French avant-garde, Deleuze and Guattari have produced (separately and together) many of the most provocative and overtly political texts of contemporary French poststructuralism. Utopian articulations of the future share textual space with incisive critiques of the structure and operation of Euro-American modernity. It is precisely Deleuze and Guattari's emphasis on breaking out of or rupturing dominant social practices that both inspires and irks critics, leading to praise for their utopian vision as well as critiques of their tendency to romanticize the subjects of criticism.[38]

Deleuze and Guattari's texts vitally engage the context of Euro-American modernist experimentations in language and textual innovation even as they can be seen to be in tension with that very tradition. Indeed, their politically committed theorization of power relations challenges the dominant structures and practices of modernity. In their effort to imagine differently the social spaces and sites of subjectivity, Deleuze and Guattari theorize alternative kinds of identities and modes of dwelling that counter the fixed commodifications

of capitalist relations. Unanchored to any specific historical formation, the radical displacement that is continually evoked in these texts
is most often referred to as "deterritorialization." First theorized in
Anti-Oedipus to describe the dislodging and dispersal of desire in
modern capitalist formations, the notion of deterritorialization appears throughout the collective texts, including *A Thousand Plateaus*
and *Kafka: Toward a Minor Literature.* Linked to deterritorialization
(and its corollary, reterritorialization), the production of "nomad" or
"nomadic" theory signifies the importance of modes of displacement
in Deleuze and Guattari's work.

Deleuze and Guattari appropriate a number of metaphors to
produce sites of displacement in their theory. The botanical metaphor of the rootlike "rhizome," for example, enacts the subjectivities
of deterritorialization: burrowing through substance, fragmenting
into simultaneous sprouts, moving with a certain stealth, powerful
in its dispersion. Rejecting the classic, Western humanist metaphors
of family trees and genealogies, the rhizome destabilizes the conventions of origins and endings: "A rhizome has no beginning or end;
it is always in the middle, between things, interbeing, *intermezzo.* The
tree is filiation, but the rhizome is alliance, uniquely alliance."[39] As a
metaphor for politics, then, the rhizome constitutes an anarchic relationship to space and subjectivity, resistant to and undermining the
nation-state apparatus.

From the rhizome to the nomad is not a far leap in the poetics of Euro-American poststructuralist theory. Like the rhizome, the
nomadic subject symbolizes displacement and dispersion. In Deleuze
and Guattari's work, the site of the desert, traditional home of the
nomad, is not unlike Baudrillard's sublime, *sidéreal* space: empty, liberatory, and a margin for linguistic, cultural, and political experimentation. For example, in their study of Kafka's poetics of alterity,
Deleuze and Guattari make repeated reference to the desert as border or margin, linked to "underdevelopment," "*patois,*" and a "third
world."[40] Similarly, the nomad is likened to the "immigrant" and
the "gypsy."[41] In all of these allusions, modernity and postmodernity collapse into undifferentiated cultures; Euro-American (or even
solely European) culture structures the point of view, erasing temporal and spatial differentiations. European gypsies and Third World
immigrants share the same theoretical spaces not through structural

relations of historically specific diasporas but through a kind of generalized poetics of displacement.

In making recourse to the metaphors of marginality and displacement, Deleuze and Guattari attempt to displace the sedimented bulk of European humanist traditions. Their antihistoricism seeks to deconstruct classical lineages even as it may tend to homogenize or blur the kinds of differences upon which contemporary identity politics insist. Yet the utility of their methodology (which appears to be much more useful to Europeans and some North Americans—that is, to those who occupy the sites of domination in modernity) is always generalized. The Third World functions simply as a metaphorical margin for European oppositional strategies, an imaginary space, rather than a location of theoretical production itself. This kind of "othering" in theory repeats the anthropological gesture of erasing the subject position of the theorist and perpetuates a kind of colonial discourse in the name of progressive politics.

In their emphasis upon linguistic "escape" and "lines of flight," Deleuze and Guattari roam into realms of nostalgia, searching for a way to detour Western civilization. Their theory of "becoming minor" evokes this Euro-American modernist move of utopian flight from the worst excesses of capitalism. "Becoming minor" is a strategy that only makes sense to the central, major, or powerful, yet it is presented as an imperative for "us all." Constructing binaries between major and minor, between developed and undeveloped, or center and periphery, in Deleuze and Guattari's collaborative texts modernity provides borders and zones of alterity to tempt the subversive bourgeois/intellectual. Becoming minor, a utopian process of letting go of privileged identities and practices, requires emulating the ways and modes of modernity's "others." Yet, like all imperialist discourses, these spaces and identities are produced through their imagining; that is, the production of sites of escape or decolonization for the colonizer signals a kind of theoretical tourism. For these spaces of alterity are not the symbols of productive estrangement or disengagement for any other subjects. These imagined spaces are invested with subversive or destabilizing power by the "visitors," as it were. This theoretical activity doubles the metaphorical colonization of modernity's margins and marginals—here colonial space must symbolize the imperialist past as a zone of utter alterity as well as the site of the liberation of the Euro-American subject. "Becoming minor" refers to the center-periphery geopolitics of modernity rather than the complex, transnational circuits of capital and power in postmodernity.

Thus when Deleuze and Guattari pose a "nomadology" against "history" they evince nostalgia for a space and a subject outside Western modernity, apart from all chronology and totalization. Their celebration of deterritorialization links the Euro-American modernist valuation of exile, expatriation, defamiliarization, and displacement and the colonial discourses of cultural differences to a philosophy that appears to critique the foundations of that very tradition. Deleuze and Guattari can be read as "high modernists," then, privileging language experimentation over all other strategies. Their model of deterritorialization, like most Euro-American modernist versions of exilic displacement, stresses the freedom of disconnection and the pleasures of interstitial subjectivity. Yet deterritorialization itself cannot escape colonial discourse. The movement of deterritorialization *colonizes,* appropriates, even raids *other spaces:* "Write, form a rhizome, increase your territory by deterritorialization, extend the line of flight to the point where it becomes an abstract machine covering the entire plane of consistency."[42] Deterritorialization is always reterritorialization, an increase of territory, an imperialization.

The nomad serves as the site of this romanticized imaginary entry into the "becoming minor" of deterritorialization. In going "from one point to another" in the process of distributing "people (or animals) in an open space," nomads have "absolute movement," as distinct from migrants, who move in more determined and located ways. Paradoxically, the nomad can be seen to be the one who "does not move" in that the nomad's movements cannot be tracked or linked to a starting or end point. Like the metaphor of rhizome, nomadism signifies the inverse of dwelling or being and celebrates the *intermezzo* zone. As a symbol of utter and complete deterritorialization, the nomad does not engage in the reterritorialization that Deleuze and Guattari describe as a necessary component of language (the return of sense after the experimentation of "becoming minor"). The nomad in Deleuze and Guattari's texts embodies the practice of shifting location, vectors of deterritorialization, a "*local absolute*": "an absolute that is manifested locally, and engendered in a series of local operations of varying orientations: desert, steppe, ice, sea."[43]

Desert, steppe, ice, sea: some of the primary sites of the Euro-American aesthetic sublime; as Lisa Bloom's work on representations of the North Pole demonstrates, such open and arid spaces are prerequisites for the imperialist imaginary.[44] What are we to make of the celebration of these colonial zones in the production of poststructuralist theory? Can colonial spaces be recoded or reterritorialized without producing neocolonialisms? If we examine the history of representations of nomads in Euro-American traditions, will we find any answer to the question of the power of its current signification?

Throughout Euro-American modernity, nomads, bedouins, and other mobile tribes have been geographically located outside metropolitan locations (in the desert or forest) or on the peripheries of metropolitan locales (gypsies, for example, who are portrayed as liminal, moving in and out of towns and always staying on the outskirts). These romanticized figures are always positioned in colonial discourse as closer to nature, purer or simpler, and near to vanishing. Within this context, the nomad participates in the discourse of the "other," signifying the opposite of Euro-American metropolitan modernity. More specifically, the nomad has been characterized as patriarchal and warlike as well as migratory. As a sign of pure circulation or deterritorialization, no historical people will probably fill the requirements to perfection. The nomad as a metaphor may be susceptible to intensive theoretical appropriation because of a close fit between the mythologized elements of migration (independence, alternative organization to nation-states, lack of opportunity to accumulate much surplus, etc.) and Euro-American modernist privileging of solitude and the celebration of the specific locations associated with nomads: deserts and open spaces far from industrialization and metropolitan cultural influences.

In his discussion of *A Thousand Plateaus,* Paul Patton argues that Deleuze and Guattari's representation of nomads is historically grounded in that "historically, as well as conceptually, nomads have a particular affinity with the line of flight, since it is along lines of technological flight that they invent new weapons to oppose those of the State."[45] Yet it is difficult to discern exactly which nomadic people Patton is referring to in his discussion. Stephen Muecke has grafted sections of *A Thousand Plateaus* to his own analysis and recording of aboriginal culture in Australia, making a much more convincing argument for nomadic strategies. Yet, even as Muecke argues that

Deleuze and Guattari's philosophy of nomadology enables us to "take on board the concept 'nomad' without having recourse to anthropological definitions," I would query how "we" can "take on board" such charged metaphors and figures without accounting for them as sites of colonial discourses, as spaces constructed by specific power relations by theorists who do not usually position themselves self-reflexively within the field of those very social forces.[46]

These questions assume more importance as Deleuze and Guattari's work has undergone synthetic adaptation in Euro-American literary and cultural criticism, generating numerous versions of theories of deterritorialization and nomad thought while often reproducing the neocolonial conditions of theoretical articulation. The subject of the critic's positionality vis-à-vis the history of the production of margins and centers in Euro-American poststructuralist theories is rarely or insufficiently addressed. An emphasis on deterritorialization over and above reterritorialization in this body of criticism suggests that nomadology both raises and suppresses the question of location through the production and consumption of theory in Euro-American contexts.

Euro-American Nomadic Subjects: Postmodern
Literary and Cultural Studies

Euro-American poststructuralist and postmodern critics have fastened upon nomadic deterritorialization to articulate challenges to disciplinary limits, canonical restrictions, and hegemonic critical practices. For example, Dominique Grisoni celebrates nomad thought as a link between "street" politics and philosophy, signifying the abandonment of established codes and methods.[47] Rosi Braidotti proposes a "new nomadism" in which ideas function as "ruses and mobile, specific strategies, which are resistant to systematization" in order to develop "multiple, transverse ways of thinking women's becoming."[48] Braidotti terms this new feminist subjectivity "interconnected nomadism."[49] Teshome Gabriel has theorized "nomadic aesthetics" in relation to black independent cinema, arguing that the figure of the nomad spans diverse cultures but symbolizes universally the "lifestyle of a free people": "Nomads have thus developed a way of life, and an aesthetic attitude, which defy and critique both the settlement and art inspired by the state."[50]

Gabriel captures closely the subversive romance of nomad thought that Deleuze and Guattari's nomadology disperses throughout Euro-American postmodern critical practices. Diverse fields, from Grisoni's European philosophy to Braidotti's politicized poststructuralist feminism to Gabriel's emergent aesthetics of black independent cinema seize upon the emancipatory metaphor of nomadism, its offer of a kind of cultural guerrilla warfare and the promise of escape from the oppressive reproductive machinery of capitalist nation-state formations. In this sense, poststructuralist and postmodern critics who have been searching for alternatives to purely nationalist or modernist critical strategies have embraced enthusiastically the generalized figure of the nomad as a symbol of hybridity, mobility, and flux; in short, the metaphorical nomad and theories of nomadology counter assertions of purity, fixed dwelling or being, and totalitarian authorities and social practices.

The translation and circulation of Deleuze and Guattari's collaborative texts in the United States in the early and mid-1980s generated a plethora of references to key terms such as "deterritorialization" and "nomadic subjects" in contemporary literary and cultural studies. One important response occurred at the University of California at Berkeley in 1986, when the organizers of a conference on "The Nature and Context of Minority Discourse" asked participants to consider Deleuze and Guattari's recently translated "What Is a Minor Literature?" The conference organizers, Abdul JanMohamed and David Lloyd, directly referenced Deleuze and Guattari in their critique of liberal pluralism, calling for the "marginalizing of the center."[51] The 1987 publication of the Berkeley conference papers in special issues of the journal *Cultural Critique* and their 1990 reissue in book form contributed to an energetic process of cultural translation as Deleuze and Guattari's terms engaged North American cultural and political concerns.

Thus Deleuze and Guattari's discussion of minor literature has been borrowed by North American literary critics to contribute to theoretical challenges to the mainstream canon of national literatures. For example, in the essays collected in the volume *The Nature and Context of Minority Discourse,* critics and theorists from a variety of institutional and cultural locations addressed the academic politics of theory as well as the grounds of literary critical production. Arlene Teraoka's and David Lloyd's essays interrogated the terms of European minorities, Allogan Slagle addressed Native American subjects, Elaine Kim situated Asian American literary practices, and Josaphat B. Kubayanda linked African diaspora communities to an emerging notion of minority discourse. Taken as a whole, the nineteen essays opened up the terms of the North American debate on canonicity to considerations of European poststructuralist theories of subjectivity and language. Such a complex and challenging task produced many disagreements as well as a variety of new alliances. Barbara Christian's important critique of the institutional politics of theoretical language, "The Race for Theory," marked a resistance to the hegemonizing tendencies of poststructuralist terms. Renato Rosaldo's "Politics, Patriarchs, and Laughter" took issue more specifically with Deleuze and Guattari's Eurocentrism, arguing that Chicano/a struggles relate less to deterritorialization than the formation of a "creative space of resistance" he terms the "border." [52] My own essay in the collection formed the germ of what has become this chapter. Writing within the context of Euro-American feminist literary production, I critiqued the concept of "becoming minor" as available only to the privileged, arguing that such "theoretical tourism" constitutes the margin as a "linguistic or critical vacation, a new poetics of the exotic." [53]

While Alice Jardine's feminist discussion of Deleuze and Guattari appeared in the North American journal *SubStance* in 1984 and numerous other essays addressed Deleuze and Guattari's collaborative texts throughout the '80s, the essays that were produced for the Berkeley conference and collected under the rubric *The Nature and Context of Minority Discourse* formed an eclectic yet bounded discursive space. These critics welcomed theories that undermined generic categories, styles, and interpretative authorities. Deterritorialization and nomadic subjects appeared to open up the discourse of textual production and reception in ways that signaled postmodern critical practices, meeting the emergent multicultural and feminist interest in hybrid identities and cosmopolitan, diasporic communities. Critiques of poststructuralist Eurocentrisms or of Deleuze and Guattari's positionality within the politics of critical production were themselves somewhat marginalized.

In keeping with this overall trend, the 1993 publication of a double issue of *Yale French Studies* on "Post/Colonial Conditions: Exiles, Migrations, and Nomadisms" suggests that critiques of post-structuralist Eurocentrisms and exoticizations remain marginal to celebrations of Euro-American modernisms. The essays collected in "Post/Colonial Conditions" draw explicitly on Deleuze and Guattari's notions of "deterritorialization" and "nomadism," yet there are some significant differences between interpretations. For example, while certain critics call for historically specific applications of the term "nomad" (cf. Lowe, Raybaud, Mehrez), others appear content to recycle a more mystified and generalized notion that only emphasizes the homogenizing tendencies in Deleuze and Guattari's theory. Thus, for the latter group of critics, deterritorialization itself is an end point, releasing both writing and reading from the restrictions of culture, nation, gender, and so on. Such a celebration of "escape" or total deterritorialization certainly can be found in Deleuze and Guattari's texts. Yet the notion of reterritorialization also circulates in their theoretical projects, arguing for contingency and historically grounded identity practices. Since Deleuze and Guattari can be read as indeterminate or avoiding a complete statement vis-à-vis the relationship between de- and reterritorialization, the Anglophone critics who adopt their terminology appear to opt one way or the other; that is, the political choices may appear to be more overt in the U.S. context where identity politics is one of the most pressing concerns in cultural and literary studies.

"Post/Colonial Conditions" offers numerous explicit connections between "deterritorialization" and "exile." For example, Winifred Woodhull's essay "Exile" argues for a delineation of distinctions between modes and historical instances of displacement, yet the very title of her essay suggests quite powerfully that "exile" is the most valued term in her study. As I argued in the introduction, the celebration and valuation of exile in Euro-American modernist critical practices privileges distance and separation as aesthetic benefits even while simultaneously deploring any political or psychological crises that such conditions may engender. Despite a concerted effort to make distinctions between modes of displacement, Woodhull's essay primarily critiques the theorizing of displacement by theorists such as Deleuze and Foucault, while valuing the deterritorializing effects of non-European or culturally hybrid writers; North African, Franco-phone writers such as Tahar Ben Jelloun and Leila Sebbar, for example, are presented alongside "immigrants" whose "textual nomadism stands in relation to *real* changes in the writers' geographical location" (my emphasis).[54] While I strongly agree with Woodhull's stated objective to make historical distinctions between modes and kinds of displacement, posing "real" exiles against "false" ones does not adequately address the subject positions that arise in the complex circulations of transnational cultures in postmodernity.

While Woodhull's discussion focuses much-needed attention on the role of immigrants and émigrés in changing French national culture, the binary nature of her distinctions undermines the ostensible theme of "postcolonial nomadics." Woodhull seeks to highlight the "symbolic status of immigrants" as "effective speakers and actors on a particular social scene" without "speaking for them."[55] Yet her essentializing tendency in marking "real" from "nonreal" immigrants leads to a determinist theory of colonial discourse where marginalized "writers" are always already the source of "ethnic" realism and "theorists" are always already the nonethnic center. A more transnational model of cultural production would argue that destabilizations from "within" can be as complexly linked to those from "without" (and vice versa). If certain immigrant writers challenge the cultural hegemony of French national culture (the home of academization and other forms of Franco-European standardization and valuation), there may be others who strive to consolidate modern national affiliations with the former colonial power.

In his essay on the Maghrebian postcolonial novel, Antoine Raybaud argues that there is a danger in "identifying the nomadism of the text with a return of the archaic," likening this move to the "return of the repressed" in nationalist rejections of colonial education.[56] Raybaud, however, romanticizes his subject, celebrating an essentialized, transcultural, ahistorical notion of writing in the service of valuing Maghrebian literature in the French canon. In the same issue, Samia Mehrez powerfully challenges such exoticization of the nomadic, arguing that deterritorialization alone "stops short." "The crucial task," she writes, "is to go beyond such a stage to trace new territories which minority discourses are acquiring, and to examine the strategies by which they seek to legitimate themselves."[57] Mehrez's critique demonstrates how colonial structures of power continue to operate in some "postcolonial" literary critical spaces, asking critics to acknowledge their participation in the territorializing functions of critical production.

Lisa Lowe's essay in the "Post/Colonial Conditions" collection proposes a historically grounded practice of literary nomadics. Discussing the postcolonial Francophone allegories of Pham Van Ky and Tahar Ben Jelloun, Lowe argues that "nomadic practices are and were of central importance to the histories of Cochinchina and Vietnam, and of Morocco and the Maghreb."[58] In addressing historically specific geographies in relation to strategic methods of nomadism, Lowe's work marks a significant departure from the celebration of generalized marginal metaphors. Like most critics who are drawn to Deleuze and Guattari's theories, Lowe emphasizes heterogeneity over essentialized identities and simultaneity over chronological or hierarchical principles. Working from Fanon's notion of a "third alternative—neither neocolonialism nor a nativist inversion," Lowe rejects any romanticization of exile and indeterminacy in search of a critique of colonialism that will "neither reproduce nor be bound in binary logic to cultural domination."[59] Recognizing the need for "strategically fixed fronts, boundaries, and centers," Lowe acknowledges tactical, political exigencies.

Considering the diversity of the essays from these collections, I would argue that within the field of postmodern discourses of displacement, these literary critical engagements with deterritorialized nomadics have produced not only emulations of Deleuze and Guattari's theories but significant reworkings that rigorously address the transatlantic, if not transnational, relations between intellectual communities. What we are witnessing is the production of a diverse and contested field in the context of U.S. reception of European poststructuralist theories. Within this context, some uses of "nomad" remain more nuanced and historically grounded than others. In order to avoid the reproduction of neocolonialisms in postmodern theories, then, the location and situation of the critic become crucial factors in the politics of theoretical production.

Deconstructing the Position of
Poststructuralist Theorist

In the midst of Euro-American theorization of nomadic subjects in the late '8os, Gayatri Spivak published an essay critiquing Western representations of "the third-world subject." In "Can the Subaltern Speak?" Spivak examined how "the theory of pluralized 'subject-effects' gives an illusion of undermining subjective sovereignty while often providing a cover for this subject of knowledge."[60] Such theories of "becoming minor" reterritorialize in the name of deterritorialization, an intrinsically reactionary move, constructing exoticized "others" in the service of unexamined cultural superiority. Spivak charged that Euro-American poststructuralist theorization stresses the heterogeneity of the micropolitics of desire but evades analysis of the theorist's own "implication in intellectual and economic history":[61]

> It is impossible for contemporary French intellectuals to imagine the kind of Power and Desire that would inhabit the unnamed subject of the Other of Europe. It is not only that everything they read, critical or uncritical, is caught within the debate of the production of that Other, supporting or critiquing the constitution of the Subject as Europe. It is also that, in the constitution of that Other of Europe, great care was taken to obliterate the textual ingredients with which such a subject could cathect, could occupy (invest?) its itinerary—not only by ideological and scientific production, but also by institution of the law. However reductionistic an economic analysis might seem, the French intellectuals forget at their peril that this entire overdetermined enterprise was in the interest of a dynamic economic situation requiring that interests, motives (desires), and power (of knowledge) be ruthlessly dislocated. To invoke that dislocation now as a radical discovery that should make us diagnose the economic (conditions of existence that separate out "classes" descriptively) as a piece of dated analytic machinery may well be to continue the work of that dislocation and unwittingly help in securing "a new balance of hegemonic relations."[62]

Demonstrating the economic grounds that produce this "overdetermined enterprise," Spivak moves the discourse from the level of individual blame to a more structural examination of inequities in the division of labor in postmodernity. This does not obviate her critique of particular critics, however. For example, Spivak specifically addresses the collaborative work of Deleuze and Guattari, noting their "failure" to consider the "relations between desire, power, and subjectivity" which "renders them incapable of articulating a theory of interests."[63] Deleuze and Guattari's rejection of ideology, then, stems from their inability to theorize their various positions: as Europeans, as men, as citizens of France, and so on. In denaturalizing bodies in the service of a radical social agenda, Deleuze and Guattari have, in effect, removed the conditions for resistance and opposition that most people in the world have no choice but to struggle for. Most grievously, poststructuralist theories of "becoming minor" and radical deterritorialization "valorizes the concrete experience of the oppressed" while remaining "uncritical about the historical role of the intellectual."[64] Thus "minority" discourse becomes a social site that is only available to those who can travel to it, as it were, and is denied as "ideology" to those who already occupy that space.

Spivak's defense of ideology is not dissimilar to Lowe's insistence upon strategic identities or Mehrez's emphasis upon reterritorialization. Spivak argues that there is no pure space of postrepresentation that evades essentialism. How does one account for the "micrological texture" of power without recognizing that subject formations stage representations? Spivak's tactics are basically deconstructive: "In the face of the possibility that the intellectual is complicit in the persistent constitution of Other as the Self's shadow, a possibility of political practice for the intellectual would be to put the economic 'under erasure,' to see the economic factor as irreducible as it reinscribes the social text, even as it is erased, however imperfectly, when it claims to be the final determinant or the transcendental signified."[65] Spivak has been practicing such a politics for some time now, from her "French Feminism in an International Frame" and "Scattered Speculations on the Question of Value" to "The Political Economy of Women as Seen by a Literary Critic" and "The Post-Colonial Critic."[66] In the interviews collected in *The Post-Colonial Critic,* for example, Spivak herself becomes a dialogic subject, situating her work in relation to the queries and comments of intellectuals from diverse locations. This movement of critical discourse from a singular style of monolingual utterance to the more interrupted and dispersed technique of the collected interviews leads to a multiply situated—even "nomadic"—critical subjectivity.

In this sense, Spivak's critical practices range from the rewriting of critical subjectivity to the reconfiguration of the objects of "literary," "English," or "women's" studies. But the field of reception for these critical productions is, perhaps, more nuanced and contested than Spivak's comments in "Can the Subaltern Speak?" may allow for. For example, in essays published in 1988, Janice Radway and Larry Grossberg use the term "nomad" to stage critiques of Euro-American modernity. Writing in the context of a discussion of power and agency in audience studies, in "Reception Study: Ethnography and the Problems of Dispersed Audiences and Nomadic Subjects," Radway moves cultural production away from the sole agency of the "artist" to a more differentiated process of more diverse participation. Rather than privileging "alternative" enunciations that represent "others" but remain locked into high art conceptions of "literature" or "criticism," Radway calls for "nomadic subjectivities" that "articulate *together* many ideological elements, discourses, and practices across the terrain of daily life."[67] Radway's utilization of "nomadic" acknowledges the "concreteness" as well as the "fluidity" of these forms of subjectivity: "Can we, in short, manage a study of the dispersed construction of everyday life by beginning with the multitude of practices engaged in by actual, historically situated social subjects who are neither stable nor unified?"[68]

In "Wandering Audiences, Nomadic Critics," Larry Grossberg situates historically the "complexity of intellectual alliances and disputes."[69] In a reading of Meaghan Morris's groundbreaking theorization of intellectual production through the prism of "travel," Grossberg moves through various models of displacement in postmodernity, arriving at an amalgam configuration: the nomadic cultural critic: "neither the tourist looking for authenticity, the native looking for a home, nor the subculturalist looking for pleasure."[70] Grossberg argues that mobility is not relativistic or disconnected from economic and sociocultural vectors. Rather, displacement cannot be considered apart from questions of "who is acting and from where" because "the critic is already within the spaces of the field, implicated in his or her own stories."[71]

Without collapsing any differences between Radway and Grossberg as irrelevant, I cite their work here as examples of an emergent, syncretic Euro-American critical practice. Through tracing the dispersal and circulation of "nomadic" subjects in U.S. intellectual contexts, I have been arguing that conflicted spaces of critical practice have arisen in response to ethnic and women's studies, in particular, challenges to literary and other disciplinary canons and traditional authorities of taste and value. These movements meet Euro-American poststructuralist destabilizations of humanist discourse on uneasy and contradictory grounds of alliance in the work of some critics who embody these diverse political and academic interests and investments. In the chapters that follow, I will examine such syncretic, contemporary critical productions, following Spivak's call for the analysis of the positioning of theorists and theorization.

This work represents dynamic transformations and negotiations of modernist and postmodernist impulses in Euro-American production and reception of critical practices and theories. The primary terms of displacement and movement construct this critical space, but their deployment is less romanticized and more responsive to the histories of imperialism and economic and cultural hegemonies in modernity and postmodernity. Far from replicating Baudrillard's world-weary cultural relativism that masks an aggressive Eurocentrism or Deleuze and Guattari's desire for a non-European alterity, many of the critical practices that I will analyze conscientiously engage poststructuralism as a complex production that spans modernist and postmodernist agendas, requiring further deconstruction of the colonial discourses of Euro-American theory.

3 TRAVELING THEORISTS

Cosmopolitan Diasporas

Distance is not a safety zone but a field of tension.
—Theodor Adorno[1]

Yet it is no exaggeration to say that liberation as an intellectual mission, born
in the resistance and opposition to the confinements and ravages of imperialism, has now shifted from the settled, established, and domesticated dynamics of culture to its unhoused, decentered, and exilic energies, energies
whose incarnation today is the migrant, and whose consciousness is that of
the intellectual and artist in exile, the political figure between domains, between forms, between homes, and between languages. From this perspective
then all things are indeed counter, original, spare, strange.
—Edward Said[2]

There are over 23 million refugees in the world today.[3] Figures con-
cerning refugees do not include *gastarbeiters,* the so-called temporary
workforces imported by European industrial nations, nor do they include the foreign domestic and child care workers or seasonal agri-
cultural workers whose employment in Western countries is often
undocumented. Approximately 24 million people live as citizens in
nation-states under conditions of "internal displacement" characterized by homelessness and chronic hunger.[4] If these great numbers do
not give us pause then we might consider the impact of immigration
in countries such as the United States or Brazil where almost everyone hails from somewhere else. The twentieth century can be characterized as a time when increasing numbers of people have become
disengaged or dislocated from national, regional, and ethnic loca-

tions or identities. As travel, changing locations, and leaving home become central experiences for more and more people in modernity, the difference between the ways we travel, the reasons for our movements, and the terms of our participation in this dynamic must be historically and politically accounted for.

In the midst of these displacements, new concerns over borders, boundaries, identities, and locations arise. In most theoretical accounts, the influx of immigrants, refugees, and exiles from the "peripheries" to the metropolitan "centers" both enriches and threatens the parameters of the nation as well as older cultural identities. Yet definitions of locations as "centers" and "peripheries" only further mystify the divides between places and people. Centers are not impermeable, stable entities of purely defined characteristics that come simply to be contaminated or threatened by "others" from elsewhere. Rather, the large metropoles that draw waves of new populations are dynamic, shifting, complex locations that *exchange* goods, ideas, and culture with many other locations. In the context of transnational economies these exchanges cannot be characterized as utopian or neutral transactions. Yet the social model of powerful, unified centers and vulnerable, crisis-ridden peripheries obscures the vital and complicated nature of diverse local economies and cultures which produce and exchange materials, practices, and value on a global scale.

Euro-American modernist discourses of displacement mystify and homogenize the terms of these historically specific exchanges, travels, and circulations, masking the economic and social differences between kinds of displacement in a homogenized "cosmopolitanism" and generalizing nostalgia through a celebration of the condition of exile. Just as all forms of representation can only allude to materiality in partial and invested ways, the discourses of displacement that circulate in theory and criticism cannot serve as more than "signs" of cultural and political concerns. Thus the argument that "real" refugees and exiles are harmed or erased by the generalized appropriations of their experiences by cultural theorists of diaspora and exile seems to me to be not exactly to the point. Creating a moralizing opposition between "real" and figurative exiles (or between politics and aesthetics) simply bolsters rather than deconstructs the elite foundations of Euro-American modernisms. In pressing for a more historically accurate and geographically specific representation of displacement in modernity and postmodernity, I am calling for an examination of the power of representation in "high" culture in general, an examination that will reveal myriad ways in which the "unhoused" and the powerless are disenfranchised by social formations that include but are not limited to arts and letters. Since metaphor is a strong part of communication that we can never truly avoid, my questions become: How does the metaphor of exile *work* in particular kinds of cultural criticism, and to what (or whose) ends? And how does the critical articulation of diasporic subjectivity either support or destabilize the Euro-American discourse of exile? In addition, how can the distinctions between exile, expatriation, diaspora, and immigration be made meaningful in historically and culturally specific ways? Rather than glossing the terms, how can their temporal and spatial dimensions be understood as linked elements in colonial discourses of travel?

Euro-American poststructuralist and postmodern critical practices have been slow to acknowledge this transnational material context. The subject position of the critic (or the multiplicity of subject positions available to the critic) has not received significant attention, either dismissed as vulgar and essentialist "identity politics" or erased through the Eurocentric rhetoric of universality. Nor has the "travel" of theories and theorists been fully considered as part of the legacy of imperialism nor as part of the politics of cultural production in transnational modernities and postmodernities.[5] In the United States, for example, it is only recently, as feminist, ethnic, and queer studies have produced dynamic theories of "border" cultures and subjects, that such "identity politics" have engaged the terms of poststructuralist theories. The position of the theorist has been theorized in ways not entirely dissimilar to that of the author in Euro-American modernism; as cultural producers of written texts, the author and the critic are represented as singular, unique, and existentially estranged or alienated from a "home" or point of origin. The terms of that estrangement may have shifted from modernist expatriation and exile to postmodern cosmopolitan diasporas, but the emphasis on dislocation or displacement as an aesthetic or critical benefit remains.

Although diaspora and the cosmopolitan subject as migrant have become the more prevalent terms by which displacement and travel are discussed in Euro-American cultural studies, exile remains a crucial term. For example, in his recent book, *The Making of Exile Cultures,*

Hamid Naficy theorizes exile in a postmodern, transnational context of Iranian immigrant communities in Los Angeles as "a process of becoming, involving separation from home, a period of liminality and in-betweenness that can be temporary or permanent, and finally incorporation into the dominant host country."[6] What marks this experience as different from conventional immigration? Naficy argues that particular communities in North America cannot be understood only through the paradigms of class and ethnicity but must also be comprehended in terms of the nature of their migration and settlement. Examining the representational strategies and cultural production of Iranian community television and music videos produced for immigrant populations in the United States, Naficy marks as "exilic" the demonstration of "ambivalences, resistances, slippages, dissimulations, doubling, and even subversions of the cultural codes of *both* the home and host societies."[7] In this sense, Naficy's definition of exile acknowledges the "continuing problematic of multiple locations," arguing for theories of cultural production that can account for these shifting and simultaneous identities and affiliations.

A similar concern with multiple subject positions in the context of displacement can be found in Ella Shohat's articulation of Arab Jewish identities. Yet Shohat's discussion of exile deconstructs the paradigm, arguing that its conventions are not uniformly available to Arab Jews in either Israel or the United States. As Shohat points out, "the notion of 'in-gathering from exile' does not allow for a narrative of Jews feeling exiled even in the Promised Land."[8] Further, the paradigm of exile requires a coherent, recognized identity or point of origin. It is Shohat's contention that the erasure of Arab Jewish culture and identity in mainstream representations of Jewish existence in both Israeli and Euro-American contexts makes "exile" not yet attainable, as it were: "Stripped of our history, we have been forced by our no-exit situation to repress our collective nostalgia, at least within the public sphere. The pervasive notion of 'one people' reunited in their ancient homeland actively dis-authorizes any affectionate memory of life before Israel. We have never been allowed to mourn a trauma which the recent images of destruction of Iraq have only intensified and crystallized for some of us."[9] Shohat seeks to find a mode of articulation for a complex, nonbinary mode of identity, refusing " 'neat' national and ethnic divisions."[10] As Shohat points out: "My anxiety and pain during a scud attack on Israel, where most of my family lives, does not cancel out my fear and anguish for the victims of the bombardment of Iraq, where I also have relatives."[11]

Avoiding the "neat" divisions between nations and ethnic groups becomes a complicated task at this moment in history. An overgeneralized and utopian notion of transnational diasporic subject can only further erase the very distinctions and forms of recognition that Shohat, for example, is calling for. On the other hand, without theories of subjectivity that can account for the constructed paradoxes of nation and race, for example, only the "binarisms of war" await us. Thus, contemporary theories of exile must delineate the material conditions of displacement that generate subject positions. Here it becomes possible to differentiate between involuntary political refugees and voluntary expatriates, not in the service of a moralizing hierarchy that grants value to the figure in greatest terror or danger but in the struggle to grasp histories that almost always elude representation and to make links between diverse agents in transnational culture. Thus the alienation of writers or intellectuals from the abuses and injustices of their "home" location can generate an "unhousedness" or displacement that brings them in solidarity, if you will, to meet the involuntary exile on the terrain of textual and political affiliation. Such a solidarity or affiliation is political, however, and cannot simply be assumed through the articulation of aesthetic principles of literary exile or the deployment of generalized metaphors. It is, perhaps, one task of cultural criticism to participate in the formation of practices that will make these political links more visible and meaningful.

Heroic Exiles and Cosmopolitan Expatriates

I shall continue to dwell at the edge of the world, a land far removed from my own . . . Here it is I that am a barbarian, understood by nobody.
—Ovid [12]

Although one often links a person in exile to a faraway locality, the fact is I felt joined more to my writing than to any country with a specific territoriality.
—Nurrudin Farah [13]

In his study of two hundred years of English Canadian exile literature, Hallvard Dahlie notes that the "negative or punitive" aspects of exile, so frequently expressed in classical Western literature, increasingly disappear.[14] This lessening of the experience of exile as a drastic amputation from the social body of the nation or community coincides with the rise of the notion of expatriation, the *voluntary* displacement undertaken for any number of reasons without entailing legal or state-sponsored banishment. Dahlie's study shares with so many Euro-American literary studies of displaced modern authors a tendency to gloss this distinction by first drawing attention to it. In fact, most studies of literary displacement finesse the difference between exile and expatriation, creating a fund of metaphors of loss, distance, nostalgia, and anomie without historicizing the representation and practice of authorship.[15]

Yet overemphasizing the differences between exile and expatriation can often bring about an overgeneralized and moralizing evaluation of motives, intentions, and behaviors. A counterdiscourse to the modernist conflation of exile and expatriation arises in several contexts: Marxist or socialist critiques of the erasure of class relations from histories of literary production and aesthetics as well as analyses of decolonization that link displacement, authorship, and repression. This counterdiscourse often situates the "exile" as a heroic vanguard over and against the false consciousness and bourgeoisification of the voluntary expatriate.

Typical of the moralizing approach to distinctions between literary exiles and expatriates is an essay published in 1971 by Mary McCarthy. Noting that the term "exile" "easily lends itself to metaphorical inflation," McCarthy nonetheless pointedly insists that exile refers to a political condition of singular and irrevocable absence. Refugees, according to McCarthy, are a mass category and can be resettled. Expatriates come in for some scorn: "The expatriate is a hedonist. He is usually an artist or a person who thinks he is artistic. He has no politics or, if he has any, like the Brownings he has acquired them from the country he has adopted. The average expatriate thinks about his own country rarely and with great unwillingness. He feels he has escaped from it. The expatriate is a by-product of industrialism. At the same time, of course, he owes his presence abroad to the prosperity induced by the factories and manufactures he is fleeing from."[16] McCarthy expresses a suspicion of the cosmopolitan expatriate and all well-traveled, willful poseurs who have not *earned* their sobriquets. A not-so-subtle strain of puritanism runs through critiques of expatriates and cosmopolitans—if not literally forced out of their place of origin by formidable political opponents, the faux exiles are seen to be reaping the social and artistic benefits of displacement without *paying* for them, without undergoing the anxiety, fear, and uncertainty that "true" exiles must always experience.

One of the more recent critiques of rhetorical conflations of exile and expatriation and the evils of cosmopolitanism can be found in Aijaz Ahmad's *In Theory.* Throughout the text, Ahmad examines the erasure of class relations in contemporary critical and literary production and the bourgeoisification of Third World elites. In particular, he singles out Salman Rushdie and Edward Said for closer scrutiny and critique, charging both writers with a cosmopolitanism that undermines the socialist project that Ahmad himself endorses. Ahmad's controversial critique of Said has elicited a vociferous critical response and I won't rehearse that debate in detail here.[17] Nevertheless, Ahmad's queries into the metaphorical operation of terms of displacement in contemporary literary and critical production deserve careful consideration.

Ahmad makes one of the clearest and most spirited counterattacks on the generalized discourse of displacement prevalent in Euro-American modernist, poststructuralist, and cultural criticism milieus. In Ahmad's view, "exile, immigration and professional preference" have become "synonymous and, indeed, mutually indistinguishable."[18] The word "exile," he notes, has been deployed "first as a metaphor and then as a fully appropriated descriptive label for the existential condition of the immigrant as such." In this ideological process, exile becomes a "condition of the soul, unrelated to facts of material life."[19]

The question of just what material conditions produce which displaced or located subjects leads Ahmad to construct a fairly rigid definition of both exile and diaspora. Diasporic intellectuals who have emigrated and fostered an "opportunistic Third-Worldism" in Western universities, for example, may use words such as "exile" or "diaspora" in reference to themselves, but Ahmad wants to place them in a category constituted through "personal convenience."[20] *Exiles,* the real, material, true signifieds of this sign of displacement, are "people who are prevented, against their own commitment and desire, from living in the country of their birth by the authority of the

state—*any* state—or by fear of personal annihilation." Against "privilege" Ahmad poses "impossibility"; against "profession" he proposes
"pain."[21] This is a very stark taxonomy. And given the degree to
which universalizing metaphors can be seen to have appropriated the
experience of those who often cannot speak or write for themselves
due to the very kinds of epistemic violence the metaphors tend to in-
voke, the agents of that appropriation—critics and writers—may be
held accountable for the worst excesses of rhetorical conflation, inflation, and erasure.

Ahmad's sharpest rebukes are saved for those who, even inadver-
tently or "with the greatest degree of personal innocence," emigrate
to the metropolitan locations for professional gain. The privileging
of the "migrant intellectual" by figures such as Said, then, inscribes
personal resonances on the page of contemporary cultural criticism.
I will discuss Said's imbrication in this scene of cultural production
and reception later in the chapter. Suffice it to say here that Ahmad's
overall critique, although problematic at best, demands that we assess
the material conditions of literary and cultural criticism in the context of imperialism and capitalist expansion. In the face of Euro-
American modernist aestheticization of displacement, Ahmad's critique provides a useful reminder that class relations play as important
a role in cultural studies as race, ethnicity, gender, and sexuality. Un-
fortunately, his emphasis on class rests within classic Marxist methodologies and cannot make links with these other crucial categories of
critique.[22]

My primary discomfort with Ahmad's analysis lies in his binary
construction of true and false exiles, of true and false consciousness.
Most telling is Ahmad's reliance upon the hallmarks of the Western
liberal political tradition. Thus "choice," "intention," and "privacy"
are the criteria that Ahmad uses to bracket the critique of cosmopolitanism in relation to particular figures. In his discussion of subaltern
studies school intellectual Ranajit Guha, for example, Ahmad writes:
"With personal choice one has absolutely no wish to quarrel, and I
certainly neither know nor wish to judge the circumstances which lead
any individual to emigrate from one country to another; those are
strictly private matters."[23] When we are examining the construction
of culture, what functions do distinctions between private and public serve? And how do choice and intention operate in any way other

than the very workings of elite privileging that Ahmad is supposedly concerned with? It seems to me, then, that Ahmad has constructed such a rigid taxonomy that he is forced to bend it constantly for figures who either do not make a perfect fit on either side of the divide or for whom it is expedient or pleasant to make exceptions. And where would Ahmad himself fall in this mapping of a field of class war that turns on displacement terminology and intellectual practice?[24]

Examining the complicities between radical intellectuals in the West or in elite locations globally and their ostensible institutional enemies is a task of urgent necessity. As Rey Chow puts it, the positioning of guilt and lack against each other leads many so-called postcolonial intellectuals to "speak with power but identify with powerlessness."[25] Such a "circuit of productivity" draws its capital "from others' deprivation while refusing to acknowledge its own presence as endowed."[26] Surely this aspect of neocolonialism requires the closest critical attention and concern, even when it brings many of us uncomfortably close to our greatest guilt, fears, and lack. But Ahmad seems content to "guilt-trip." That is, *In Theory* points its textual finger at theorists, sending each to his or her side of the line drawn by the omniscient critic—this one goes to the gulag of class elitism while another joins the author in socialist solidarity. My question becomes: If Ahmad can see immigration as contradictory in critical and material practice, how can he seek to construct pure categories that are free of paradox and contradiction? In Ahmad's configuration, exile is an almost exalted form of travel, forged in pain, cleansed by a singular glory, and made sacred by its purity. It may never be confused with the contaminated indulgence that characterizes the cosmopolitan. In the face of such energy to establish a strict division, I would argue that we will find only further complications, contradictions, and blurrings of borders. If we can identify a desire for a strict division between exile and cosmopolitan diaspora, what material relations might produce that desire itself?

In worrying the exile/expatriation divide in this manner we can lose sight of a greater and more overarching binary configuration: the opposition between exile and immigration. That is, between the ostensible "real" and "false" exile there are degrees of return that may or may not be possible; political regimes may change, financial limits may be overcome, or some other move may become possible. But what separates the exile/expatriate from the immigrant in many contemporary discourses of displacement is the commonplace belief that immigrants *intend* to assimilate: they leave their homes without reluctance and they face a new situation with an eagerness to become as much a part of the nation or community as possible. In addition to this rather simplistic notion of intention to assimilate, I would argue that immigrants are associated with financial or material gain rather than aesthetic gain; in moving to improve their material circumstances, immigrants do not offer a romantic alternative to the exile, who may be seen to be displaced for spiritual, political, or aesthetic survival alone.

The modes of displacement that come to be attached to the figure of immigrant, therefore, are counter to those most valued by Euro-American modernism: rather than embodying the desire to return to a lost origin, the immigrant is represented as eager to reject that origin; instead of a spiritual or creative identity or profession, the immigrant is associated with less romantic forms of labor—even, simply, with purely material motives, ranging from physical survival to elite careerism. Neither political refugee nor exiled artist, the immigrant, in such a mystified and unified characterization, cannot participate in the terms of Euro-American modernism and cannot be recuperated or professionalized in terms of cultural production. In this sense, just as the tourist forms an antithesis to the exile in Euro-American modernism, so, too, does the immigrant. The fact that the material conditions of displacement for many people blur these distinctions or that many modern subjects may participate in any number of these versions of displacement over a lifetime—never embodying any one version singly or simplistically—requires material histories of cultural production that would emphasize emergent subject positions and critical and cultural practices that are more responsive to transnational conditions.

Just as histories of immigration help to deconstruct the Euro-American modernist mystique of exile, histories of decolonization also point to contradictions in these prevailing narratives of authorship and cultural production. For example, in his most recently published collection of essays, *Moving the Centre,* Ngugi wa Thiong'o describes his resistance to the category of exile in terms that destabilize the modernist link between displacement and authorship. Describing his surprise in the late '70s at finding himself anthologized in a British text on writers "in exile," Ngugi explores his deeply rooted resistance to the Kenyan government's efforts to drive him out of his country as well as his distaste for the cosmopolitan identity of "exile writer"; "I could not bring myself to use the word 'exile' in reference to myself." [27] Noting that other writers in the British anthology include Katherine Mansfield and V. S. Naipaul, Ngugi attempts to make the familiar division between "voluntary exile" (expatriation) and "forced exile" (a victim of state terror). Yet he finds that this distinction is difficult to manage when considering what some might call the "postcolonial" subject. The very institutional practices of high colonialism that sent Africans to Europe to further their education, for instance, created a culture of alienation that privileged travel and displacement. While physical exile has been "part and parcel of twentieth-century African literature," Ngugi argues, "the state of exile in the literary landscape reflects a larger state of alienation in the society as a whole . . . The people themselves have been in exile in relationship to their economic and political landscape." [28]

Ngugi has explored the ramifications of alienation and decolonization in both prose and fiction over the years. In *Decolonizing the Mind,* for example, he argued that in writing his novels in English, he worked in de facto exile. Both the genre and language prevented his work from being read and received by most of his compatriots. In *Moving the Centre,* Ngugi ends his essay on exile by asking whether or not there can be a "successful homecoming" for African literature. It is only through breaking out of linguistic "prison," Ngugi argues, that is, through a refusal of English and other colonial lingua francas, that such a homecoming can be achieved.

Valorizing or making central his "native" language, Ngugi disrupts imperialist hegemony through inversion of two terms of a binary opposition that reflects the material realities of colonial relations. In resisting the cosmopolitanism of "external" exile as well as protesting the silencing of "internal" exile, Ngugi's work destabilizes the repressive politics at work in a former colony, representing Kenyan cultural practices both linked to and separate from the metropolitan centers, internally fragmented in resistance to numerous levels of repressive state tactics on both local and global levels. Yet Ngugi's use of exile as a metaphor for the exploitation and oppression of colonialism in a supposedly postcolonial era remains rooted in a center-periphery model of global culture, constructing essentialist notions of "native origin" and "nation." Ngugi's cultural and critical practices reflect his particular historical formation. In the context of decolonization, Ngugi's rejection of cosmopolitanism is linked to a resistance to modernization and other colonial legacies. For a displaced writer such as Ngugi who privileges the local, the cosmopolitan metropole can only signify the pitfalls of globalization and hegemonic Western effects. If Ngugi has a "choice," however, between "writer in exile" and "writer at home," can his critique of cosmopolitanism work across the board for every instance of displacement? Ngugi's resistance to the Euro-American modernist construction of cosmopolitan authorship raises questions about figurative and literal territorial affiliations. His essay on exile reminds us that imperialism produces diverse subjects and, therefore, our considerations of discourses of displacement must take into account different political and geographic contexts.

Writing as an Exile: Edward Said's Critical Displacements

What does it mean, at the end of the twentieth century, to speak like Aimé Césaire of a "native land"? What processes rather than essences are involved in present experiences of cultural identity? What does it mean to write as a Palestinian? As an American? As a Papua New Guinean? As a European? From what discrete sets of cultural resources does any modern writer construct his or her discourse? To what world audience (and in what language) are these discourses most generally addressed? Must the intellectual at least, in a literate global situation, construct a native land by writing like Césaire the notebook of a return?
—James Clifford [29]

The critical discourse of the diasporic cosmopolitan intellectual draws upon both Euro-American modernist exile formulations and post-modern theories of location, most often dehistoricizing specific contexts through a celebration of migration and displacement. Edward Said's writing on exile is difficult to position within this matrix of modernism and postmodernism, global and local. It oscillates between criticial positions. At its most historically specific moments, when the discussion focuses on contemporary history, it converges with postmodernism, enacting a powerful critique of modernist aesthetics and politics. At other moments his concerns remain intimately linked with modernist traditions and cultures. These contradictory elements demonstrate not only the complex historical, cultural, and geographic points of identification of a figure such as Said but also the strong links between Euro-American modernism and its supposed aftermath—postmodernism. That Said is now as reknowned for his activism on Palestinian issues as he is for his literary criticism suggests that he is a multiply positioned critic; his reception is not homogeneous.[30] Thus, rather than place Said in one camp or another, literary or political, I would read his work as a particularly visible instance of the way both modernist and postmodernist tendencies privilege discourses of displacement. In this critic's work, both tendencies come into play, straining political and poetic agendas, illuminating the continuities between diverse Euro-American critical traditions.

Much of Said's writing has centered on the relationship between worldly events and aesthetic concerns. In particular, in a series of essays that span the last twenty years, he has vigorously questioned the condition of exile in both personal and historical terms. Increasingly, his writing on exile has explored the terrain of his own displacement, forming a powerful fusion of autobiography and criticism. As an engagement with the structuralist critique of the subject position of the author as well as with the poststructuralist critique of fields of power in Western institutions, Said's writing on exile poses a provocative methodological challenge to critical practice. The personal and the political are continually theorized in his recent work to forge an emerging practice that Said terms "post-colonial secular criticism."

In "Secular Criticism," the essay that introduces the collection *The World, the Text, and the Critic,* Said discusses the precise division of labor that constructs the field of literary criticism in the world today. Said's comments echo Lukacs's admonition in "Writer and Critic" that specialization leads to a cult of professional expertise. Following Lukacs, Said argues that a separate realm of literary expertise is specifically organized around a principle of noninterference. That is, literary critics enact their specialization by refraining from acting in worldly affairs, by remaining silent about history and politics, and by encouraging a belief in the division between art and action. A system results where "the cultural realm and its expertise are institutionally divorced from their real connections with power."[31]

Throughout the essays collected in *The World, the Text, and the*

Critic Said attempts to counter this version of aesthetics by arguing for the "worldliness of texts," tracing links between Lukacs, Benjamin, Adorno, and other humanist Marxist theorists. Given the oppositional nature of Marxist and poststructuralist positions on issues such as objective reality and representational practices, Said's negotiations of this complex, contradictory, and multiple critical legacy are necessarily synthetic and paradoxical. Said's emphasis on practice links his work to dialectical materialism even as his focus on the shifting terms of discourse in culture binds his work to the more overtly political practitioners of poststructuralism such as Foucault. In order to sort through both the theoretically valuable challenges and the negative effects in the practice of poststructuralist textuality, Said proposes a structure of cultural production based on relationships between locatable elements. Writing is produced by *someone* as opposed to no one, he argues, and at a particular time as opposed to no time. Without endorsing monumental essences or transhistorical myths of person or creation, Said argues for two complementary concepts of critical practice: affiliation and worldliness: "My position is that texts are worldly, to some degree they are events, and, even when they appear to deny it, they are nevertheless a part of the social world, human life, and of course the historical moments in which they are located and interpreted." [32]

The formulation of literary critical practice as a process of displacement and creative affiliation is illustrated in the introduction to *The World, the Text, and the Critic* by Said's discussion of Erich Auerbach. A European Jewish exile in Istanbul during World War II, Auerbach wrote *Mimesis,* his treatise on Western literary traditions, under conditions of scholarly hardship: inadequate libraries and resources, separation from colleagues, and so on. Said argues that it is precisely the isolation of this situation that infused Auerbach's work with its particular value and meaning. Separated from the "authentic" markers and materials of his home culture, Auerbach wrote to assuage his sense of loss. In the wake of poststructuralism, Said reads this activity as a willed act of cultural construction in the face of dissolution and displacement. It is cultural displacement that Auerbach forged into a principle of critical action and that Said puts to his own use in "Secular Criticism" and the essays that follow: "In other words, [*Mimesis*] owed its existence to the very fact of Oriental, non-Occidental exile and homelessness. And if this is so, then *Mimesis* itself is not, as it has so frequently been taken to be, only a massive reaffirmation of the Western cultural tradition, but also a work built upon a critically important alienation from it, a work whose conditions and circumstances of existence are not immediately derived from the culture it describes with such extraordinary insight and brilliance but built rather on an agonizing distance from it."[33]

The maxim at work here seems to be that one needs to be situated on the boundary that marks the division between home and away in order to produce a truly resistant as well as affirmative study—a powerful theory for a theorist who identifies himself as alienated and distanced as well as deeply tied to both Western and non-Western cultural elements. This boundary or border zone signifies the limits of culture in modernity. Said defines culture as "an environment, process, and hegemony in which individuals (in their private circumstances) and their works are embedded, as well as overseen at the top by a superstructure and at the base by a whole series of methodological attitudes."[34] Such a notion of culture implies not just passive belonging but a more active connotation of possession. The significance of culture as "possessing possession," Said writes, is its power to "authorize, to dominate, to legitimate, demote, interdict, and validate."[35] That is, culture works to make evaluative distinctions. Due to the fact that Western culture tends to erase all signs of this operation of construction and to naturalize concepts of belonging and identity, the best manner of recognizing the organizing principles or elements of a culture is to embrace displacement. Thus, exile becomes the situation par excellence for the cultural critic—distance and alienation enable profound insight: "On the one hand, the individual mind registers and is very much aware of the collective whole, context, or situation in which it finds itself. On the other hand, precisely because of this awareness—a worldly self-situating, a sensitive response to the dominant culture—that the individual consciousness is not naturally and easily a mere child of the culture, but a historical and social actor in it. And because of that perspective, which introduces circumstance and distinction where there had only been conformity and belonging, there is distance, or what we might call criticism."[36]

If distance and displacement operate at the heart of Said's theory of critical practice, then producing relationships across or in spite of distance is just as integral a part of the practice of imagining a world in which that criticism takes place. In order to theorize both distance and the constructive, critical bridging of distance, Said distinguishes between filiation and affiliation, locating filiation with the traditions of generation more closely associated with nineteenth-century culture and affiliation with the reworking of relationship in the aftermath of modernist estrangement. Affiliation is above all nonbiological, that is, nonessentialist. As a description of connection it is, then, deeply modern, produced out of alienated, reified relations of modern culture. Affiliation is compensatory, but it is also vitally generative of new systems, even a new authority. Thus there is a conservative process embedded in affiliation that authoritatively replicates the structure and function of filiation. Said relies on the "verbal echo" between the two words to underscore their relationship as transitional and overlapping, not oppositional. As an "expert," the critic may legitimate the more reactionary aspects of filiation through the institutional affiliations required by the activity of professional criticism. The critic may also work as a historian of affiliation, that is, of the social relations that construct the mystification of affiliation: "The second alternative is for the critic to recognize the difference between instinctual filiation and social affiliation, and to show how affiliation sometimes reproduces filiation, sometimes makes its own forms. Immediately, then, most of the political and social world becomes available for critical and secular scrutiny."[37]

Said turns the borders or boundaries of culture into that zone of willed homelessness that will rework filiation into affiliation in the sense of critical distance. Rather than reinforcing the aspects of culture that "require mere affirmation and orthodox compliancy from its members," secular, worldly criticism seeks to produce concrete, materially relevant connections.[38] As Lukacs wrote, writers and critics are caught up in the material conditions of modern culture, yet they generally refuse to examine those very conditions, constructing, instead, a separate citadel of art and culture. When Said argues that texts are always "enmeshed in circumstance, time, place, and society," he is extending Lukacs's critique into a politics of location, locating criticism firmly in the material world of conflicting views and troubled categories of social analysis.[39] Yet, as contemporary history demonstrates, "secularism" is not always the solution for nationalist troubles, and "worldliness" can operate in elitist forms as well.[40] Thus even Said's theory of exile as authorial and critical agency can reproduce Euro-American modernisms.

The Uses of Exile

Exile is the unhealable rift forced between a human being and a native place, between the self and its true home.

I am speaking of exile not as a privileged site for individual self-reflection but as an *alternative* to the mass institutions looming over much of modern life.
—Edward Said[41]

The tensions between worldliness and homelessness, between neutrality and affiliation, can be read through the lens of exile in Said's writing over more than a decade. In Said's texts, the term "exile" mediates the diverse and complex elements of identity and location, serving as a metaphor for a multilayered investigation of the modern condition. As in the two sentences cited above, the term has different uses in Said's work, signifying both cataclysmic loss and critical possibility. The relationship between exile as a metaphor of modernity and exile as a series of specific events and conditions in time and place is productively stressed in this body of work to tease out the meanings of this critical term. Exile, then, functions as a reading strategy, a definition of a historical condition, a precept, a political or cultural program, and a specific zone for the exploration of the relationship between nation, identity, and location. In Said's writing throughout the '80s, exile is a term that makes the study of literature and culture "worldly"; that is, it links politics and art through the practice of criticism. Yet the contradictory pull between modernism and postmodernism is always evident in these essays.

"Reflections on Exile," one of Said's most sharply focused essays on exile, relies upon many of the arguments for or against displacement that characterize the modernist attitude. Thus exile is a "norm" as well as a compensatory artistic standpoint. Exile is emblematic of human estrangement and longing as well as specifically inhuman and intolerable. In negotiating the binary oppositions of modernist representations of exile, Said draws upon the critical theory of radical displacement developed by Frankfurt School theorist Theodor Adorno in his memoir, *Minima Moralia*. Just as Auerbach's distanced literary work appears emblematic for Said, Adorno's exilic writing operates as a kind of road map toward secular critical practice.

First published in German in 1951, *Minima Moralia: Reflections from a Damaged Life* was written during World War II when Adorno emigrated to North America. Desperately unhappy and increasingly alienated, Adorno's meditations on displacement constitute a sort of *ur*text of Euro-American modernist angst. Exile's "mutilations," Adorno argued, include the expropriation of the writer's language, the estrangement from culture and place that "nourish knowledge," and an awareness that, on a certain level, the new world will remain "incomprehensible." Thus the "intellectual in emigration" must forge a new critical consciousness beyond or through melancholy in order to apprehend a form of objective reality—distance brings understanding. Much like Auerbach's, Adorno's response to forced displacement provides Said with a powerful theory of critical practice. "There is no remedy," Adorno wrote, "but steadfast diagnosis of oneself and others, the attempt, through awareness, if not to escape doom, at least to rob it of its dreadful violence, that of blindness." [42]

In addition to reinforcing his Hegelian belief in the objective value of displacement, Adorno's exile in North America underscored his view that the predicament of modern life lies in a tortured relationship to mass culture; that is, change or revolt against the past is inevitable, but something of substance is always irretrievably lost. For example, in the aphorism entitled "Refuge for the Homeless," Adorno writes: "Dwelling, in the proper sense, is now impossible." In this passage Adorno does not suggest that a return to the traditional notion of home is even fully desirable: "The traditional residences we grew up in have grown intolerable: each trait of comfort in them is paid for with a betrayal of knowledge, each vestige of shelter with the musty pact of family interests." His tone is grimly nostalgic: "The house is past." [43] Modernity has brought both bombs and technology to eliminate the middle-class, European comforts that Adorno once knew. He describes a culture that produces progress in order to destroy itself. In a wartime apocalyptic mood, Adorno declares modern private life and the terms of habitation to be insubstantial, effectively rootless. This response to displacement might be viewed as quintessentially modernist: it embraces distance and estrangement as require-ments for critical insights. Since "dwelling" is now impossible, the solution is to make a "home" in writing: "For a man who no longer has a homeland, writing becomes a place to live."[44]

Adorno neither sentimentalized nor idealized the vocation of writing as "home." Yet his identification of an artistic practice as "refuge for the homeless" intersects with modernist preoccupations with displacement and the creative act. It is not surprising, then, that in "Reflections on Exile," Said cites Adorno on the impossibility of dwelling and the possibilities of writing, building an argument for a critical practice based on perpetual displacement: "The exile knows that in a secular and contingent world, homes are always provisional. Borders and barriers, which enclose us within the safety of familiar territory, can also become prisons, and are often defended beyond rea-son or necessity. Exiles cross borders, break barriers of thought and experience."[45] The compelling force of writers such as Auerbach and Adorno lies in the use they make of their political fate—a practical, worldly philosophy of separation and distance that forges new affilia-tions between past and present, home and away, that are no longer based on Western organic categories of religion and family ties. That an artistic or professional vocation provides the safety net that re-places older bourgeois filiations is not problematized in this instance by Said. The redemptive power of writing (understood as specialized labor) is assumed without investigating the conditions of production that often govern such a craft. The absence of women writers from the discussion of exile as redemptive authorial practice and the crucial issue of class in both exile and literary/artistic communities suggest that the question of writing a "home" may be even more complex than Adorno's and Auerbach's exilic paradigms allow.

Though Said uses exile to construct a worldly, or cosmopolitan, set of linked affiliations that can destabilize nationalist or religious identities, his primary construct is still linked to modernist aesthetic principles. This contradiction can be clearly read in the tension be-tween the figure of the solitary exile and the multiple subjects that are signified by the term "refugees." In "Reflections on Exile," Said draws upon images of refugees for inspiration, linking the solitary exile to a mass, global experience of displacement. The distinction between earlier exiles and those of today, Said argues, lies in the scale of the phenomenon. This is, he writes, "the age of the refugee, the displaced person, mass immigration."[46] Yet throughout the essay Said often abandons his reference to a global phenomenon and returns to a mystified figure—the solitary exile. Rather than elucidating the modes of representation that arise in an age of refugees, immigrants, and the homeless, Said returns to a figure more closely associated with classical Western traditions as well as modernist myths of authorship.

The rhetorical slippage between refugees and exiles is not accidental. Just as exiles and expatriates are often conflated in modernism, here refugees and exiles perform a similar operation. The plight of historically constituted refugees might be said to *authorize* Said's discourse on exile (just as exile authorizes the activities of expatriation in other instances), yet the relationship between the exile (or "border intellectual") and the ever-expanding numbers of displaced persons remains uneasy and unresolved. Salman Rushdie has described the trajectory of the concept of exile in Said's work as moving between the privileged, literary reflections of the middle class and the complicated, unexpressed experience of large-scale displacement: "In the West everyone has come to think of exile as a primarily literary and bourgeois state. Exiles appear to have chosen a middle-class situation in which great thoughts can be thought. In the case of the Palestinians, however, exile is a mass phenomenon: it is the mass that is exiled and not just the bourgeoisie."[47]

"Reflections on Exile" performs several contradictory functions in light of this tension between singular and mass experience, oscillating between, conflating, and even transforming the oppositional terms. Said clearly understands the stereotypes at work in any differentiation between refugee and exile: "Refugees . . . are a creation of the twentieth-century state. The word 'refugee' has become a political one, suggesting large herds of innocent and bewildered people requiring urgent international assistance, whereas 'exile' carries with it, I think, a touch of solitude and spirituality."[48] In this representation, the refugee is a faceless political construct outside the sphere of literature and aesthetics. The exile, on the other hand, is a romantic figure that can be readily identified and positioned in an aestheticized world of creativity and loss. Refugees, Said implies, are undocumentable. They are, in fact, often without documents, or they must fabricate them. Their existence is often statistically unverifiable or marginal.

Disenfranchised, they are "people suddenly lost, without a tellable history."[49] Criticism, Said seems to suggest, cannot follow this faint trail. Once moved, a mass of people becomes ghostlike, disappearing off the map of literature and culture: "To reflect on exiled Muslims from India, or Haitians in America, or Bikinians in Oceania, or Palestinians throughout the Arab world means that you must leave the modest refuge provided by subjectivity and resort instead to the abstractions of mass politics. Negotiations, wars of national liberation, people bundled out of their homes and prodded, bussed, or walked to enclaves in other regions: what do these experiences add up to? Are they not manifestly and almost by design irrecoverable?"[50]

To follow Said at this moment is to claim that a poetics of "mass politics" is impossible. Yet his own work within the same essay and in other texts argues that these experiences may participate in a poetics of displacement. Most of Said's recent work, in fact, argues that there are cultural practices that do reflect these material relations, practices that are at once related to modernism as well as distinctly separate from it.

Once the category of exile is historicized, it is impossible to traffic in stereotypes and mystified constructions. "Exile," Said writes, "is irremediably secular and unbearably historical; . . . it is produced by human beings for other human beings."[51] Thus Said's own commitment to secular criticism and the worldliness of texts propels him beyond his attachment to modernist configurations of authorship and subjectivity. His task becomes more complex, more inventive, and more critically risky. The representation of mass displacement as irrecoverable and beyond cultural expression reduces the refugee to ultimate victim, pinned in lumpen opposition to the recoverable memoirs and fictions of the exiled, bourgeois modernist. Historicizing refugee experience might bring a previously invisible category back from the wilderness of the margins of criticism and literature, perhaps through the inclusive mantle of the term "diaspora."

By the mid-'80s Said appears torn between the multiply located identities that a term such as "diaspora" makes possible and the meaningful structure of sentiments that attach themselves to his preferred term, "exile." In a conversation with Salman Rushdie in 1986, Said describes Palestinian existence as a series of local instances linked less to a specific geography than to people's memories, distinct traditions, and the bonds between immigrant communities in other countries. "The idea that there is a redemptive homeland," Said states, "doesn't answer to my view of things."⁵² This is a radical statement to make in the face of Palestinian nationalist efforts to resecure *land* in equally nationalist Zionist Israel. Said's predicament is that his position is more cosmopolitan than local, more closely connected to the perennial dispersions that comprise postmodern definitions of diaspora than to the modernist model of exile and return. Said embodies a series of contradictory positions or views, whose permutations we can read as a map of Euro-American criticism in the midst of profound changes, linking traditions and practices. Thus a cosmopolitan intellectual, schooled in the same elite Euro-American institutions as his most vehement critics, producing theoretical interventions that draw attacks from the political Right as well as the Left, writes criticism that can only reflect the tensions and complexities of this social history. While Said's writing can be said to articulate a cosmopolitan sensibility, among other things, the reception of this designation is shifting rapidly as Euro-American cultural criticism comes to grips with material histories of displacement and a pressing interest in dismantling Eurocentric discourses. A growing body of critical writing on cosmopolitan diasporas, spurred by the emergence of "postcolonial" literary and cultural studies, continues to reproduce the vexed links between modernist and postmodernist discourses of displacement.

Cosmopolitan Subjects

And while it would be the rankest Panglossian dishonesty to say that the bravura performances of the intellectual exile and the miseries of the displaced person or refugee are the same, it is possible, I think, to regard the intellectual as first distilling then articulating the predicaments that disfigure modernity—mass deportation, imprisonment, population transfer, collective dispossession, and forced immigrations.
—Edward Said⁵³

Against the arguments for a literal notion of exile as the emblematic metaphor for the displaced intellectual, a notion of cosmopolitan or diasporic subject has emerged in Euro-American criticism over the last decade. For example, Hamid Naficy describes such figures as having "more in common with their exilic counterparts at home and in the West than they do with their fellow citizens—either at home or in the host country."[54] This displaced intellectual constitutes a "universal category," "cutting across geographical cultural boundaries."[55] Beyond the older socialist paradigm of the "international," the cosmopolitan intellectual as migrant figure signals for many either the liberatory or negative effects of an increasingly transnational world.

Tim Brennan argues that this "new" cosmopolitan figure signals a "world supposedly exempt from national belonging," thereby creating "spokespersons for a kind of perennial immigration, valorized by a rhetoric of wandering."[56] This vanguard of postmodern transnationalism could be seen to constitute the contemporary "stars" of world literature; Brennan's study refers to such "celebrity" authors as Salman Rushdie, Mario Vargas Llosa, Bharati Mukherjee, Derek Walcott, and Isabel Allende. Brennan argues that writers who can parlay what appears to be an "authentic native attachment to a specific Third World locale" into a career in letters in the First World are the high-profile avatars of a massive wave of immigration that has reshaped and destabilized the national identities of Western countries. The production and reception of contemporary "world" or "postcolonial" literature, therefore, must be read through the lens of "economic and cultural inequalities, wholesale labor recruitments and legal arrangements set up on the basis of the former Empires."[57] In this manner, the emergence of the cosmopolitan subject as celebrity author or critic is materially linked to the weakening of nation-states in the advent of transnational capital configurations even as such shifts in cultural and national identity pose the "national question more strongly than ever," that is, "within the Western countries to which the new 'immigrants' now only half belong—countries which are being forced to account for the new composition of their collective make-up."[58]

Thus, if the cosmopolitan writers appear to signal the dissolution of the nation-state in favor of a new pluralism, it is crucial to keep in mind that this "pluralism" is warmly welcomed in metropolitan cultural capitals that may be less interested in recognizing more overtly revolutionary nationalist struggles in former colonial locations. As Brennan points out, a Western literary establishment selects as "interpreters" of geopolitical change those writers who are as similar and sympathetic to Western values and concerns as they are different. That is, reviewers and critics construct "authentic public voices of the Third World" by celebrating cosmopolitan authors who can appear exotic even when they have similar "tastes, training, repertoire of anecdotes, current habitation"[59] as those very same reviewers and critics. In other words, the writing of the cosmopolitan celebrity author can be appropriated for hegemonic uses to manage diversity in the context of globalization mainly on the basis of social and economic class affiliations.

Yet it is important not to overgeneralize a complicated scene of literary and cultural production. For example, unlike overtly conservative cosmopolitan writers, the authors whom Brennan singles out also produce texts that can be read in subversive or progressive ways: "But for all their differences, they seem to share a harsh questioning of radical decolonisation theory; a dismissive or parodic attitude towards the project of national culture; a manipulation of imperial imagery and local legend as a means of politicizing 'current events' and a declaration of cultural 'hybridity'—a hybridity claimed to offer certain advantages in negotiating the collisions of language, race, and art in a world of disparate peoples comprising a single, if not exactly unified, world."[60]

While I am less convinced of the benefits of generalized "hybridity," Brennan points out just how complex and mediated literary production can be. Rather than accuse the "cosmopolitans" of a betrayal of nation, Brennan first establishes the social context of immigration and transnational technologies; that is, the world is no longer strictly organized by either rational markets or nation-states. If the "new" cosmopolitan literature accommodates liberal as well as radical interests and if it traffics in the gestures of progressive multiculturalism while enacting cultural appropriations, then this is not so much the fault of individual writers as it is a map of the social relations of cultural production and reception. Here is where our critical practices must focus—not on the canonical virtues of individual texts, not on the aesthetic properties of seemingly "found" objects, but on the dissemination through publishing, telecommunications, and entertainment industries of products whose conditions of production can be analyzed and made more meaningful.

What is at stake in ignoring these material and social relations? As Rob Nixon has argued in relation to Euro-American critical reception of V. S. Naipaul, the "confusion of dislocation with detachment" and the dehistoricizing of the writer's connections with diverse national and political identities give a writer such as Naipaul a "rhetorical advantage" (and, I would add, a professional and financial advantage, as well). Nixon points out that "despite the evidence of his primary affiliations to metropolitan culture on the London–New York axis," Naipaul constructs himself as an eternal migrant.[61] As I have argued, Euro-American modernist literary conventions have encouraged such a stance. Yet Nixon contrasts Naipaul's aloofness and seemingly ontological rootlessness to other Caribbean writers such as Derek Walcott, George Lamming, C. L. R. James, and Edward Braithwaite, who have also experienced displacement and complicated issues of cultural and national identity. Unlike these other writers who have maintained powerful connections to immigrant histories and cultural production, Naipaul has identified with the universalizing gestures of mainstream Euro-American literary establishments — in effect, profiting from the very cultures he refuses to affiliate himself with. As Nixon writes: "The irony is not to be missed: Naipaul, secure, esteemed, and integrated into the high culture of metropolitan England, asserting his homelessness, while considerable numbers of genuinely disowned people battle to be acknowledged as legitimate members of the society he is at liberty to reject rhetorically although he depends upon it in every way."[62]

Naipaul fits less conveniently into the complex positioning that Brennan mapped out for his set of cosmopolitan celebrity authors. Is there any difference between Rushdie and Naipaul? Some would argue that Naipaul's explicitly conservative politics sever him from the diasporic predicaments explored in a more admittedly progressive writer such as Rushdie. A. Sivanandan charges Naipaul with "selling out," describing him as profoundly centered in English culture and utterly co-opted by the former colonizers: "For the moment 'they' accept you, you are finished, completed; the moment they adopt you, you have sold out, you have become the object of their history, you have no evidence apart from them. Even to lay claim to their language and render it more exquisite than they is an act of self-betrayal — because they re-claim you in their language."[63]

As we have seen in Ngugi's critical practice, among others, opting for purism in language effects is one way to counter the hegemonic impact of imperialist modernization and global homogenizing. But such a construction of national or cultural separatism cannot accurately account for the political, social, and cultural formation and ongoing experiences of ever greater numbers of people. In a cultural struggle for political survival, a figure such as Naipaul, so powerfully ensconced in the Euro-American world of letters, can serve, then, as the negative nth degree of the cosmopolitanism that Ahmad, Ngugi, and Sivanandan so vehemently warn us against and that Brennan and Nixon contextualize in more measured but equally skeptical tones. If the cosmopolitan in this negative sense is not only privileged but hypocritical—gaining from other people's difficulties—then this term can serve as a more global and current substitute for "bourgeoisie," for the emergent power brokers who know and see nothing but their own self-interest yet legitimate and rationalize their actions by recourse to the rhetoric of humanism. If the cosmopolitan subject is a "'citizen of the world' by virtue of independent means, high tech tastes, and globe-trotting mobility,"[64] then the cosmopolitan intellectual or writer is especially culpable, proclaiming liberation politics from that safety zone of privilege, traveling to accrue and *control* knowledge in the name of multiculturalism.

In Bruce Robbins's argument for a progressive critical practice of cosmopolitanism, he points out that cosmopolitanism does not exist in a purely negative sense except in our textual articulations of identity politics. He suggests that the positive aspects of cosmopolitanism reflect the transnational conditions of globalization just as much as the negative aspects do. That is, rather than pose absolute homelessness against absolute locatedness, or absolute antinationalism against absolute nationalism, Robbins argues for a "density of overlapping allegiances rather than the abstract emptiness of non-allegiance."[65] Borrowing the term "discrepant cosmopolitanisms" from James Clifford's work, Robbins critiques the overvaluation of the local in contemporary cultural criticism, particularly when such localization opposes any and all generalization or theorization: "The anti-cosmopolitan jargon of the authentically particular and the authentically local provides no escape from or political alternative to the realm of the professional. It simply conceals the exemplification, representation, and generalization in which any intellectual work, professional or not, is inescapably involved, its own included."[66] In arguing for cosmopolitanism of a certain sort, Robbins is not arguing that anyone can ever be a cosmopolitan in "the full sense of belonging everywhere."[67] Such a will to power, the belief that the entire world is equally available to be occupied or represented or identified by any subject, is just another manifestation of imperialism. When globalization enacts these imperialist cosmopolitanisms we would do well to resist them. Robbins is searching for something else, another critical tool to articulate a critique of the moralizing qualities of identity politics without doing away with politics or with any complex notion of identities. Reading Robbins's call for a viable practice of cosmopolitanism via professionalism alongside Ahmad's rejection of cosmopolitanism suggests that, between the two, other critical practices remain to be elucidated.

From Travel to Diaspora: James Clifford's Critical Peregrinations

We are all Caribbeans now in our urban archipelagos . . . Perhaps there's no return for anyone to a native land—only field notes for its reinvention.
—James Clifford[68]

The cultural criticism of James Clifford investigates the possibilities and limits of cosmopolitan modernities. Throughout the early to mid-'80s, Clifford explored what he termed a "Caribbean" world, "hybrid and heteroglot."[69] Using poetics as a template of social formations, Clifford was clearly drawn to writers who strained and reworked language—Aimé Césaire, Michel Leiris, and Victor Segalen, for example —writers whose vexed relationship to French cultural traditions and the colonial legacy could be read through their textual experimentations. While Clifford is, perhaps, better known as a historian of anthropology who has destabilized the discipline by strenuously attending to the social construction of written narratives in the field, his engagement with literary modernism is a linked but less discussed aspect of his oeuvre. In emphasizing the *writing* of culture, Clifford has theorized the connections between Euro-American literary modernism and the rise of particular schools of ethnography, mapping fields of social texts and sites of cultural production. The strong concern with poetics and linguistic inventiveness in Clifford's work operates in uneasy but productive tension with articulations of postmodern concerns and critiques of modernist versions of colonial discourses. In this sense Clifford's project, not unlike Said's, bridges structuralism and poststructuralism, modernism and postmodernism, and poetics and politics.

As a theorist of modern travel, Clifford disrupts the conventional disciplinary organization of study in the human sciences, bringing into practice the self-reflexive study of the history of the disciplines themselves. In this sense, as Clifford historicized the "writing" of culture through the development of anthropology during the modern period, a simultaneous history of cultural articulations of Euro-American colonization emerged as well. Throughout the late '70s and '80s, Clifford's essays probed the intertwined legacy of institutional disciplinization, economic practices dominated by Euro-American interests, and the cultural production of written texts. Collected in 1988 in *The Predicament of Culture,* this body of writing problematized ethnographic textual strategies and modes of power, drawing upon poststructuralist critiques of authorial intention and narrative coherence. In these essays the influence of both Roland Barthes and Michel Foucault in particular can be traced through attention to the poetics of language as well as the politics of power relations. As a transliteration of such French poststructuralist approaches to the field of anthropology, Clifford's essays enact a kind of traveling theory or, to stretch the metaphor even further, a form of disciplinary expatriation.

For example, in an essay on Aimé Césaire's intellectual formation, Clifford links the poet's memories of colonized Martinique and metropolitan Paris to the poetic possibilities of imagined communities. Reading Césaire's neologisms as inventive challenges to colonial strictures, Clifford asks: "How does one grasp, translate a language that is blatantly making itself up?" In tracing Césaire's "hybrid" and "heteroglot" Caribbean world, Clifford enacts a similar critical practice. Césaire's poems "make demands," so Clifford constructs critical imperatives: interdisciplinary readings, interpretive twists and turns. Playing against the romance of fixed or native origins, Clifford observes that Césaire's neologisms open up significance: "Césaire does not restore the 'meanings' of language, culture, and identity; he gives them a turn."[70]

In making Césaire an exemplary forerunner of postmodern hybridity, Clifford relies upon linguistic inventiveness—a modernist preoccupation. It is Césaire's language—its "radical indeterminacy" and resistance to easy translation—that constitutes a "Caribbean" practice of pastiche: "Césaire still sends readers to dictionaries in several tongues, to encyclopedias, to botanical reference works, histories, atlases. He is attached to the obscure, accurate term and to the new world. He makes readers confront the limits of their language, or of any single language. He forces them to *construct* readings from a debris of historical and future possibilities."[71]

In a similar vein, discussing Leiris and Segalen as well as Césaire, Clifford stressed the heteroglossia of French colonial discourses and celebrated the dynamism of a "poetics of displacement." In emphasizing the poetics of colonial discourses, Clifford linked the texts of ethnographers such as Griaule, Conrad, and Malinowski to diverse kinds of writing, producing a theory of textuality *in* as well as *of* imperialism. For Clifford's work in this period, creole contexts provide an ideal example of colonial and postcolonial hybridity. In the diverse tongues, neologisms, and mixed influences of "creolité," Clifford found a model of the poetics that characterizes the potential of a postmodern critical practice.

Throughout contemporary Euro-American criticism from the late '70s to the present, a universalized concept of creolization or hybridity has come to reflect a postmodern turn in cultural criticism. Both critiques and celebrations of such a turn have produced significant interpretations of Clifford's work, contributing to an expansion of the field of cultural studies as well as reactions against it.[72] Clifford's essays from the late '80s and early '90s can be read, in part, as a response to these interpretations. They constitute, therefore, both a critique of liberal relativism in the Euro-American academy as well as a theorization of the cultures of travel in modernity.

For example, in an essay published in 1989 in the journal *Inscriptions*, "Notes on Theory and Travel," Clifford offers a new series of questions and comments on the relationship between global and local cultures:

> Theory is no longer naturally "at home" in the West—a powerful place of Knowledge, History, or Science, a place to collect, sift, translate, and generalize. Or, more cautiously, this privileged place is now increasingly contested, cut across, by other locations, claims, trajectories of knowledge articulating racial,

gender, and cultural differences. But how is theory appropriated and resisted, located and displaced? How do theories travel among the unequal spaces of postcolonial confusion and contestation? What are their predicaments? How does theory travel and how do theorists travel? Complex, unresolved questions.[73]

Drawing upon and radically reconfiguring Said's notion of "traveling theory," Clifford proposes a "crucial research agenda," asking: "How do different populations, classes and genders travel? What kinds of knowledges, stories, and theories do they produce?"[74] The figures that most concern Clifford remain the male intellectuals who best combine a modernist, writerly sensibility with a comparative eye toward geopolitics and world history: Malinowski, Said, Leiris, and, most recently, Paul Gilroy. In mapping "discrepant cosmopolitanisms" through these writers, Clifford focuses on reception as well as production. Such writers, he argues, "move theories in and out of discrepant contexts, addressing different audiences": "Theirs is not a condition of exile, of critical 'distance,' but rather a place of *betweenness,* a hybridity composed of distinct, historically-connected postcolonial spaces . . . Theory is always written from some 'where,' and that 'where' is less a place than *itineraries:* different, concrete histories of dwelling, immigration, exile, migration."[75]

In this essay, Clifford is much less concerned with the poetics of displacement per se and much more interested in the politics of theory as a historical relationship between cultural production and reception. The hybridity Clifford investigates is less generalized and stresses "historically-connected" sites that are not essentialized. In marking the necessity of analyzing histories of "dwelling," Clifford is also moving away from the aestheticized tendencies of poststructuralist nomadologies and theories of displacement.

The same year brought the publication of a closely related essay, "Traveling Cultures," in the widely disseminated Routledge anthology, *Cultural Studies.* In "Traveling Cultures," Clifford has exchanged the more universalizing "we" of global cosmopolitans for more particularized statements: "I'm not recommending that we make the margin a new center (e.g. we are all travelers) but rather that specific dynamics of dwelling/traveling be comparatively analyzed."[76] This statement marks a shift from "we are all Caribbeans now" to a critical practice that Clifford refers to as "comparative, intercultural studies." Yet "Traveling Cultures" remains attached to travel as a kind of *un*metaphor even though the term cannot deconstruct fully the burden of a Euro-American historical context. That is, "travel," as it is used in Euro-American criticism, cannot escape the historical legacies of capitalist development and accumulation, of imperialist expansion, and of inequities of numerous kinds. bell hooks has argued that "travel," as she has read the term in Clifford's work, is overdetermined, produced from a "center" of Western social and political power. She writes that while she appreciates his efforts to make the term more "inclusive," "Travel is not a word that can be easily evoked to talk about the Middle Passage, the Trail of Tears, the landing of Chinese immigrants, the forced relocation of Japanese-Americans, or the plight of the homeless."[77]

In Arnold Krupat's sympathetic but rigorous critique of Clifford's terms of travel, the Western nature of travel is destabilized through a comparison to Native American histories of placement and movement. Like hooks, Krupat reads Clifford's main body of work from the '80s as endorsing "oscillation" or "free play." Noting that Clifford's "strongest leanings" are "oriented toward narrating cultural change in inventive, emergent, and politically progressive modes," Krupat argues nevertheless that Clifford's language can convey a "decided nostalgia," not for "cultural purity" but for "that fuller empowerment, that greater 'ethnographic authority,' of an earlier generation."[78] Krupat is interested in such ironic tensions in Clifford's work in order to demonstrate the challenges in clearing out hegemonic practices in cultural criticism in favor of what he terms "ethnocriticism." Such a practice concerns "critical movement" that cannot simply be termed either "travel" or "placement": "Criticism may be considered the product of restlessness; centered people don't produce it in forms recognizable to the West. Thus ethnocriticism cannot strictly be based on the rootedness and sacralized sense of place that the indigenous people of this continent had and continue to have. Its decentered center is indeed the 'West,' but its movement is not in the interest of going places; rather it is a tentative feeling-around to encounters with Others who—for whatever reasons, less securely centered than some of their contemporaries or their ancestors—are also feeling their way around."[79] Both hooks and Krupat engage Clifford's work in an effort to expand the theorization of displacement in historical and cultural specificity. While their primarily U.S.-based examples do not address fully the uneven nature of the study of imperialism in ethnic studies, their critiques point toward imaginative and useful reworkings of the terms of displacement. That this process is a dialogue that engages Clifford in turn can be seen in key shifts in his recent work.

In "Traveling Cultures," for example, Clifford acknowledges that his theories of cosmopolitan hybridity have not sufficiently addressed class differences, gender issues, and geopolitics. Using the image of the hotel as a privileged site for the productive tension between dwelling and displacement, Clifford deconstructs that vantage point, making it particular and historically grounded rather than universal and abstract: "As I abandon the bourgeois hotel setting for travel encounters, sites of intercultural knowledge, I struggle, never quite successfully, to free the related term 'travel' from a history of European, literary, male bourgeois, scientific, heroic, recreational, meanings and practices."[80] Yet the metaphor of the "bourgeois hotel" *can* engender critical examinations of the power relations in cultural production and reception. If the "hotel" can represent the site of a diverse set of particular, historical subjects, perhaps it should not be so quickly abandoned as an analytical tool. That is, if Euro-American cultural critics acknowledge that such images and institutions have multiple meanings that operate within and through diverse traditions and histories, is the "hotel" to be left behind in search of other travel accommodations, or does it become, itself, a site of historical archaeology? One way to "travel" into sites of "intercultural knowledge" is to take a closer look at the social construction of the "hotel." But the notion of "travel" as an organizing principle for the research may come to be less and less meaningful as this kind of inquiry proceeds.

In examining critiques of "travel," I am not suggesting that Clifford's theorizations are naive or unaware of ongoing debates. Clifford's interdisciplinary investigations have opened a new field for discussion, a dialogue that links a wide variety of scholars. And while hooks has made a valuable intervention in colonial and postcolonial discourse studies in claiming that "holding on to the concept of 'travel' as we know it is a way to hold on to imperialism,"[81] I do not read Clifford's work as simply reproducing the epistemic violence of the past. In his writing from the late '80s, Clifford makes a case for "travel" rather than "displacement" in order to *avoid* ahistorical glosses and critical abstraction: "I hang onto 'travel' as a term of cultural comparison, precisely because of its historical taintedness, its associations with gendered, racial bodies, class privilege, specific means of conveyance, beaten paths, agents, frontiers, documents, and the like. I prefer it to the more apparently neutral, and 'theoretical,' terms such as 'displacement,' which can make the drawing of equivalences across historical experiences too easy."[82]

Clifford's argument for an affirmative deconstruction of "travel" in its historical contexts is persuasive. Yet, in the rigorous straining of a term under deconstruction, marginalized and previously unconsidered terms and histories become more primary. Thus migration, immigration, homelessness, and other more collective experiences of displacement in modernity become more important elements in Clifford's work at the moment he is making the strongest argument for the term "travel." Increasingly, the terms of "dwelling" concern Clifford, mitigating against the romanticized nomadology of much Euro-American postmodern poststructuralism during the same period. In moving toward more collective experiences and in theorizing the histories of dwelling as well as displacement, Clifford cannot be said to be reproducing a fascinated gaze on imperialism and its discontents. Rather, Clifford's work in this period emphasizes the social construction of identities and communities in resistance to the historical effects of Euro-American imperialism. And, for Clifford as for many other critics, the question becomes how to use terms in the full knowledge of their historically laden construction in transformative and admittedly partial ways.

This very problematic informs Clifford's recent essay, "Diasporas." Here Clifford's engagement with the question of cosmopolitanism, traveling theories, and cultures of displacement finds its most extended articulation vis-à-vis a more contemporary postmodern, transnational context. Clifford describes "diaspora" as a "traveling term" in "changing global conditions," in order to examine what is at stake, "politically and intellectually," in contemporary articulations of diaspora: "How do diaspora discourses represent experiences of displacement, of constructing homes away from home? What experiences do they reject, replace, or marginalize? How do these discourses attain comparative scope while remaining rooted/routed in specific, discrepant histories?"[83] Focusing on two distinct, paradigmatic instances of diaspora, black British cultures and articulations of anti-Zionist Judaism, Clifford argues that these examples demonstrate "non-exclusive practices of community, politics, and cultural difference."[84]

In "Diasporas," Clifford works to open a critical space for identity and community formations that negotiate the historically produced tension between movement and dwelling. Thus the "old localizing strategies" (bounded communities, organic cultures, region, nation, race, etc.) can no longer account for transnational circuits of culture, populations, and capital. Clifford is interested in a specific if widespread phenomenon of contemporary life: What are the "diasporic dimensions" that create links between people in diverse locations, constituting identities that do not reproduce nationalisms, for example, or that bridge and deconstruct the essentialist constructions of modernity?

Here Clifford proposes resistance culture along the lines of Birmingham School theorization of subaltern communities in relationship to hegemonic capitalism.[85] The Birmingham School, the group of sociologists and other academics and activists associated with the Centre for Contemporary Cultural Studies, has mapped cultures of resistance through disparate sites of cultural production, including the diasporic communities of color in Great Britain. Clifford draws upon Paul Gilroy's *The Black Atlantic* in order to illustrate a powerful theorization of transnational cultural effects upon the formation of contemporary identity. Gilroy's notion of the black Atlantic posits a vibrant set of diasporic experiences that draw upon the material conditions engendered by technologies of transport, divisions of labor, and cross-cultural effects of moving back and forth and around the Atlantic Ocean. In the process of mapping this transnational and transethnic terrain, Gilroy dislodges essentialist identities in favor of more hybrid ones.[86] As Clifford describes this emergent critical practice: "Identifications not identities, acts of relationship rather than pre-given forms: this 'tradition' is a network of partially-connected histories, a persistently displaced and reinvented time/space of crossings."[87]

In a similar vein, Clifford reads the theory of anti-Zionist Jewish identity proposed by Daniel and Jonathan Boyarin in their essay "Diaspora: Generation and the Ground of Jewish Identity" as profoundly destabilizing of nationalist discourses. In their efforts to articulate "group identity" without recourse to either essentialized genealogical or geographic origins, the Boyarins propose a "flexible and nonhermetic critical Jewish identity."[88] Uncoupling Judaism from the "fascism of state ethnicity" here requires historically specific inquiries into the difference between diasporic and rooted practices. Diaspora, the Boyarins claim, encourages "mixing," cultural creativity, and a theory and practice of identity that would "simultaneously respect the irreducibility and the positive value of cultural differences, address the harmfulness, not of abolishing frontiers, but of a dissolution of uniqueness, and encourage the mutual fructification of different lifestyles and traditions."[89] While some aspects of the Boyarins' essay resonate with poststructuralist celebrations of nomadology, Clifford reads this piece empathetically, linking this tracing of a rabbinical Jewish anti-Zionism to the theory emanating from black British cultural studies.[90] Such formulations of group identity seem to be resistant to the machine of the nation-state, and they create complex connections between diverse cultures as well as multiply sited subjectivities. Thus, writes Clifford, the Boyarins' "critique of teleologies of return to a literal Jewish nation in Palestine parallels Gilroy's rejection of Afrocentered diaspora projections." Both critical instances provide Clifford with examples of practices of dwelling as "positive transnationalism."[91]

The transnational aspects of diasporas signal both positive and negative elements of migration: the destabilization of nationalisms, the production of dynamic border zones, and reconfigurations of identities as well as the hegemonic aspects of globalization and transnational corporate exploitation.[92] As Khachig Tölölyan writes, transnational communities are "sometimes the paradigmatic Other of the nation-state and at other times its ally."[93] Similarly, diasporas can function through and against global corporate sponsorship. Roger Rouse points to "increasingly polarized economies" and "contradictions in development" as forces that stretch diasporic communities "beyond their limits" and produce "the chronic reproduction of their incongruities."[94] In this context, the utopian elements of transnational diasporas require a tempered acknowledgment of the uneven distribution of capital and resources and the exploitative divisions of labor that construct contemporary communities. Modernist privileging of distance and exile formations that interpellate cultural criticism can obscure these material conditions, constructing theories that celebrate hybridity and a poststate era.

While "Diasporas" constitutes a significant shift in the terms of critical practice for Clifford, moving beyond "travel" to the transnational qualities of "diaspora," one strand of the argument can be read as reproducing modernist exile formations in the midst of a postmodern articulation. Although diaspora interests this critic precisely because it "involves dwelling, maintaining communities, collective homes away from home," and because it does not reproduce exile "with its frequently individualistic focus,"[95] a formal strategy in his essay resists deconstruction, repressing an important term—"immigration." Although Clifford does not construct the conventional modernist opposition between immigration and exile, his theorization of diaspora depends upon a contrast to Euro-American normative definitions of immigration. Thus, even though Clifford does not necessarily reproduce this definitional distinction as absolute, the representation of distinctions between discourses of immigration and diaspora has a tendency to reinforce rather than deconstruct a conventional ideological practice.

Representations that pose immigration and diaspora as historically or culturally distinct often construct a binary division between nationalism and globalization. In such a scenario, the subjects of displacement are constructed through the judgment of the progressive critic—immigrants are seen to replace one nationalist identification for another while diasporic émigrés confound territorial and essentialist nationalisms in favor of transnational subjectivities and communities. This valorization of generalized hybridity is presumed to construct a global or cosmopolitan set of identities that are superior to the nineteenth-century conventions of nation, race, and gender that immigrants negotiate in their efforts to assimilate. Something beyond historical specificity is at stake in representing the diverse and complex shifts in the organization of capital, geographies, and populations in such a simplistic dualism. In the terminological and conceptual distinctions drawn between subjects of displacement, perhaps we learn more about the social construction of Euro-American theory in the present moment than about the historical and cultural conditions of migration.

Clifford's essay does not draw such a crude opposition, and he is careful to contextualize his descriptions of immigrants. In an endnote he writes: "The distinction between immigrant and diasporic experiences . . . should not be overdrawn. There are diasporic moments in classic assimilationist histories, early and late, as new arrivals maintain and later generations recover links to a homeland. Diasporic populations regularly 'lose' members to the dominant culture."[96] Yet these "diasporic moments" could be further plumbed, rather than marginalized, for links between the historical experiences of migration and displacement. I am not suggesting that there are no differences between historical time periods and kinds of displacement in modernity. Rather, I am arguing that monolithic categories and mystifying definitions obscure relevant and nuanced histories. For example, assumptions that all earlier immigrants to the United States uniformly and enthusiastically embraced voluntary assimilation are historically inaccurate and should not be used as counterexamples to the distinct experiences of slaves, Native American removals, political refugees and exiles, and other involuntary displacements.[97] Clifford also cautions that distinctions between old and new immigrants should not be "overdrawn," but these cautions are contained in the essay's endnotes. Cultural studies still needs to center the definitional and conceptual problems of "old" and "new" histories in diverse locations. Otherwise, the antiteleological aspects of diaspora notwithstanding, a new hierarchy of migrancy emerges that draws upon strands of modernist aesthetics to rationalize representations of differences.

In his discussion of Gilroy, Clifford cites a significant critique posed by Kobena Mercer based on Mercer's view of diaspora consciousness as "entirely a product of cultures and histories in collision and dialogue." Critical of the privileging of African origins in Gilroy's work, Mercer proposes a more radically antiessentialist reading of diasporic conditions. Clifford finds value in both critics' versions of diaspora but leans more toward Gilroy's "routing of diaspora in specific maps/histories." Yet the difference is not in the route, as it were, but in the reconfiguration of origin. Although his work is hardly essentialist in a naive vein, Gilroy's diaspora recuperates an identity while Mercer is resisting the authorities that come along with the history of that identity. Here I would agree with Clifford that this difference is finally not resolvable and the specific cultural contexts of diasporic communities may make a significant difference. That is, the histories that "origins" and "destinations" as well as "routes" may accrue will vary in their political and cultural effects.

For example, Nalini Natarajan cautions that for South Asians the term "diaspora" holds both promise and problems. Writing of the "Indian diaspora," Natarajan notes that conservative alliances between consumerism and fundamentalism result in homogenized notions of national origin. Thus, in metropolitan contexts, subversive aspects of diaspora can "interrupt the hegemony of cable TV," but conservative elements "reinforce the hegemonies of religion, caste, and class within the diasporic community."[98] Natarajan's comments remind us not to get overenthused about the possibilities of media and technology practices that destabilize nation-state discourses. On the other hand, the usefulness of a term such as "diaspora" lies in its ability to link new and diversely peopled communities: "In managing knowledge, as Foucault has shown us, one of the most effective ways of holding together disparate images is that of nomenclature. Thus domestic workers in Kuwait and Saudi Arabia, software technologists in the United States, retail store owners or sugarcane workers in the Caribbean are part of the medley of signifiers denoted by the single signifier 'Indian diaspora.'"[99]

The work, then, that diaspora does as a term is similar to the operation of creolité: constructing identities from the "debris of historical and future possibilities." This practice of hybridity, writ large in collectively lived experience, establishes "transregional" identities through contemporary technologies and new critical histories. Rejecting the critical distancing of modernist exile formations and their attendant binary oppositions, the practice of diaspora in Clifford's essay addresses the "place of betweenness," the neither/nor situation. More than a valorization of the predicament of multiple locations, such a view of diaspora illuminates continuities and discontinuities between temporal fields such as modernity and postmodernity as well as spatial fields such as nations, territories, locations, and bodies. In its current usage in contemporary cultural criticism, exemplified in Clifford's recent essay, diaspora as cosmopolitan hybridity displaces expatriation, represses immigration, and reworks exile all at once. It does not do any of this work absolutely or evenly. Read as a cultural production of the social forces it describes, diaspora discourse articulates both generalized migrancy or nomadism as well as a strenuous call for particularized histories of specific sites of hybridity as the contemporary articulation of postmodern transnationalism.

Postmodern Migrants: Tracing Modernist Exile

[T]o travel implies movement between fixed positions, a site of departure, a point of arrival, the knowledge of an itinerary. It also intimates an eventual return, a potential homecoming. Migrancy, on the contrary, involves a movement in which neither the points of a departure nor those of arrival are immutable or certain. It calls for a dwelling in language, in histories, in identities that are constantly subject to mutation. Always in transit, the promise of a homecoming—completing the story, domesticating the detour—becomes an impossibility.
—Iain Chambers [100]

When Adorno wrote in the 1940s that "dwelling, in the proper sense, is now impossible," he articulated the despair and the promise that cataclysmic historical events induce. The exilic subject of Adorno's *Minima Moralia* wanders in a cultural desert, mourning the past to write in and through the apocalypse of loss. In the early '90s Iain Chambers's evocative charge that homecoming becomes an impossibility deploys a migrant subject-in-transit. Dwelling is now reworked as the possibility of the impossible—a thoroughly postmodern tour de force—that is, as the practice of resistance to Euro-American Enlightenment principles of time, space, and subjectivity. In this scenario, the migrant (who both is and is not reducible to all other displaced subjects in contemporary culture) signifies mobility and habitation simultaneously.

Rey Chow in *Writing Diaspora* links diasporic conditions to subject positions of migrancy, specifically those produced in relation to the cultural practices of telecommunications and computer technologies. For example, the user of the internet is described as a kind of postmodern traveler: "The practical behavior of the hypertext user will be like the air traveler who covers large stretches of space in little time . . . while sitting in one spot. This user is no longer a reader or writer in the traditional or even poststructuralist sense but a passenger-in-transit, whose sedentariness is a factor of his/her rapid motions through time and out of time."[101] In the "race for speed" that Chow identifies as characteristic of the present moment, globalization wins out over localized interests primarily through dislodging human beings from their originary sites, creating displaced subjects who can less effectively resist new, hegemonic circuits of power. In Chow's account, migrants are not only the cosmopolitan intellectuals but the "surplus" humans of electronified divisions of labor—alienated workers of the global economy.

In both Chambers's and Chow's recent work, migrants people the theories of diaspora, giving figurative substance to claims about emergent subjectivities. As Chambers writes, the contemporary moment "compels us to recognise the need for a mode of thinking that is neither fixed nor stable, but one that is open to the prospect of a continual return to events, to their re-elaboration and revision."[102] If Chambers's theory of migrancy embodies a more celebratory moment in cultural criticism, both Chow and Chambers propose displacement as fraught with risks but somehow critically required in formulating contemporary critical practice. Is the figure of the diasporic migrant in Euro-American criticism simply a postmodern version of modernist exile? Inasmuch as political and economic circumstances that produce cultural representations have specific characteristics across time as well as across space, the two figures cannot be the *same*. Yet similarities exist that suggest that there are continuities between the cosmopolitan subject or "migrant" and the "exile." In the contemporary Euro-American theoretical or critical practices that I have discussed in this chapter, a slippage occurs between the modernist figuration of authorship as a form of exile and what could be called a more "postmodern" manifestation of existential homelessness. This link is most clearly demonstrated in the professional consolidation of the identity of author or artist (or critic) through access to a universalized "experience" of displacement. In an age that appears to be characterized by movements of populations, diasporas, and travel of many kinds, such gestures can take on the appearance of truth. Like all generalizations, however, such appearances operate as truisms, obfuscating and even erasing the representation of social relations in historically grounded and politically meaningful ways.

How can we pose the question of widespread displacement in

such a way as to render it historically and politically viable? How can we theorize the emergence of specific subjects in the midst of vast changes in the economic and social order? One part of such a project can take as its task the mapping of continuities and discontinuities between critical practices, between the ideological formations that structure representations. If modernist exile operates in some fashion in and through postmodern migrancy, the good news is that we can trace this link to fashion new histories of critical practices. In this way, we can distinguish between *kinds* of postmodernisms and modernisms as well as between different cultural politics. The recognition and historicizing of such distinctions inevitably shifts the ground of critical practice, creating opportunities for new alliances as well as reaffirming ongoing affiliations. It is also an opportunity to actively decide what kinds of critical tools we need to address which questions.

The differences between modernist exile and postmodernist migrancy, then, are just as important as the similarities. For example, the prevalence of references to immigration in contemporary theories of displacement and diaspora speaks to a profound shift away from the more aestheticized criteria found in modernist criticism. In this sense, my critique of Euro-American modernism's erasure or suppression of both tourism and immigration is made possible by the disruptions of master narratives that "postmodernism" signifies. That the postmodern must be thought of as fractured, uneven, and diversely produced and distributed in contemporary cultures does not obviate this important change. Nor does the impoverishment and mystification of much of what could be considered postmodern contemporary criticism undercut the powerful possibilities of this historical moment.

When critics write of exile, they refer to an experience that triggers strong responses. To be separated from the person or location that one loves best or knows most intimately is an unbearable condition. Because each living being knows the pain of separation and loss on some level, the deployment of exile as a metaphor cathects modern subjects in a profoundly primal way. To raise questions about how the representation of displacement from a home location is used as an ideological construct does not diminish movements that struggle to restore to individuals and groups what is most important to them. If anything, investigating the critical uses of exile may reinvigorate activism and resistance to state-sponsored terror by fostering a politically responsible cultural criticism. When criticism admits to its power to narrate history and represent culture, it can utilize its self-reflexive and deconstructive capacities with greater accuracy.

Deconstructing the discourse of exile requires imagining distance in less binary and more complicated ways. In the age of telecommunications and transnational cultural production this might mean that distance does not inevitably lead to exile or war but to new subjectivities that produce new relationships to space as well as time so that distance is not only a safety zone or a field of tension but a terrain that houses new subjects of criticism.

4 POSTMODERN GEOGRAPHIES

Feminist Politics of Location

A whole history remains to be written of *spaces*—which would at the same time be the history of *powers* (both of these terms in the plural)—from the great strategies of geopolitics to the little tactics of the habitat.
—Michel Foucault[1]

A place on the map is also a place in history.
—Adrienne Rich[2]

This book's project concerns itself with the discourses of displacement that arise in the cultural production of Euro-American criticism in postmodernity. Yet each metaphor of displacement includes referentially a concept of placement, dwelling, location, or position. Thus exile is always already a mode of dwelling at a distance from a point of origin. Tourism is travel between points of origin and destinations. Diaspora disperses the locations of dwelling into an interstitial habitus. Nomadism is the most attenuated concept in relation to location. Yet even theories of nomadic rhizomes include "nodes"—those sites of intersecting movements or "lines of flight." Thus most notions of displacement contain an oppositional notion of placement and vice versa. In this chapter, I want to address the other end of the binary of displacement/placement: the cultural production of theories of location in Euro-American critical discourse, particularly the dynamic discussion of the politics of location in feminist theories of identity and subjectivity. For many Euro-American feminist theorists, the concept of location offers a solution to the universalizing gestures of masculinist thought, providing a way of rearticulating marginality or particularity. Yet these feminist theories of location do not arise in a vacuum, as it were, but can be linked to movements and tendencies in contemporary Euro-American criticism in general.

In fact, theories of placement abound in contemporary critical thought. Increasingly, as part of an effort to avoid the abstract aestheticization of theoretical practices, the terms of cultural criticism have drawn from spatial as well as temporal concepts. Maps and borders are provocative metaphors, signaling a heightened awareness of the political and economic structures that demarcate zones of inclusion and exclusion as well as the interstitial spaces of indeterminacy. Topography and geography now intersect literary and cultural criticism in a growing interdisciplinary inquiry into emergent identity formations and social practices. Geographers who believe that all modes of description and analysis follow narrative conventions and are, therefore, highly constructed and historically contingent articulate various versions of "geographic imaginations." For example, James Duncan and David Ley call for the theorization of a "situated geographic imagination" that can problematize description, unpack dominant ideologies of space and time, and deconstruct "hidden geographies" such as the social formation of boundaries.[3] Derek Gregory argues for a rigorous critique of Archimedian knowledge by deconstructing "maps, landscapes, and spaces *and also* images of location, position, and geometry."[4] Gregory believes that more "open forms of cartographic discourse" are possible, emerging from the examination of the field's own historiography and the critical practices that transform disciplinary conventions. Gregory insists, however, that none of the conceptual and terminological tools at hand are absolute or neutral. If the new geographers are going to challenge successfully dominant hegemonies, they must "recognize that different people in different places are implicated in time-space colonization and compression in different ways."[5]

Thus terms such as "borders," "maps," "location," "space," and "place" do not necessarily liberate critical practices from the very conundrum of aestheticization and universalization that spurred a search for alternative metaphors and methods in the first place. In fact, as geographers Neil Smith and Cindi Katz argue, the widespread appeal to spatial metaphors appears to result from a "decentering and destabilization of previously fixed realities and assumptions" that leaves space "largely exempted from such skeptical scrutiny." According to this argument, space provides coherence and order for an "otherwise floating world of ideas."[6]

The very operation of metaphor lends powerful credence to Smith and Katz's analysis. Metaphor proceeds by drawing upon a familiar and concrete set of meanings to clarify or explain another set of meanings that are far less familiar or distinct. As literary and cultural studies have destabilized meanings, rendering certainties uncertain and placing Enlightenment categories "under erasure," spatial metaphors have increasingly served to create new meanings, often through abstraction and allusion.[7] Smith and Katz point to the unexamined and even dehistoricized function of space in this process of metaphorization. This "absolute space," marked by "fixity and inertness," becomes a given in critical discourses that utilize spatial metaphors.[8] In marking the gap between materialist and metaphorical treatments of space, Smith and Katz argue for a renewed attention to the historical production of space in modernity and postmodernity, not to suppress or do away with metaphorical operations but to explore the "interconnectedness of metaphor and materiality" to advance the "shared project of a spatial politics."[9]

How to negotiate or mediate space with time or vice versa? These questions engage the proponents of "spatial politics" and the "politics of location" alike. In Euro-American philosophy and social theory, the analysis of space and time has preoccupied both materialists and idealists. Most recently, the discipline of geography has produced dynamic theories of the relationship between space and time, raising historically attuned questions of representation and scientific description. The "conversation" between geography, poststructuralist destabilizations of rationality and humanism, and feminist theories of subjectivity takes place in the midst of profound shifts in the organization of industries, technologies, and cultures. The era of flexible accumulation with its rapid circulations, destabilized nationalisms, and ever-increasing inequalities poses particular challenges to those who would attempt to come to terms with it. The transnationalization of culture as well as industry brings with it profound possibilities for forging new alliances and identities. The same conditions also induce neoconservative consolidations of power. Against the homogenization of globalism, the qualities of the local or regional are frequently championed. And in the face of exclusivist tendencies in specific locations, recourse is made to the international or transnational.

In this chapter, I will argue that the global and the local are two spatialized articulations of modernity that have taken on specific resonances in the midst of the shifts in economic, political, and cultural realms that are associated with postmodernity. The mapping of these seemingly oppositional spaces as a global-local nexus cuts across numerous disciplines and critical practices. Unexamined ideologies of travel and displacement pervade the burgeoning literature of postmodern geographies. A renewed emphasis on local, regional, or particular sites and positions in Euro-American feminist theories of subjectivity valorizes the local as the practice of political and cultural resistance. The privileging of the local in this body of feminist work is produced in a context of increased concern about hegemonic cultural and economic practices, practices most visibly fomented and disseminated by transnational capital and its diversely pervasive effects in postmodernity. In examining the emergence of the "local" as the site of resistance to globalization in general, I want to focus on the ways in which Euro-American feminist critical practices produce postmodern discourses of placement as well as displacement. Often more urgently tied to material analyses of lived experience and gendered divisions of labor, Euro-American feminist theories have challenged implicitly or explicitly the abstractions and aestheticizations of poststructuralist practices. Yet problems arise when authentic sites of identity formation become celebrated. Since feminist theories are just as heavily implicated in the transnational politics of cultural production as other forms, I will argue that some of the transformative critical practices that can rewrite the way subjects view themselves and their links with each other can emerge from feminist debate and theorizing. Looking at the siting of the local and the politics of location in contemporary Euro-American feminist criticism foregrounds the history of an oppositional critical strategy, one that works to destabilize hegemonic social formations but often operates in the service of its "other": multinational capitalism as globalization.

The Production of Space in Euro-American Modernity

Space can now be recognized as an active constitutive component of hegemonic power . . . It tells you where you are and it puts you there . . . The problem is this: where do we want to be, and how do we want to get there? What
kind of political spaces are there to be occupied? And who is this "we" anyway?
—Michael Keith and Steve Pile [10]

The European tradition takes a certain notion of space for granted.
The great open emptiness of the desert, sea, or sky has inspired metaphors of infinity and timelessness that alternately terrify and soothe
the post-Enlightenment subject. Regardless of the emotion that is
engendered, space is assumed to be *there:* a substance that is relatively immune to the workings of time unless culture perpetrates its
crimes against space by spoiling, crowding, polluting, and inscrib-
ing its presence onto or into that blank expanse. Time, and its social
practices, have been very much of the essence, as it were. Periodi-
cally, questions are raised about this relationship between active time
and deadened space, posing the relationship as a dynamic interaction
of material, historical issues. In the current moment, space is in the
midst of a renaissance. It finds a new reassertion in the postmodern critical practices that have emerged in Euro-American academies
since the post–World War II era, taking on a specific intensity in
the period following decolonization and the increasing flexibility and
mobility of capital that mark the last two decades.

Most of the current Euro-American theorists of the representation of space acknowledge an intellectual debt to Henri Lefebvre, the
French Marxist theorist who linked the production of space to the
rise of capitalism. Lefebvre situates the Enlightenment as a pivotal
moment in the codification of space into physical, mental, and social
domains. With the rise of philosophy and mathematics, among other
disciplines and sciences, codified space rationalized bourgeois hegemony through the state and its ancillary institutions. Lefebvre points
to the absolute nature of space in Cartesian thought as well as the advent of the Kantian transcendental category to demonstrate the social
construction of a dominant set of social practices. In this formulation,
the rise of a specific class and its hegemonic practices produce systems
of knowledge, modes of representation, and social relations that include the production of "space" and the reproduction of modernity.

This new, rational space contains its other—time—in historically specific ways. Equally fetishized, solidified, and fixed in the service of the liberal bourgeois state, time remains the weaker category until the binary begins to reverse itself in the nineteenth century. Lefebvre cites Marx's reinstatement of historical time as revolutionary time along with Bergson's delineation of consciousness as mental duration as precursors of a philosophical tradition that stretches from Husserl to Deleuze. At stake in the struggle between time and space for Marx (and for Lefebvre) is the suppression of history, "transformed from action to memory, from production to contemplation." Time, "dominated by repetition and circularity," is "overwhelmed by the establishment of an immobile space which is the locus and environment of realized Reason." In this social practice, time "loses all meaning."[11] Such an analysis of alienation and passivity in the face of immobile space and fetishized time gives rise to an entire chain of philosophical and critical responses.

Doreen Massey has argued that the explanatory narrative of the production of space that I have outlined above is culturally and politically limited, economically determinist, and resolutely modernist. As a feminist geographer, Massey struggles to account for the pervasive effects of late capitalism without positing either a universal class or a generalized masculinism. Massey's critique is produced in the context of a contemporary school of spatialization theorists who work in and around the discipline of geography, utilizing contemporary Euro-American Marxist, poststructuralist, and, in some instances, feminist critical practices. This group, which includes David Harvey, Edward Soja, Derek Gregory, Neil Smith, John Urry, Liz Bondi, and Mona Domosh, among numerous others, concerns itself with the materialist histories of the production of space in modernity and postmodernity. Accepting basic Marxist tenets of dialectical materialism, this loosely defined school of thought also critiques the humanist historicism of nineteenth-century intellectual thought (including some versions of Marxism). Exploring poststructuralist theories of subjectivity and identity, these writers also argue for versions of materialist standpoints and modes of description. While there are significant differences of approach and emphasis among the geographers to whom I refer as a "group," not the least of which involves their engagement with raced and gendered cultural studies, they are linked through their interest in analyzing the material histories of the powerful effects of capitalist modes of production through nuanced examinations of the representation of space.

If Lefebvre provided a history of the suppression of time in favor of space throughout the rise of modern capitalism, David Harvey and Edward Soja have contributed histories of new forms of social relations and representations—the space-time compressions that marked the turn of the century and the current moment. Harvey's influential text *The Condition of Postmodernity* investigates the spatial and temporal representations of Euro-American modernism as the productions of specific material practices such as imperialist expansion, Fordism, the internationalization of money, and new systems of credit. In this context, Harvey examines the privileging of time over space in the social theories of Marx, Weber, Adam Smith, and others, theories that assume a pre-given spatial order within which time functions. Linking the notion of progress to this aspect of modernity, Harvey notes the emphasis on *becoming* rather than *being* as the conquest of space enhances the agency of the temporal actor.[12]

In marking pivotal moments in the unification of European space through an analysis of representational "crises," Harvey seeks to "highlight the material links between political-economic and cultural processes."[13] Harvey argues that the latest round of time-space compression began in the early '70s in response to fiscal crises, both emulating and distinguishing itself from the earlier phenomenon at the turn of the century that fueled much of the practices of modernism. In both instances, space is "annihilated" through time as the speed-up in the turnover times of capital increases the effects of volatility and emphemerality in "fashion, products, production techniques, labor processes, ideas, ideologies, values, and established practices."[14] Thus Harvey examines postmodernism not as an isolated bundle of aesthetic effects or as a rejection of modernist values and practices. Rather, Harvey ties the emergence of postmodern forms in architecture, art, and philosophy to the transition from Fordism to "more flexible modes of capitalist accumulation via the mediations of spatial and temporal existence."[15] Here, space-time compression becomes not just a series of instances in the speed-up of the circulation of information, goods, and populations through a static and unchanging notion of space. Harvey's analysis demonstrates how absolute or universalized space remains unexamined in most inquiries into the "postmodern condition," leading to a revival in the aestheticization of politics, a renewed rise in nationalism, and the "restoration of the hegelian state."[16]

Modernism is defined by Harvey as a set of practices that negotiate place and space, present and past, universality and particularism in specific ways. He identifies two primary responses to space-time compression that manifested themselves as ambivalence toward the unification processes of globalization and anxiety about proximity. In the first case, unity was relaunched as an "Enlightenment project of universal human emancipation in a global space bound together through mechanisms of communication and social intervention."[17] This new version of spatial rationality divided and portioned space into exterior and public as well as interior and private locations in the service of a supposed break with the past. The other response resisted such unifying spatial practices, privileging instead a whole range of fragmentations and diversifications. This version of modernist concerns emphasizes the uniqueness of place in the face of homogeneity, entailing a set of identificatory practices that detail the local, locale, and positionality: "By enhancing links between place and the social sense of personal and communal identity, this facet of modernism was bound, to some degree, to entail the aestheticization of local, regional, or national politics. Loyalties to place then take precedence over loyalties to class, spatializing political action."[18]

That capital induced two such responses is not inexplicable in Harvey's analysis. He identifies universalism and particularism as "two currents of sensibility" that coexisted in the same cultures and even in the same person "even when one or the other sensibility became dominant in a particular time and place."[19] This puts the current emphasis on spatialized particularity, on the local, in a specific context. The emergence of identity politics since the late '60s, then, can be linked to the most recent round of space-time compression as capital has increasingly organized itself to enhance the qualities of mobility and fragmentation. Place and identity, Harvey points out, become key when "everyone occupies a space of individuation."[20] In the face of apparent global homogenization, regional specificity may be asserted. Resistance to mass movements and communitarian identities that cross or subvert national or local boundaries may be expressed as individualism. Tradition and heritage also function in opposition to time-space compression and globalism. Harvey argues that "place" becomes the locus of social identity, fixing social relations into a static, if seemingly secure, state. Such attachments to "place-bound identity" may begin as oppositional movements but, Harvey reminds us, they also become part of the "very fragmentation which a mobile capitalism and flexible accumulation can feed upon."[21]

Thus the reassertion of space in postmodernity can be seen as a radically mixed bag. Simply reversing binaries does not transform social relations. If modernist internationalism heralds globalized capitalist domination, localism can signal the formation of ethnocentrisms, racisms, and fascism. Harvey's critique of the mystification of space in modernity moves us in the direction of theorizing alternative critical practices and politics. Edward Soja, another primary theorist in geography, would term such a set of practices a "radical political culture of postmodernism." Deeply influenced by Marxist, materialist methodologies, both Soja and Harvey evidence extreme skepticism toward ludic poststructuralist critical practices and what Soja refers to as "neoconservative postmodernism." Yet both theorists labor to come to terms with the conditions of postmodernity, including the complicities of institutional structures, intellectual positions, and progressive politics. Their writings, therefore, contribute to a growing body of critical work that proposes syncretic, interdisciplinary methods of analysis.

Edward Soja's primary argument in *Postmodern Geographies* allies itself with Harvey's claim that the nineteenth-century privileging of time over space has been increasingly countered by a reassertion of space. Both Soja and Harvey mark the 1850s and the 1970s as major points of crisis in social, economic, and political practices that generate transitions in industrialization, the circulation of money, information, and goods, and the production of systems of meaning and representation. Soja urges us to demystify representations of space as inert and undynamic and time as fluid and dialectical in favor of critical methods that combine and refigure "time and space, history and geography, period and region, sequence and simultaneity."[22] Calling for a rejection of doctrinaire Marxist historicism, ideologically bound empirical methods, as well as "simplistic anti-Marxism," Soja, like Harvey, seeks a materialist critical practice. Drawing on Jameson's notion of "cognitive mapping," Soja seeks "a new way of seeing through the gratuitous veils of both reactionary postmodernism and late modern historicism to encourage the creation of a politicized spatial consciousness and a radical spatial praxis."[23]

The explanatory narratives of Harvey and Soja revolve around an irreducible origin in the rise of industrial capitalism. In "Flexible Sexism," Doreen Massey details an extended critique of the unexamined masculinism implicit in Soja's and Harvey's work.[24] Her assertion that their dominant view is "assumed to be the universal, and that view is white, male, heterosexual, western," is not limited to Soja and Harvey but extends to the conditions of the production of theory in the Euro-American academy.[25] While Massey does not dispense with a materialist analysis of class and capitalism, she strenuously argues that there are "other axes of social power relations by which our current societies are characterized"—such as gender.[26] Both Soja and Harvey refer to feminist concerns in a "laundry list" of contemporary identity politics and social movements, references Massey charges with a superficiality of analysis. Noting the absence of any close reading or citation of Euro-American feminist theory in both primary texts by Soja and Harvey, Massey makes a key point: Such exclusions do not simply constitute a local problem (reductively stated as "no women") but signify the absence of a "whole line of argument central to the relationship between modernity, space, and social relations."[27] Soja and Harvey, as theorists of contemporary conditions, produce partial accounts through a rhetorical guise of generality.

Massey draws upon Griselda Pollock's and Janet Wolff's work on the spatial politics of gender in Euro-American modernity to argue that gender- and race-blind analyses can only produce limited accounts.[28] Arguing that women experience modernity in varied and complex ways, feminist theories of spatialization and modernity deconstruct the new master narratives of time-space compression. Thus sites such as "the city" have to be analyzed with more than class relations in mind. Women have varied histories of mobility and habitus in Euro-American metropoles. For instance, immigrants, people of color, and poor people all have significantly distinct relationships to what has been misleadingly termed "the" postmodern. Indeed, as Massey argues, "different social groups, and different individuals belonging to numbers of social groups, are located in many different

ways in the new organization of relations over time-space."²⁹ Massey
is skeptical of the claims for a pervasive "new, disturbing placeless-
ness." It is only from an elite vantage point that such time-space compression can appear utterly dominant. Who is it, Massey asks, that in
these times feels "dislocated/placeless/invaded"? Are these articulations of the refugee, the homeless person, or the sexually assaulted?
Or are these metaphors devised for the use of those whose power has
become dislodged, adjusted, or threatened?

While Harvey and Soja have narrowed the field of space-time
compression to the circulation of capital per se, Massey works to recuperate the concept in the context of diverse social effects:

> If time-space compression can be imagined in that more socially
> formed, socially evaluative and differentiated way, then there
> may be here the possibility of developing a politics of mobility
> and access. For it does seem that mobility, and control over mo-
> bility, both reflects and reinforces power. It is not simply a ques-
> tion of unequal distribution, that some people have more than
> others, and that some have more control than others. It is that
> the mobility and control of some groups can actively weaken
> other people. Differential mobility can weaken the leverage of
> the already weak. The time-space compression of some groups
> can undermine the power of others.³⁰

The "crisis" in modernity comes to be seen as a series of destabilizations of power and privilege for a specific population, a collective identity that has assumed a power to generalize its point of
view. The absence of other points of view is not haphazard. The
feminist theorists whose work interests Massey are those who argue
that modernism is deeply invested in its absences; indeed, they are
structuring absences. Thus, Massey argues, the experience of mod-
ernism/modernity and its cultural productions and definitions "are
all constructed on and are constructive of particular forms of gender
relations and definitions of masculinity and of what it means to be a
woman. This is not ('just') to say that modernism was or is patriarchal
(this would hardly be news, nor differentiate it from many other periods in history); it is to say that it is not possible fully to understand
modernism without taking account of this."³¹

An impoverished field results when influential cultural theo-

rists publish studies of contemporary society that structurally con-
strain race, gender, and sexualities through their marginalization and
"othering" vis-à-vis the privileging of modes of production. Massey
argues strenuously for a skeptical reading of some versions of postmodern inclusivity, pointing to the rhetorical strategies of token
mentions and structural absence: "But if the problem of the postmodernists is that while celebrating the existence of the Other most
of us are consigned to being means of constructing the identity of
white, heterosexual men, the problem of the modernists is that they
do not see us, really, at all. Or, if they do, it is as somehow deviations from the norm, troubling exceptions to the(ir) rule."[32] Here
Massey is pointing to the links between postmodern and modern cultural articulations. The blinkered vision of the modernists finds its
opposite moment in the wide scanning of the postmodern approach.
Massey reminds us that the lived experience of these social formations is filled with contradiction and contests for interpretive power
and social privilege. Indeed, "most of us" are consigned to positions
that we would wish to resist, shift, and reconfigure. Our ability to
analyze these conditions, to write and circulate their histories, and to
transform them vary drastically according to economic, cultural, and
political resources. Attention to materialism, Massey notes, entails
far more than an emphasis on money and capital circulation. Questions of gender, among other diverse aspects, require a broader and
more complex materialism that addresses the powers and the limits of
hegemonic formations. Feminist critiques of modernism offer powerful alternatives to the notion that only one "true" story can be told
about advanced capitalism. As Julie Graham writes:

> From a critical feminist perspective, existing theories of Ford-
> ism and Post-Fordism offer a "totalizing" rendition of capitalist
> development which fails to acknowledge multiplicity and differ-
> ence in social life. Telling the story of the postwar period from
> an "objective" viewpoint or from the perspective of a collec-
> tive subject actively marginalizes those whose experience fails to
> conform to the contours and emphases of the narrative—those,
> for instance, who are excluded from mass consumption, paid
> employment, capitalist class processes, or even citizenship. And
> when such a narrative is used in articulating the goals and visions

of progressive movements, discursive silences become political exclusions.[33]

As Graham's critique demonstrates, gender inevitably raises questions of locale, the specifying gesture of difference *from* something or someone else. Searching for the grounds of theory, the body, region, home, nation, and particularity of location presents compelling evidence or testimony. Recently, Euro-American feminist geographers have asked questions not only about how gender has an impact on mobility but also about how gender produces location. Such spatializations of identity and subjectivity can be interpreted as responses to the temporal accounts of modernity that cannot account for complex and differentiated subjects. Yet, increasingly, geographers seem to be advocating an examination of the *uneven* operations of postmodernity that produce possibilities for some and delimit or obstruct opportunities for others.[34] For example, in his discussion of Harvey's work, Derek Gregory argues that a modernist attachment to distance or a centered point of view will produce master narratives that function, finally, to obscure the historical conditions and spatial politics of postmodernity:

> For some, these processes undoubtedly present new opportunities and demand larger responsibilities, reveal wider horizons and enhance geographical imaginations; but for others they impose additional burdens and raise higher barriers, create further distinctions and diminish individual capacities. This means that a critical human geography must not only chart the differential locations and the time-space manifolds that are created through these processes—a project for which some of the concepts of spatial science might still be reclaimed—but also draw out the multiple, compound, and contradictory subject-positions that they make available. The production of space is not an incidental by-product of social life but a moment intrinsic to its conduct and constitution, and for geography to *make* a difference— politically and intellectually—it must be attentive *to* difference.[35]

Power constructs these differences, of course, and, keeping in mind Foucault's comment about the common history of spaces and the history of powers great and small, it is clear that the recourse to the local, whether feminist or not, is linked to this representational matrix. Does attention to local or regional particularities resist universalization and totalizing theories? Can spatial politics or politics of location address the need to account for difference that Gregory and Massey raise as urgent priorities for their discipline? The arguments for or against the local must be understood within the context of a global-local nexus: the spatialized oppositional construct that organizes perceptions of identities, cultures, and places in postmodernity.

The Global-Local Nexus

Global and local are two faces of the same movement from one epoch of globalization, the one which has been dominated by the nation-state, the national economies, the national cultural identities, to something new.
—Stuart Hall[36]

The "something new" that Stuart Hall refers to is that vast and complicated shift in the organization of capitalism that is referred to as flexible accumulation or specialization. Articulated by Mandel as "late capitalism," further delineated as the suppression of distance by speed and mobility in telecommunications, rapid transfers, immediacy, and ahistorical "shock" by Jameson, Baudrillard, and Virilio, among others, this phase is variously pinpointed as emerging in the late '60s or early '70s. In the aftermath of over a decade of debate and publication about the "postmodern"—is it utopian or reactionary?—the changes in modes of production and distribution, the destabilizing of national identities and delegitimation of state functions and institutions, and the proliferation of fragmented "alternative" politics are now taken as givens. The primary mode of explanation is a shift from "Fordist" to "post-Fordist" production, resulting in the radical reorganization of national industries, the movement "offshore" of primary production, the overturning of organized labor and the "feminization" of workforces, and massive shifts in "superpower" alliances and alignments. These changes have not boded well for the world's poorest. Environmental hazards have increased while worker safety standards have plummeted. Transnationalization has altered but not undermined middle-class dominance globally.

This process is not unitary or coherent. Hall points out that there are now at least two forms of globalization that are in tension with each other. The older form continually makes recourse to nationalism and national cultural identity in a defensive move. The newer form makes use of differences in order to contain and incorporate them. What looks like a postmodern flux of diversity, then, can also be seen as a complex management of contemporary modes of production, distribution, and consumption: Global mass culture "is now a form of capital which recognizes that it can only, to use a metaphor, rule through other local capitals, rule alongside and in partnership with other economic and political elites. It does not attempt to obliterate them; it operates through them. It has to hold the whole framework of globalization in place and simultaneously police that system: it stage-manages independence within, so to speak."[37]

What happens to space and time in this context? The model of capital accumulation relies upon increasing territory and expanding markets and opportunities for production and consumption. If one axis of this process depends upon growth or expansion, in the post-Fordist conditions that aim can be best gained by increasing mobility and flexibility of location and fragmentation of operations. Moving industry "offshore" (that is, out of the United States and Europe and into areas that have been underdeveloped) to export processing zones that have regulations extremely favorable to transnational corporations, changing workforces regularly to keep labor costs as low as possible, and dividing corporate labor and tasks across geographic space all follow this logic. The second axis could be seen as temporal, represented as the simultaneity of communications through electronic technologies, the increasing rapidity of transactions that microprocessing computers make possible, and the new aesthetics and forms of entertainment that emphasize speed and immediacy. These two axes, taken together, can only be understood through a global-local nexus whereby the older modernist models of accumulation, expansion, experimentation, and change are mediated by current conditions.

Kevin Robins and David Morley argue that new technologies not only make a new relationship between time and space but between place and space. That is, *locale* or place is a specific form of spatialization in postmodernity that creates networks, communities, and identities. They point out that more and more people are connected electronically than by conventional geographic proximity. In their view, communities constituted by World Wide Web sites, for example, or by television or radio transmissions are increasingly vital locales. Speaking of the challenges to nation-state policing of "national space" by satellite broadcasting in Europe, Robins and Morley argue that such transgressions of frontiers and subversions of territories transform the relationship between boundary and space. Inevitably, these destabilizations and "crossings" delegitimate the borders themselves, raising questions about national and ethnic identities. Yet even as technologies promote the dissolution of national borders and the destabilization of modernity's political mappings, they are also associated with the "increasing transnationalization of accumulation" that unevenly develops the regions in question.[38]

Such a globally managed science of differentiation reaches its apotheosis in the practice of target marketing. Target marketing utilizes sophisticated geomapping software to create databases that can identify and define extremely discrete sets of consumers across dispersed populations. As the maxim from '80s advertising giant Saatchi & Saatchi has it, there are greater differences between midtown Manhattan and the Bronx than between Manhattan and the seventh arrondissement of Paris.[39] Robins points to the growing importance of targeting consumers on the basis of "demography and habits rather than on the basis of geographical proximity" as part of corporate objectives to combine "mobility and flexibility with the control and integration of activities on a world scale."[40] Peter Childers reminds us that these geography-driven systems derive from military technological applications that "target" the "enemy."[41] Such "geographic information systems" track so-called personal data through census and credit card records to construct "imagined communities" of consumers with micro-identities. Childers points to the dramatically uneven nature of this new spatial logic: "The problem today is that capital is able to map the subject within postmodern space but the subject is unable to map him or herself spatially. Hispanic children of middle-income families in Miami don't know how to map (much less determine or change) their differential position within urban space or how to capitalize on it, but Arby's does, and Wal-Mart does, and Philip Morris does, and government police forces and military intelligence units do."[42] Although we should not overestimate the hegemony of Wal-Mart, target marketing practices remind us to approach claims about the powers and possibilities of local specificity with some skepticism. Robins points out that the surge in interest in local economies, local economic strategies, and local consumers "may reflect a new valuation of difference and particularity, but it is also very much about making a profit from it."[43] Thus the heady cosmopolitanism of the transnational cultures of exchange and circulation that seem to bypass national boundaries and constraints is highly provisional, tied to a bottom-line corporate profit margin: "It may well be that, in some cases, the new global context is recreating sense of place and sense of community in very positive ways, giving rise to an energetic cosmopolitanism in certain localities. In others, however, local fragmentation . . . may inspire a nostalgic, introverted and parochial sense of local attachment and identity. If globalization recontextualizes and reinterprets cultural localism, it does so in ways that are equivocal and ambiguous."[44]

Stuart Hall also argues that the destabilization or dissolution of frontiers and boundaries engendered by postmodernity can result in the formation of "exclusivist and defensive enclaves." Such rediscoveries of identity can function as forms of fundamentalism, leading to local ethnicities that are as "dangerous as national ones."[45] How, Hall asks, can one avoid becoming trapped in the place from which one begins to speak? What seems like a necessary point of enunciation, a rediscovery of place, a past, a context, a grounding, can become exclusive, limiting, closed, and essentialized. If all enunciation "comes from somewhere" and is always "positioned" in discourse, a radical analysis of place, locale, and location is needed. Otherwise, the reclaiming of identitarian territory mystifies the very workings of subjectivity and politics in postmodernity. As Hall writes: "The homeland is not waiting back there for the new ethnics to rediscover it. There is a past to be learned about, but the past is now seen, and it has to be grasped as a history, as something that has to be told. It is narrated. It is grasped through memory. It is grasped through desire. It is grasped through reconstruction. It is not just a fact that has been waiting to ground our identities."[46]

One could say, then, that the "local" is not really about a specific intrinsic territory but about the construction of bundles or clusters of identities in and through the cultures of transnational capitalism. Whether the "local" is seen to be fluid and relational or fixed and fundamentalist depends upon one's position or enunciatory situation vis-à-vis economic, political, and cultural hegemonies. This is, perhaps, one of the greater paradoxes of the global-local nexus: The local appears as the primary site of resistance to globalization through the construction of temporalized narratives of identity (new histories, rediscovered genealogies, imagined geographies, etc.), yet that very site prepares the ground for appropriation, nativism, and exclusions. This condition may be paradoxical but it is by no means mysterious or ineluctable. As Armand Mattelart and Jean-Marie Piemme describe this process: "The local seems to signify a return to the concrete, at the same time as the concrete it rediscovers takes us . . . further away from the possibility of understanding a vaster reality from which the concrete takes its meaning . . . The local is of real interest only where it permits . . . a better grasp . . . of the dialectic between the abstract/universal and the concrete/experienced."[47]

If we can grasp the local in this way and understand its role in the construction of knowledge and cultural production, for example, then we have improved our analysis of the global-local nexus in postmodernity. It is probably no accident that Euro-American feminist theory has engaged this question with great vigor and urgency over the last decade. The issue of enunciation, its powers and possibilities, its *locations* and sitings, and the relational politics of discourse vis-à-vis sexual difference and gender have concerned a great number of critics and theorists. For example, feminist cultural critic Elspeth Probyn analyzes location as a question of "where we speak from and which voices are sanctioned."[48] In an important essay published in 1990, "Travels in the Postmodern: Making Sense of the Local," Probyn argues that reference to location is not transformative in and of itself. In fact, Probyn points out, specifying location is a standard gesture in the West, part of the production of value and knowledge that creates canons, races, genders, and a host of other marked categories. In Probyn's work, the term "local" signifies a more particularized aspect of location — deeply connected to the articulation of a specific time — and a potentially transformative spatial practice. The local does not exist in a pure state. Retrieving or recuperating the local cannot immediately transform the contradictory politics of feminist theory, nor is recourse to the local an instant panacea. Probyn writes: "Living with contradictions does not necessarily enable one to speak of them, and in fact for concrete reasons, it may be dangerous to do so. The recognition that the subaltern works across her positioning does not immediately entail a form of free agency." [49]

The question of agency is not unrelated to the issues of accountability and responsibility. Indeed, throughout the '80s, Euro-American feminist theories of subjectivity either opted for mobility (thereby homogenizing difference) or location (often overlooking transnational or global links or affiliations). Just how to negotiate these claims (with their attendant politics and institutional/critical practices) has preoccupied feminist theorists for the better part of fifteen years at the very least. The literature is now widely multidisciplinary, deserving of a close reading.

The Limits of Global Feminism

"For," the outsider will say, "in fact, as a woman, I have no country. As a woman I want no country. As a woman my country is the whole world."
—Virginia Woolf [50]

In creating our own centers and our own locals, we tend to forget that our centers displace others into the peripheries of our making.
—Elspeth Probyn [51]

In the winter of 1936–37, Virginia Woolf fashioned her now famous pacifist declaration against fascism and nationalism as the enunciation of a gendered standpoint. In the decades since Woolf wrote these words, Euro-American feminists have extended them to justify the dream of a global sisterhood of women with shared values and aspirations. It is, perhaps, no accident that the author of these lines about a common world of women also wrote the essay "A Room of One's Own," the classic exposition of modern Euro-American feminism's efforts to expand the conditions for work and a life of the mind to women. Juxtaposing these two images, a world of women and a room of one's own, underscores Woolf's modernist concern with space and location, with articulating the need for physical place as a matter of material and spiritual survival as well as with the expansion and contraction of colonial worlds. Such a concern with location and space, with rooms of one's own, with expanding "home" from the domestic to the public sphere, has been one of the hallmarks of Euro-American feminist practice. Drawing upon Woolf's powerful metaphors of claiming and imagining space for women, Euro-American feminists have conceptually refurbished rooms and staked out worlds in the name of women everywhere.

The claiming of a world space for women raises temporal questions as well as spatial considerations, questions of history as well as place. Can such claims be imagined outside the conceptual parameters of modernity? Can worlds be claimed in the name of categories such as "woman" in all innocence and benevolence, or do these gestures mark the revival of a form of feminist cultural imperialism? Chandra Mohanty has argued that any "naturalization" of analytic categories such as "woman" that are supposed to have cross-cultural validity ends in a mystification of difference, more particularly in the production and reproduction of discourses of difference between men and women, between women, and certainly between countries and peoples.[52] Euro-American discourses of "global feminism" have naturalized and totalized categories such as "Third World women" *and* "First World women." If such naturalizations have begun to be deconstructed in the name of an anti-imperialist and antiracist feminism, what conceptions of location replace Woolf's worlds and rooms?

It is in the complex and often paradoxical practices of a "politics of location" that the postcolonial and postmodern discourses of feminism emerge as intertwined subjects of criticism. First coined by Adrienne Rich in a series of essays presented and published in the early 1980s, the term "politics of location" has been picked up as a useful way to articulate the concerns of regional, particular, and local interests in a number of different fields and disciplines. As sketched out in Rich's work throughout the early '80s when she most forcefully examined the limits of feminism and the effects of racism and homophobia in the women's movement in the United States, her notion of a politics of location deconstructed hegemonic uses of the word "woman" within a context of U.S. racism and elite or academic feminist practices. As this concept moved beyond Rich's articulation, it began a process of cultural translation and transformation. At the present moment, it functions as both a marker of Western "interest" in other cultures and signals the formation of diasporic identities. Whether it encourages resistance to hegemonic formations, whether it becomes its own academic reification—turning into an instrument of hegemony itself—or whether it marks important shifts in discourses of location and displacement depends, not surprisingly, upon who utilizes the concept in what particular context.

The term "politics of location" emerged in the early 1980s as a particularly North American feminist articulation of difference and even more specifically as a method of interrogating and deconstructing the position, identity, and privilege of whiteness. Adrienne Rich's examination of a concept of a politics of location stems from more than a decade of struggles over the defining and positioning of feminism in the United States. Racism and homophobia in the U.S. women's movement in general, and in academic feminist discourses in particular, brought such painful splits between women that the white feminist mainstream was pressed to turn its attention away from assertions of similarity and homogeneity to examinations of difference. The uneven, divisive, and slow process of these shifts, shifts that remain incomplete and unfinished, testifies to the difficulties mainstream academic feminism has encountered in accounting for institutional, class, and race privilege in the formation of "theory." Simultaneous to struggles within U.S. women's movements and the emergence of an activist agenda of articulating difference within the category of gender, the introduction of poststructuralist methodologies also brought new value to explorations of difference within academic feminism. Rich's essays on a politics of location, therefore, can be read as eruptions of "difference" in both activist and academic discourses at a pivotal moment in white, North American feminist practices.

Poet, political activist, pedagogue, and publisher: Adrienne Rich has acquired a cultural influence that stems from several decades of interaction with the most pressing social issues in North American life. Emerging as a poet during the civil rights struggles and the nascent second-wave Euro-American women's movement, Rich's prose writing has moved from the academic to the more popular realm of cultural commentary.[53] Although Rich has explored positions of marginality within U.S. cultures of gender, race, and sexuality for close to thirty years, her work has currency and cultural legitimacy to a larger degree than many of the other writers and activists with whom she allies herself. It is within the context of the complex relationships between cultural assertions of collectivity (constituting "we" and "us") and the experience of marginality and exclusion that the question of location becomes politicized in contemporary U.S. feminist theory.

In several essays published in her collection *Blood, Bread, and Poetry* in 1986, Rich describes how she began to formulate the concept of a politics of location during her travel as a delegate from the United States to a conference in Sandinista-governed Nicaragua in the early '8os. She is quite explicit about the effects of this material displacement on her consciousness of power differences between countries and between people. Rich argues that "going there" changed her perception of her location as a North American. Particularly throughout the first essay written after her return, Rich lists what she has learned from her conversations with Nicaraguans in the midst of a revolution: food, health, and literacy are as important, if not more important, than free contraception and abortion. Her primary ideas about social change have not altered; she still believes that "you build from the ground up," empowering the most disempowered. What has changed is her perception of *who* constitutes the powerless: the ranks of the powerless include some men as well as women. Recognizing that her citizenship makes her more powerful in the world at large than either women or men in Nicaragua causes Rich to return with a new agenda: "I came home, feeling that feminists in the United States, *because we are here,* have a special reason to help try to get the foot of the United States off Central America. The women of Central America will then have room to move and name their own priorities as women, and this possibility affects us all."[54]

This passage illustrates Rich's evolving conviction that by working to change conditions at "home," women in the United States can have a direct effect on the lives of people in other places. Rather than conduct missionary movements to dictate correct feminist attitudes and practices in other countries, Rich argues for U.S. feminists to mobilize around a much broader range of issues than ever before, including foreign policy. In the early '8os this line of argument was new to many white, Euro-American feminists, marking a rupture with neocolonial Western modernities.

Each of Rich's essays on a politics of location revolves around the same core realization: that North American feminism, dominated primarily by white, middle-class women, has failed to acknowledge that women in other circumstances and in different geographic locations may have separate agendas and other priorities. Rich now sees that her feminist practice has been limited in general and even more particularly it has been ideologically constituted by U.S. foreign policy. "Some of us," Rich writes, "calling ourselves radical feminists, never meant anything less by women's liberation than the creation of a society without domination . . . The problem was that we did not know whom we meant when we said 'we.'"[55]

The construction of "we" as a questionable category marks Rich's essays on location as a dramatic departure from earlier radical feminist discourse: "How do we actively work to build a white, Western feminist consciousness that is not simply centered on itself, that resists white circumscribing?"[56] In the latter sentence, the "we" is clearly meant to signify "white, Western feminists," and this self-conscious marking of "we" signals Rich's new interest in differentiating a dominant feminist center from margins. This move, a kind of decentering through centering, a self-conscious review and rejection of the power of dominant feminist centrality, is a complex one and worth exploring in more detail. For, like other kinds of theoretical deterritorializations, the decentering or destabilization of power remains on the level of discourse; built on words and images, the effects of such rhetorical strategies are neither insignificant nor wholly transformative. They constitute partial shifts in the dynamics between women in different relations of power and thereby construct a particular moment in the histories of these relationships.

The key to Rich's politics of location, then, lies in her recognition that as marginal as white, Western women appear to be in relation to the real movers and shakers in this world—white men—there are others made marginal by white, Western women themselves. Rich desires "us" to take responsibility for these marginalizations, to acknowledge "our" part in this process in order to change these unequal dynamics: "The movement for change is a changing movement, changing itself, demasculinizing itself, de-Westernizing itself, becoming a critical mass that is saying in so many different voices, languages, gestures, actions: it must change; we ourselves can change it."[57] How does a feminist movement for social change "de-Westernize" itself? Rich proposes a politics of location in which white, North American feminists explore the meaning of "whiteness," "recognizing our location, having to name the ground we're coming from, the conditions we have taken for granted."[58]

Although Rich had been moving in the direction of such a deconstructive moment for some time, without the critiques of Audre Lorde, Barbara Smith, Michelle Cliff, and other U.S. women of color with whom Rich worked throughout this period, her notion of a politics of location would not have been as fully formulated. "De-Westernizing," then, could be seen to begin at "home." Yet her full-est critique of her earlier "chauvinism" is written out not within the parameters of domestic conversations but in the aftermath of a trip abroad. In its first articulation as a term, therefore, a politics of loca-tion could be seen as a *suppression* of discussions of differences between white women and women of color *within* the geographic boundaries of the United States in favor of a new binary: U.S. white women and the victims of U.S. foreign policies. This floating boundary between "us" and "them" is set by Rich depending upon her travels, her femi-nist agendas, and her point of view. The subject of U.S. women of color and their disparate and linked histories of diaspora and im-migration along with contradictory and complex political positions vis-à-vis U.S. nationalist identities and agendas have no place in this formulation.

Thus, despite her efforts to account for the politics of location, Rich remains locked into the conventional opposition of the global-local nexus as well as the binary construction of Western and non-Western. She deconstructs the equalizations of "global feminism" (the "common world of women" scenario) by homogenizing the loca-tion of "North American feminist." Yet in her earlier deconstructions of North American differences between women Rich had seemed to ignore or discount global distinctions. Such oscillations are pre-dictable in binary constructions that depend upon generalized polar opposites. The root of the particular problem at work in Rich's essays on a politics of location can be traced to her attachment to the con-vention of travel as transformation. Unable to critique the inherently binary nature of Western travel paradigms, Rich completely rewrites her "home" in terms of "away." Yet over ten years of coalition work with women of color in the United States might account for many of the ideas found in the politics of location essays. The issue of ac-countability is not only between North and South American women, then, but among women at home in the United States as well.

Rich's deconstructive practice appears to have captured the imagination of a range of Euro-American critics who seek to bridge poststructuralist destabilizations of master narratives and materially based political concerns.[59] Sensitive to poststructuralist charges of essentialism toward any fixed positions, the theorists of location seek to negotiate between ahistorical mystifications of identity made in the name of political movements and antihistorical universalizations made in the name of philosophical purity. Thus Rich's essays on the politics of location have encouraged decentering moves as critics examine their positions vis-à-vis geopolitics. For example, Neil Smith and Cindi Katz point to what they term a crucial "double shift" in Rich's critical practice: "The brilliance of Rich's formulation is that it maintains the relationality of social identity without slipping into a formless relativism, and at the same time disarranges the received fixity of social *and* geographical location."[60] Rich, they argue, questions the "very process through which the base map of different locations" is drawn, linking social and geographical location in a dynamic relation. Parting ways with Euro-American "global" feminism's vision of a unitary world of women, Rich acknowledges the problematic power of mapping, naming, and establishing agendas.

This practice of a politics of location, however, conflates "Western" and "white," reinscribing the centrality of white women's position within Euro-American feminism. A further danger lies in the removal of the term from the context of debates about feminist accountability to celebrations of cultural relativism, expressing a transnational "fiesta" of differences that mystify and codify power relations. While some readings of Rich (such as Chandra Mohanty's 1987 essay on the politics of experience)[61] have integrated this specific formulation into feminist, anti-imperialist cultural criticism, the circulation of Rich's notion of a politics of location does not always emphasize her concerns about race and imperialism.[62] With such homogenizations in mind, Lata Mani, in "Multiple Mediations," argues for a revised politics of location that demonstrates that "the relation between experience and knowledge is now seen to be not one of correspondence but one fraught with history, contingency, and struggle."[63] In this practice, a politics of location operates as a strenuously contested and dynamically stressed term, signaling debate and transformative theorizing.

In a similar vein, in "Notes on Travel and Theory" James Clifford draws on Rich's notion of a politics of location to question the totalizing operations of Euro-American theory, problematizing the "suppression of location and its genealogical, storytelling functions."[64] Clifford points to Rich's politics of location as a way to negotiate the claims of the particular and universal, neither "grounded" in essentialist experience nor released into transcultural and transhistorical "overview." Rather, Clifford argues that location in this critical practice is dynamic, historicized, and inherently multiple:

> "Location," here, is not a matter of finding a stable "home" or of discovering a common experience. Rather it is a matter of being aware of the difference that makes a difference in concrete situations, of recognizing the various inscriptions, "places," or "histories" that both empower and inhibit the construction of theoretical categories like "Woman," "Patriarchy," or "colonization," categories essential to political action as well as to serious comparative knowledge. "Location" is thus, concretely, a *series* of locations and encounters, travel within diverse, but limited spaces.[65]

Viewing location as a part of travel, as entailing movement or multiplicity rather than stasis and singularity, links the theorization of place to the paradoxical materiality that time-space compression can produce. Imbuing space with time leads to spatializing via the production of histories. Which histories do this work in postmodernity? Or, rather, what claims for identity and subjectivity produce histories through spatialization in Euro-American critical practices?

The notion of a politics of location, generated out of an urgent recognition of specifically U.S. racist and ethnocentric feminist critical practices, has helped to produce just such questions for Euro-American criticism. Along with the widespread circulation of Rich's essays in the late '80s and early '90s, the converging critical practices of colonial discourse, ethnic studies, and feminist studies, among others, in the U.S. academy have highlighted the theoretical status of "location" as a primary discourse. For those who are troubled by the appearance of relativism and nihilism in poststructuralist theories of the subject, "location" promises to situate the free-floating signifiers of identity in historicized sites. For those who are concerned to avoid the sentimental or naive excesses of "essentialism" (the catchword among Euro-American feminists for biological determinism or reductionism), the "local" mediates history, science, and radical contingency to propose a material but obviously constructed substance or presence. Underlying these compromises and negotiations is the recognition that political necessity, even urgency, requires the theorization of a meaningful tension between universal and particular, similarity and difference, and home and away.

The crucial questions remain: Who writes of difference, location, and travel? And who gains? As Rosi Braidotti points out, "accountability and positionality go together."[66] The struggle for accountability requires a negotiation, then, of positionality and the knowledges produced from those locations. Referring directly to Rich's essay, Vivek Dhareshwar argues that a politics of location necessitates accountability of one's actions: "That struggle, and the questioning of one's privileges and the taking of responsibility that it entails, must begin with oneself . . . That questioning, its urgency, is guided by the possibilities offered by a future 'we,' by the possibility of political community that without eliminating conflict would allow for mutually heightened vulnerability."[67]

Without such accountability, Euro-American feminist critical practices will not sufficiently examine the material conditions of "information retrieval," ignoring the politics of reception in the interpretation of texts, information, and points of view from the so-called peripheries, calling for inclusion of "difference" by "making room" or "creating space" without historicizing the relations of the global-local nexus that govern production, circulation, and exchange. Most importantly, feminists with cultural and social centrality need to investigate the grounds of their strong desire for rapport and intimacy with the "other." Examining the politics of location in the production and reception of theory can turn the terms of inquiry from desiring, inviting, and granting space to others to becoming accountable for one's own investments in cultural metaphors and values. Such accountability can begin to shift the ground of feminist practice from magisterial relativism (as if diversified cultural production simply occurs in a social vacuum) to the complex interpretive practices that acknowledge the historical roles of mediation, betrayal, and alliance in the relationships between women in diverse locations.

Gendering the Local: Standpoint Epistemologies

Thus, the dangers of postmodernism as seen by some feminists are those of both relativism and the abandonment of theory. While many reject the modernist "view from nowhere," they question whether postmodernism would not lead us to the equally problematic "view from everywhere." Are coherent theory and politics possible within a postmodern position?
—Linda J. Nicholson [68]

The question of how to negotiate the tension between displacement and placement, deterritorialization and reterritorialization, nomadism and home preoccupies Euro-American feminist critical practices.[69] Whether these concerns are articulated as the relationships between local and global, center and periphery, home and away, or national and international, a sense of inquiry into the status of boundaries, borders, and states of difference pervades theoretical discourses. Bodies of knowledge, physical bodies, and bodies of land coexist as subjects of feminist inquiry into the social construction of raced, gendered, sexed, and classed material life. Drawing upon the terms of the emerging postmodern geographies as well the multidisciplinary methodologies of cultural studies, much of this feminist work reframes and reconfigures the major Euro-American poststructuralist projects of the '70s and '80s. Debates about "sexual difference" in the context of racism, "postmodernism" in the context of neocolonial globalization, and "gender" in the wake of lesbian, queer, and transgender critiques have raised critical flashpoints in Euro-American feminist theory.

Many of these feminist theories engage the tension between difference and similarity, recognizing the limits of "global feminism" and critiquing the power moves of universalizing gender theories. Yet an attachment to a generalized notion of gender as a primary category of analysis pervades much of this apparently "postmodern" literature. This very move, the assertion of difference and diversity in an articulation of universalizing singularity, characterizes a school of thought associated with a "standpoint epistemology." The so-called standpoint school of thought has elicited a vigorous debate in Euro-American feminist theory, especially in the United States as political struggles around race and class privilege have intensified the stakes in the discussion. First coined by Nancy Hartsock to establish a ground for feminist thought and political action at approximately the same moment as Adrienne Rich's politics of location, the concept of gender as a singular standpoint is as fraught as the notion of a unitary global sisterhood. That is, the modernist idea that there is *a* standpoint that gender makes possible, linking women in a common experience-based perspective, is challenged by postmodern articulations of multiply sited subjects and diverse critical practices. While Rich's analysis of location attempts to deconstruct a unitary position, Hartsock's advocacy of a gendered standpoint reasserts a kind of global feminism—the assumption of common ground on terms defined by a specific set of interests.

Hartsock published her essay "Rethinking Modernism: Minority vs. Majority Theories" in a context of widespread concern among feminists in the United States over the incursion of French-influenced poststructuralism during the '70s and '80s, particularly in terms of divisions between feminists engendered by the "race for theory," as Barbara Christian put it.[70] The relationship between activism and the academy, between the social movement politics generated by civil rights, second-wave feminist, and antiwar efforts as well as the institutional and professional politics that produced the new "theories," was questioned rigorously (as it continues to be). At the beginning of her essay, Hartsock asks: "[W]hat kinds of knowledge claims are required for grounding political action by different groups?"[71] Her conclusion, that "postmodernism represents a dangerous approach for any marginalized group to adopt," depends upon a number of assumptions about subjectivity, history, politics, and location or positionality. That is, Hartsock refers to differences between women but cannot specify her own difference or positionality vis-à-vis women whose interests might be different from her own.

Hartsock argues that "transcendent" and "omnipotent theorizers," here understood to be nonmaterialist poststructuralists, produce objects of study—"Others"—by persuading themselves that they exist "outside time and space and power relations."[72] She identifies social movements that have rejected the totalizing powers of the "Theorizer," positioning feminists as "Others" who would rebel against such domination: "We who have not been allowed to be subjects of history, who have not been allowed to make our history, are beginning

to reclaim our pasts and remake our futures on our own terms."[73]
Implicitly and explicitly, Hartsock calls for a coalition of "liberation
movements" that would resist the race for theory and recraft political
and theoretical dialogues. But Hartsock does not query the formation
of "we" in the manner that Rich does. In her essays on the politics of
location Rich argues that assumptions about a collective identity mask
power relations. By including women, regardless of class or race privilege, in the generic categorization of "we," Hartsock produces static
terms of identity that cannot account for the complex subjectivities
and conditions of cultural production that postmodernity engenders.
Simply rejecting "the postmodern" in favor of identity politics can
only result in coalitions formed through cultural nationalism.

   The model of coalition became increasingly important in U.S.
feminist discourses throughout the '80s as the emphasis on "differences" worked through various strata of activist and academic efforts
to address the history and legacy of white supremacy, homophobia,
and class privilege.[74] Rather than assert a common world or singular female experience, many Euro-American feminists struggled to
develop alternative formations that could account for "differences"
without losing the intrinsic base of materialist feminist analysis: the
female body, the lived experience of female bodies in a masculinist
world, and the shared elements that analysis of female lives might
bring to the fore. Theorizing "location" was one strategy to ground
the specificity of female lives without biological determinism or
global feminist relativism. "Standpoint epistemology," however, asserts positionality not as a way to link geopolitics to an understanding
of how subjects become gendered in historically specific ways but
as a way to embed a point of view that is claimed to be generalizable. This mode of positioning reproduces the power relations that
generated the critique of Euro-American feminist racism and ethnocentrism in the first place. Arguing for modernism against an aestheticized postmodernism, for nationalism against transnationalism
or hegemonic globalization, and for coalitions of discrete entities,
Hartsock's "standpoint" remains linked to the Marxist tradition of
dialectical materialism. Thus, brought together by a common standpoint, women will transcend their state of oppression as well as any
significant differences between them.

   In a reading of Bernice Johnson Reagon's well-known essay on coalition politics, Hartsock argues that empowerment occurs through nationalism and social activism based on identity politics. Citing Reagon's text very selectively to propound a pro-nationalist position, Hartsock articulates her primary complaint against a generalized post-modern/poststructuralist critical practice: "Somehow it seems highly suspicious that it is at this moment in history, when so many groups are engaged in 'nationalisms' which involve redefinitions of the marginalized Others, that doubt rises in the academy about the nature of the 'subject,' about the possibilities for a general theory which can describe the world, about historical 'progress.' Why is it, exactly at the moment when so many of us who have been silenced begin to demand the right to name ourselves, to act as subjects rather than objects of history, that just then the concept of subjecthood becomes 'problematic'?"[75] Hartsock neglects to mention that Euro-American feminism initiated its claims for selfhood throughout the modern period and especially during the nineteenth century (often at the expense of poor, nonwhite, and colonized women's subjectivity), not just "at this moment." A closer look at those histories destabilizes the idealistic coalition implied in Hartsock's reference to "liberation movements." In resistance to these acts of domination, women around the world have contested any number of practices that modernity has engendered, including global feminisms, masculinist nationalisms, local elite power relations, and "underdevelopment." Indeed, in "Rethinking Modernism," Hartsock's references to "liberation movements" tend to be sweepingly generic ("women's liberation," "decolonization struggles," "racial liberation movements"), erasing the struggles within those movements against racism, class privilege, sexism, and other forms of discrimination and domination. "Our" silences, then, have been unevenly produced and experienced.

Without a clear analysis of the material relations between political geographies and cultural formations, raising questions about what counts as theory gets linked to *who* articulates and produces knowledge. "Identity" is marshaled to confer authenticity and power in resistance to powerlessness. Standpoint allies itself with concerns about positioning interests and the material conditions of knowledge production, but it recuperates the binaries of center and periphery, "us" and "them" through identity politics. For example, in order to critique the "postmodern" excesses of poststructuralist relativism in Euro-American feminist theory, Hartsock reads Reagon's coalition politics essay as pro-nationalist, that is, as calling for separatist activism. Reagon, a long-standing activist in civil rights and feminist struggles, a founder of the singing group Sweet Honey in the Rock, and a well-respected writer and U.S. social and cultural historian, articulates identity politics in much of her work. The 1983 publication and circulation of Reagon's piece in Barbara Smith's significant collection, *Home Girls: A Black Feminist Anthology* (one of the first volumes printed under the Kitchen Table: Women of Color Press imprimatur), strongly influenced the discussion of coalitions, communities, and identity politics in U.S. feminist circles throughout the decade. Reading this essay as pro-nationalist to argue against "postmodernism," however, underscores the stakes in claiming an identity through such paradigms of modernity as claiming a "self" and a "nation."

Reagon's essay was first delivered as a presentation at a U.S. women's music festival that was struggling with strategies of radical lesbian separatism and cultural nationalism in the face of racism and classism within its "woman-centered" constituency. Reflecting on the positive and negative results of separatism as a political and cultural method of survival, Reagon argued that such impulses can make spaces that are vitally necessary for the cultural and even physical survival of oppressed groups and individuals: "That space . . . should be a nurturing space where you sift out what people are saying about you and decide who you really are. And you take the time to try to construct within yourself and within your community who you would be if you were running society. In fact, in that little barred room where you check everybody at the door, you act out community. You pretend that your room is a world."[76] But, Reagon cautions, the limit of such a practice is that it is *not* the world—and the world will not tolerate your practice of separation. Thus "there is no chance that you can survive by staying *inside* the barred room . . . Nationalism at another point becomes reactionary because it is totally inadequate for surviving in a world with many peoples."[77] Although it can be terrifying to emerge from those spaces of separation that felt so urgently necessary, Reagon argues, "We've pretty much come to the end of a time when you can have a space that is 'yours only'—just for the people you want to be there . . . There is no hiding place. There is nowhere you can go and only be with people who are like you. It's over. Give it up."[78]

Reagon's critique of separatist identity politics in U.S. radical cultural feminism in the early '8os hinges on a distinction between "home" and "coalition." Our homes, she cautions, are not to be confused with the space of our communities (which must always be mixed, contentious, and changing). Even though this worldly analysis of the space of political action and affiliation still entails identity politics and a cultural nationalist "home," Reagon challenges the universalizing presumptions of a gendered standpoint. The term "woman" is a "code" that cannot be confused with a generality: it has to be made into multiple particularities through temporal struggles in the spatialized embodiment of community. "Anything," Reagon writes, that says " 'Women,' we're gonna come."[79] Making the category "woman" work, making it more historically accurate and politically viable, Reagon concludes, "Today wherever women gather together it is not necessarily nurturing. It is coalition building. And if you feel the strain, you may be doing some good work."[80]

It strikes me as interesting that Hartsock reads Reagon's essay as exclusively propounding a standpoint based on gender. Although Reagon is reclaiming the identity "woman" for those who have been excluded by white ethnocentrism and now choose to "gather together," I read the essay as a critique of standpoint epistemologies and global feminism. If Reagon's nonacademic presentation in a movement event such as a women's music festival articulates a powerful critique of the critical practices of feminism both in and out of the U.S. academy, then Hartsock's opposition between theory and activism seems reductionist. That is, the critique of white supremacy, bourgeois thinking, and Eurocentrism comes from all over or, at least, from diverse places and actors. Reagon's essay poses questions such as *Whose* standpoint constitutes identity? and From *where* does that point of view emanate? We are also prompted to ask how specific mediations produce various readings and how different sites engender particular crises of meaning that lead to new theories and modes of articulation. If activist locales and actors generate theory and contribute to the very terms and debates that constitute the crisis of meaning and communication that characterizes "postmodernism," the strict division between "academic theory" and "activism" is undermined. And the category "woman" becomes deconstructed in practice in ways that Hartsock's "modernism" cannot account for or contain.

The problem may be, as Norma Alarcón has expressed it, that when gender is the central concept in feminist theory, "epistemology is flattened out in such a way that we lose sight of the complex and multiple ways in which the subject and object of possible experience are constituted."[81] Standpoint epistemologies give us no way to inquire into *relative* mobilities and spatial imprisonments that mark diverse women's lives. Alarcón points out that while the *violence* that is part of the process of subject constitution in modernity has been acknowledged vis-à-vis sexual difference, Euro-American feminism has been less able to account for the violence that comes from women toward other women: "To be oppressed means to be disenabled not only from grasping an 'identity,' but also from reclaiming it. In this culture, to grasp or reclaim an identity means always already to have become a subject of consciousness. The theory of the subject of consciousness as a unitary and synthesizing agent of knowledge is always already a posture of domination."[82]

Who can inhabit the subject position that Hartsock wishes to save from poststructuralist deconstruction? What historical conditions structure that possibility or impossibility? What spaces or locations are recognized or erased? As Inderpal Grewal puts it, "while the disenfranchised were earlier seen as the 'other,' they must now become the Self." Both Alarcón and Grewal view the "subject" as a term that must be problematized and not recuperated ahistorically or statically. Thus Grewal argues that it becomes difficult to understand what the new subjectivities might be, "when what Hartsock seems to be calling for is the autonomous, full subject, the imperial subject that has structured both colonial power relations and Anglo-American feminism."[83]

To articulate multiplicity is not enough. Alarcón's essay on the critical production and reception of the groundbreaking anthology of writing by women of color, *This Bridge Called My Back,* argues that when the point of view is inhabited by "woman" it does not automatically alter social paradigms. Subject formation since the Enlightenment proceeds through identification into full consciousness — formally reserved for men of property, it is now claimed for women. The right to an identity is perceived to be the key to subjectivity, citizenship, and political viability. When this process remains undercritiqued or recuperated, as Hartsock, for example, would have it, the "inherited view of consciousness has not been questioned at all" and, Alarcón argues, works against the interests of nonwhite women.

Rather than identification, the complex subjects in formation

in the anthology under review in Alarcón's essay work through dis-
identification with the "prevalent formulations of the most forcefully
theoretical subject of feminism": the idea that there is a common de-
nominator between women.[84] Alarcón describes the female subjects of
This Bridge as constructed through a "crisis of meaning," through the
cognitive dissonance and epistemic violence that articulation requires
as women who cannot identify with "woman" in Euro-American
feminist contexts. Alarcón reads the writers in the anthology as displaced in their subjectivity through a multiplicity of discourses: "femi-
nist/lesbian, nationalist, racial, socioeconomic, historical, etc."[85] The
writers in *This Bridge* are "driven to grasp" their social relations. There
is no single standpoint in this reading of the texts: indeed, there are
not exactly "differences": "*Bridge* writers, in part, were aware that these
positions are often incompatible or contradictory, and others did not
have access to the maze of discourses competing for their body and
voice. The self-conscious effort to reflect on their 'flesh and blood experiences to concretize a vision that can begin to heal our "wounded
knee"' led many *Bridge* speakers to take a position in conflict with
multiple intercultural and intracultural discursive interpretations in
an effort to come to grips with the 'many-headed demon of oppression.'"[86]

   If oppression is a many-headed demon, our responses must be
just as multiple in the effort to resist appropriation and mystification.
To argue for an analysis of the compressions and reassertions of time
and space, divisions of labor, placements and displacements is not to
argue for chaos, microfragmentation, or hybridity. Attention to difference in this context of linkages augurs alternative systems of interpretation, narrative, and subjectivity. The discrete categories of identity politics cannot account for these complicated subjects. As Grewal
has argued, such postmodern subjectivities are not as "unattainable"
as they are often represented to be, "nor are they the domain of white,
male, European theorists."[87] Rather, "multiply *placed*" and "multiply
linked" subjectivities are constructed out of the complex positionings
that diasporas, for example, and other contemporary conditions produce.[88] Yet, as Alarcón argues, much Euro-American feminist writing continues to stress the placement and positioning of subjects as
a means of fixing or recognizing identity rather than an examination
of the social construction of the desire to fix identity itself.

   For example, Linda Alcoff's well-known essay "Cultural Feminism versus Post-Structuralism: The Identity Crisis in Feminist Theory," first published in 1988, is representative of efforts to formulate a theory of subjectivity that is neither essentialist nor radically indeterminate. Alcoff critiques the limits of U.S. cultural feminism's essentialist categories through poststructuralist destabilizations of metaphysics and logocentrism. But she argues for the viability of the political agenda of cultural feminism and the agency and subjectivity it signals. Alcoff draws upon Teresa de Lauretis's influential work to bridge the seemingly incommensurate gulf between politics (figured in the United States at that moment as cultural feminism) and theory (figured as French-influenced poststructuralism).[89] In her work in the mid to late '80s, rather than linking gender to an ontological nature or biology, as the early work of Adrienne Rich and Mary Daly seemed to do, de Lauretis explored a notion of experience as practice whereby gender could be seen to be a lived process of interactions, situations and gestures *in the world*. Just as importantly, gender could not be seen to be simply a language effect and thereby could not be relegated to a practice of free play. In theorizing experience in a newly complex and synthetic manner, de Lauretis opened up the terms of both cultural feminism and poststructuralism in ways that led to the formation of related concepts of gender positions. The subject that emerges in this work has agency and a capacity for analytical reflection, with a consciousness that is in the process of formation—never totally fixed and always in relation to history.

Deeply engaging de Lauretis's work, Alcoff proposes a concept of gendered identity as *positionality*.[90] Although she stresses fluid and contingent properties in these positions, her theory falls squarely into the logic of "identity politics," the notion that "one's identity is taken (and defined) as a political point of departure, as a motivation for action, and as a delineation of one's politics."[91] Referring to "points of departure" and "claiming identities," Alcoff tries to balance her stated interest in deconstructive practices and the fixed, standpoint epistemology of gender positionality:

> The concept of positionality includes two points: first . . . that the concept of woman is a relational term identifiable only within a (constantly moving) context; but, second, that the position women find themselves in can be actively utilized (rather

than transcended) as a location for the construction of meaning, a place from where meaning can be *discovered* (the meaning of femaleness). The concept of woman as positionality shows how women use their positional perspective as a place from which values are interpreted and constructed rather than as a locus of an already determined set of values.[92]

Here Alcoff performs a contradictory move. On the one hand, she argues for mobility of signification, a seemingly historicized notion of terms, and a deconstruction of the metaphysics of presence and transcendence. On the other hand, the rigidly singular aspect of her categories (*the* concept of positionality, *the* meaning of femaleness, *the* position that women find themselves in, etc.) undermines that agenda. As Norma Alarcón has described this operation: "The difference is handed over with one hand and taken away with the other."[93]

If positionality and location share many of the pitfalls of standpoint epistemology, how might feminist critical practices proceed otherwise? As the discussion of the history of representations of space in Euro-American critical practices and the production of a global-local nexus in conditions of postmodernity has shown, any utopian or celebratory promotion of the "local" or "location" per se will not contribute to the spatialized politics that challenge "scattered hegemonies."[94] If, as Elspeth Probyn suggests, we do not abandon the local but "work more deeply in and against it," we lay the groundwork for a rejection of unitary feminism in favor of affiliations that are not based on mystified notions of similarity *or* difference.[95]

To work more deeply in and against the local might require strategies that acknowledge the specific conditions of space-time compression, transnational tendencies in economies and cultures, as well as the challenges to binary oppositions such as center-periphery, global-local, self-other, and so on. Given its participation in Euro-American modernity, its articulation through subjectivity and identity politics, and the powerful positioning of its geopolitics through national affiliations, Euro-American feminist discourses have no choice but to query the locations and positions that seem to make a difference in the way women's lives are lived and represented.

Working in and against the Local

We need to think through what might be an adequately progressive sense of place, one which would fit in with current global-times and the feelings and relations they give rise to, *and* which would be useful in what are, after all, political struggles often inevitably based on place. The question is how to hold on to that notion of geographical difference, of uniqueness, even of rooted-ness if people want that, without it being reactionary.
—Doreen Massey[96]

Place, location, and position offer roots to the histories and identities that many people struggle to achieve and realize in the aftermath of the slave trade, colonial intervention and disruption, and massive migrations. I have been arguing that recent Euro-American feminist discourses of location and position can be linked to the critical geographies of postmodernity. The debates about essentialism, identity politics, standpoint epistemology, coalitions, and the politics of location have produced discourses that negotiate placement and displacement. In particular, a set of critics now link analyses of time *and* space to the histories of colonialism, racism, and feminism.

For example, in two key essays written in the last half of the '80s, Chandra Talpade Mohanty asks how location both determines and produces "experience and difference as analytical and political categories in feminist 'cross-cultural' work."[97] A sociologist who has influenced the terms of Euro-American feminist discourse through her examination of the histories of political activism, antiracist and anti-imperialist critical practices, and the theorization of the term "Third World women," Mohanty asks *how* one locates oneself in time and space. A critic of imperializing tendencies in Euro-American feminist theories, Mohanty allies herself with Rich's deconstructive project, shifting from an inquiry into the position of privilege per se to the multiple positionings that feminist critical practices engender.

In order to examine the dynamics of these positionings, Mohanty investigates both temporal and spatial dimensions. For example, in "Feminist Encounters: Locating the Politics of Experience," published in 1987, Mohanty argues that focusing on the "*temporality* of struggle" destabilizes the logic of Euro-American modernity. She identifies a static sense of place with a dominant History: all "non-identical," uneven, and diverse articulations of contemporary conditions are subsumed by a universalized master narrative. Explicitly drawing on Rich's notion of a politics of location, Mohanty negotiates history and geography to dislodge singular, privileged accounts in favor of more multiple and diverse ones. Oppositional agency occurs through a temporality of struggle, here defined as "an insistent, simultaneous, nonsynchronous process characterized by multiple locations rather than a search for origins and endings."[98] The location of critical practice that Mohanty inquires into is provided by her own experiential matrix as a South Asian woman of color in the United States, reconfiguring the link between "personal" and "political" as a challenge to rather than a recuperation of the possessive individualism of Euro-American paradigms of subjectivity: "It is this process, this reterritorialization through struggle that allows me a paradoxical continuity of self, mapping and transforming my political location. It suggests a particular notion of political agency, since my location forces and enables specific modes of reading and knowing the dominant. The struggles I choose to engage in are then an intensification of these modes of knowing—an engagement on a different level of knowledge. There is, quite simply, no transcendental location possible in the U.S.A. of the 1980s."[99]

In theorizing reterritorialization through links between women based on spatialized histories, Mohanty opens a space for the articulation of a "third world women's politics."[100] In "Cartographies of Struggle: Third World Women and the Politics of Feminism" from 1991, Mohanty utilizes Benedict Anderson's notion of "imagined communities" to support her construction of "third world women" as a "political constituency," not a "biological or even sociological one." Thus what links "third world women" or "women of color" is the potential of coalition based on a "common context of struggle rather than color or racial identifications." Mohanty argues that it is "the common context of struggles against specific exploitative structures and systems that determines our potential political alliances."[101]

Yet determining the "common context" among diverse women necessarily entails some form of identity formation. For instance, to ground her argument, Mohanty investigates the conditions of multinational production, colonialism and its aftermath, and various institutional and disciplinary practices. Arguing that an analysis of the employment of Third World women workers would form a "potential space for cross-national feminist solidarity and organiz-

ing," Mohanty identifies a site of feminist practice that confounds the
Euro-American feminist convention of Third World martyred victims
and First World saviors.[102] Rather than observing or appropriating
the "experiences" of women who people the "global assembly line,"[103]
Mohanty points toward critical practices that would form a grid of
intersecting interests, subjects, and purposes. In that multiply constituted space of critical analysis and political action, new subjects of
feminism emerge that cannot be written into the modernist narrative.

This kind of agency, "born of history and geography" combined, produces positions from which narratives, practices, and cultural articulations can be enunciated. Rather than postulating "I
am born female and therefore my experience is structured by that
fact," Mohanty argues that the intersections of "various systemic networks of class, race, (hetero)sexuality, and nation . . . position us as
'women.'"[104] Location is, then, discontinuous, multiply constituted,
and traversed by diverse social formations. One becomes a woman
through race and class, for example, not as opposed to race and class.
Third World women can be linked in the context of white racism in
the colonies and in the nation-states of Europe and the Americas as
the regulation of miscegenation made material the property relations
of the slave trade and imperialist expansion. Or one's sexuality is
constitutive of one's positioning vis-à-vis heterosexual privilege in a
homophobic culture. When immigration status, legal and civil rights,
and socioeconomic parity can be abridged based on a lack of ad-
herence to an established sexual norm, lesbians experience "gender"
in historically specific ways. One's citizenship and placement in relation to nation-states and geopolitics formulate one's experience of
gender when the threat of deportation, the lack of a passport, or subaltern status within the nation as an indigenous "native" place limits
on or obstruct mobility and modes of survival. In this cartography
of struggle, gender operates simultaneously but diversely. When an
illegal immigrant to the United States experiences a lack of access to
reproductive health services, is it the same "experience" that a middle-
class or wealthy woman has in her pursuit of similar services? Access
to reproductive health services does not automatically create "sisterhood." But an alliance between women who need such services that
did not force "sameness" upon its subjects might produce significant
results. Acknowledging power and its historical effects as constitutive of differences among women lies at the very base of theorizing

location in this way. Mohanty argues emphatically for a recognition of the relational dynamic between the terms we more usually string together in lists:

> The relations of power I am referring to are not reducible to binary oppositions or oppressor/oppressed relations. I want to suggest that it is possible to retain the idea of multiple, fluid structures of domination which intersect to locate women differently at particular historical conjunctures, while at the same time insisting on the dynamic oppositional agency of individuals and collectives and their engagement in "daily life." It is this focus on dynamic oppositional agency that clarifies the intricate connection between systemic relationships and the directionality of power. In other words, systems of racial, class, and gender domination do not have *identical* effects on women in third world contexts.[105]

A similar argument is made in Ruth Frankenberg and Lata Mani's essay, "Crosscurrents, Crosstalk: Race, 'Postcoloniality' and the Politics of Location," published in 1993. Frankenberg and Mani begin their inquiry into various axes of subject formation by questioning the totalizing effects of terms such as "postcoloniality." An overused generality can be made meaningful, they suggest, by situating a term in time and space across a range of contexts.[106] Thus different subjects are positioned differently by the social relations that a universalized use of the term works to obscure, and those positions are structured by spatial and temporal dynamics. So to ask "What about 'the colonial' is over, and for whom?" requires a locating of perspective that disrupts the temporal logic of dominant history. Whose colonialism, when, and where? Such questions summon multiple subjects and within each subject the acknowledgment of multiple axes of subject formation. Thus the "postcolonial" is constructed discursively not only as a binary opposition between colonizer/colonized, as a "dialogue with dominant white society," but through an "engagement between particular subjects, white society, region of origin and region of religious and/or political affiliation . . ."[107] Here location as an axis stages "cross-racial encounters" and could be imagined as a mode of staging many other interactions.

Thinking about location as an "axis" rather than a place helps us

imagine the contradictory and complex workings of subject formation in postmodernity. If, as Frankenberg and Mani argue, there are
"moments and spaces" in which subjects are "driven to grasp their
positionings and subjecthood" (in this case as "postcolonial"), there
are forms of oppression that make such recognition and consciousness impossible or limited.[108] This uneven, discontinuous, yet open
process allows for the alignment of identity at the intersection of
axes not as the monumental erection of a stable site but as a tempo-
rally spatialized location—a paradoxical space of historicized effects.
Thus practices "may be given new meanings and create 'new subjects'
in different locations."[109] Frankenberg and Mani's examination of the
term "postcolonial" opens up an analytical space that enables them
to argue that at "given moments and locations, the axis of coloni-
zation/decolonization might be *the* most salient one, at other times,
not so."[110]

The significance of Frankenberg and Mani's argument to Euro-
American feminist critical practice may lie in their efforts to historicize
without creating ethnocentric periodizations. Emphasizing simultaneity and multiplicity allows for an analysis of the way relationships
to different axes of domination shift and interact. Thus some women
remain attached to racist or colonialist discursive formations long
after the originary material conditions have vanished or changed. But
the powers that can be accrued from those discursive formations, the
power to maintain them, in fact, might be similar and also different
in a distinct location or time. Resistance to those formations, then,
requires a more complex analysis of these similarities and differences.
These histories might yield better materials for building coalitions
among women in diverse and unequal relations to each other.

In their study of women's lives in Worcester, Massachusetts,
Geraldine Pratt and Susan Hanson argue that geography, as the study
of the spatialization of social relations, opens up such coalitional
energies in Euro-American feminist critical practices. Noting that the
celebratory treatment of differences among women can result in static
terms that reinscribe closure and recuperate white, middle-class dominance, Pratt and Hanson are equally concerned that the valorization
of terms of exile, marginality, and nomadism can reproduce elitism
and individualism. Like Mohanty, Frankenberg and Mani, and others,
they advocate the exploration of the processes through which differ-

ences are created, "to show the ways in which gendered, racialised and classed identities are fluid *and* constituted in place—and therefore in different ways in different places."[111]

Placing the emphasis on *processes* through which differences *are created* rather than on the recognition and consolidation of discrete, primordial identities moves theory into a position of operating for affiliative subjects rather than against them. Thus Pratt and Hanson draw a distinction between "situating oneself in order to recognise and take responsibility for one's identity and actions" and a "quest for an unsituated (or continually resituated) consciousness."[112] In their study, therefore, location does not simply *reflect* identity: identities are formed through the mediating activities of places, locations, and positions. Geography, Pratt and Hanson argue, is ideally suited to investigate the spatialization of these temporal activities as lives become gendered, raced, and classed in relation to cultural and social formations. In "Geography and the Construction of Difference," they focus on the circulations of working populations, in this case of women who work not only at home but in the service and industrial sectors of a small city that has weathered the recession but not recovered its vitality as a former mill town. Arguing against the elision of discussions of labor in most Euro-American cultural studies and pointing to the significance of international labor migrations, Pratt and Hanson stress that to focus solely on tourism, mass media, or even economic globalization will overstate or overgeneralize the phenomenon of "time-space" compression: "Although the world is indeed increasingly well connected, we must hold this in balance with the observation that most people live intensely local lives; their homes, work places, recreation, shopping, friends, and often family are all located within a relatively small orbit. The simple and obvious fact that overcoming distance requires time and money means that the everyday events of daily life are well grounded within a circumscribed arena."[113] Pratt and Hanson urge us not to celebrate this intensely local nature of many women's lives but to work simultaneously in several directions: to acknowledge the local as a historically constituted phenomenon that divides women from each other and reinforces social and economic boundaries; to recognize the liberatory aspects of mobility without mystifying the social relations that determine how access to travel and the conditions of displacement occur; and to work to understand the complicities and complex positionings that arise in such critical practices. "Geographies of difference" do not only reveal divisions but can "uncover interdependencies and connections." Thus, in this study of divisions of labor and divisions between women based on race, class, language, and education, Pratt and Hanson resist reinforcing identity politics and reject standpoint epistemology altogether: "Gender is constituted differently in different places, in part because . . . places are sites where particular sets of social relations are experienced and compressed. . . In stressing the potentially transformative role of plotting relations of space that underwrite variable constructions of gender, we do not intend to imply that movement and displacement are never transformative. Our argument is that most people are fixed in and by space. Understanding these processes provides one way of seeing differences as socially constructed." [114]

Within each place there are "horizontal hostilities" between women that cannot be addressed without recognizing the partial and fractured nature of our ideological categories and critical practices. If differences between women are constructed and maintained by geographies of space and place as well as temporal enactments of identity, the challenge for critical feminist practices remains the deconstruction of the opposition between space and time, global and local, self and other. Pratt and Hanson call for a "more complicated set of geographical constructs to conceptualise adequately subjectivity and community." [115] The aim is not "cross-cultural identification" but an "informed knowledge of how the conditions of others' lives are shaped by local opportunities and in relation to each other." [116]

Pratt and Hanson's study of the social construction of differences among women in one locale offers one example of what Probyn described as "working in and against the local." Keeping in mind Gayatri Spivak's critique of the practices of information retrieval in Euro-American critical practices, it is possible to engage in inquiries into positionality and location without commodifying or objectifying subjects if both temporal and spatial axes are acknowledged and investigated. Or, as Ella Shohat argues, a "relational" approach to the study of cultures and identities would operate "at once within, between, and beyond the nation-state framework," calling attention to the conflictual hybrid interplay of communities within and across borders." [117] In this sense, investigating location becomes an opportunity to deconstruct the binary formations of modernity in favor of the complex, shifting social relations that produce cultures, subjects, and identities in postmodernity.

Questions of location are most useful, then, when they are used to deconstruct any dominant hierarchy or hegemonic use of the term "gender." Location is not useful when it is construed to be the reflection of authentic, primordial identities that are to be reestablished and reaffirmed. We have seen that discourses of location can be used to naturalize boundaries and margins under the guise of celebration, nostalgia, or inappropriate assumptions of sameness. A politics of location is also problematic when it is deployed as an agent of appropriation, constructing similarity through equalizations when material histories indicate inequities. Only when we utilize the notion of location to destabilize unexamined or stereotypical images that are vestiges of colonial discourse and other manifestations of modernity's structural inequalities can we recognize and work on the complex relationships among women in different parts of the world. This form of critical practice identifies the grounds for historically specific differences and similarities among women in diverse and asymmetrical relations, creating alternative histories, identities, and possibilities for alliances. Such a politics of location undermines any assertion of progressive, singular development and alerts us to the interpellation of the past in the present. A politics of location in this mode critiques the limits of modernity without overvalorizing the possibilities of postmodernity.

NOTES

Questions of Travel: An Introduction

1 Bishop, "Questions of Travel," in *The Complete Poems: 1927–1979*, 94.
2 This book does not argue that all culture can be read through the lens of colonial discourse. Yet it does participate in the interdisciplinary effort to link cultural studies and contemporary theory to the history of imperialism. I am mindful that some practitioners of "colonial discourse" or "postcolonial criticism" make overly general claims and totalizing arguments that mask extremely diverse and complicated experiences of domination and resistance. The critique of an ahistorical postcolonial critical practice centers around the tendency of critics in the United States and Europe to, as Michael Sprinker puts it, "ignore the complex material determinations of imperialism's history," reducing all interaction with this manifestation of capitalist expansion to the same. Such attacks on the "colonial discourse" school tend to target poststructuralists and lament the demise of Marxism. While I heartily agree that material differences often disappear, especially in the institutionalization of "postcolonial literature" in the academy, I would caution against wholesale dismissal of the alliances between poststructuralism, cultural studies, feminist theory, ethnic studies, and regional studies that "colonial discourse" signals in many instances. Rather than choose between ahistorical "culturalism" and narrowly conceived "materialism," it might be better to push the parameters of both paradigms in an effort to understand what methods can best analyze contemporary complex conditions. For recent critiques of "culturalist" totalizations in the form of "colonial discourse" and "postcolonial" studies, see Sprinker, introduction to *Late Imperial Culture;* Ahmad, "Postcolonialism: What's in a Name?"; and Dirlik, "The Postcolonial Aura."

3 For a powerful critique of V. S. Naipaul's construction as a "homeless exile" in Euro-American cultures of criticism, see Nixon, "London Calling."

4 See Stafford, *Voyage into Substance.*

5 Clifford, "Traveling Cultures," 110. I will discuss Clifford's work in more detail in chapter 3.

6 Eagleton, *Exiles and Émigrés,* 9.

7 The journal *Diaspora* has opened up a forum for considerations of the distinctions and links between displaced subjects. See Rouse, "Mexican Migration"; Lowe, "Heterogeneity, Hybridity, Multiplicity"; Castles, "Italians in Australia"; and Schnapper, "A Host Country of Immigrants." See also the two-volume "Post/Colonial Conditions: Exiles, Migrations, and Nomadisms," *Yale French Studies* 82 and 83 (1993). Although there are more discussions of the distinctions between versions of displacement in modernity and postmodernity, a great deal of homogenizing or mystification continues to be promulgated in contemporary criticism.

8 See Said, "Traveling Theory," in *The World, the Text, and the Critic,* 31–53. For elaborations on Said's initial discussion, see Clifford and Dhareshwar, "Traveling Theories, Traveling Theorists."

9 Chambers, *Border Dialogues,* 104.

10 Rich, "An Atlas of the Difficult World," 6.

11 Hall, "The Local and the Global."

12 Young, *White Mythologies,* 19.

13 Jameson, "Modernism and Imperialism," 44.

14 See Grewal and Kaplan, "Transnational Feminist Practices and Questions of Postmodernity."

15 Young, *White Mythologies,* 11.

16 Appiah, "Is the Post- in Postmodernism," 343–344.

17 Ibid., 342–343.

18 See hooks, "Postmodern Blackness," in *Yearning,* 23–32; and West, "Postmodernity and Afro-America."

19 Wallace, "Modernism," 45–46.

20 Lubiano, "Shuckin' Off the African-American Native Other," 157.

21 Ibid., 158.

22 Richard, "Postmodernism and Periphery," 10.

23 Ibid.

24 See, for example, Yúdice, Franco, and Flores, *On Edge.*

25 Appiah, "Is the Post- in Postmodernism," 346.

26 Ross, introduction to *Universal Abandon?* xvi.

27 Williamson, "Woman is an Island," 100–101.

28 Lyotard, *The Postmodern Condition,* 15.

29 Fraser and Nicholson, "Social Criticism without Philosophy," 89.

30 Ibid., 101.

31 Ibid.

32 Larsen, *Modernism and Hegemony,* xxvii.

33 Laclau, "Politics and the Limits of Modernity," 79.

34 Ibid., 80.

35 Spivak, "The Post-modern Condition," in *The Post-Colonial Critic,* 19.

36 Mohanty, "Cartographies of Struggle," 13.

37 See Grewal and Kaplan, introduction to *Scattered Hegemonies.*

38 Ong, "The Gender and Labor Politics of Postmodernity," 283.

39 Lyotard, *The Postmodern Condition,* 79.

40 Hassan, *Paracriticisms,* 47.

41 Laclau, "Politics and the Limits of Modernity," 65.

42 Aronowitz, "Postmodernism and Politics," 61.

43 Larsen, *Modernism and Hegemony,* xxiii.

44 Jameson, foreword to *The Postmodern Condition,* by Jean-François Lyotard, xvi.

45 Pred and Watts, *Reworking Modernity,* 1.

46 Ibid., xiii, 2.

47 Ibid., 6–7.

48 For important reconfigurations of the "postcolonial," see Shohat, "Notes on the Post-Colonial"; McClintock, "The Angel of Progress"; Frankenberg and Mani, "Crosscurrents, Crosstalk"; Grewal, " 'Postcolonial,' Ethnic Studies, and the Problem of the Diaspora"; and Appiah, "Is the Post- in Postcolonial."

49 See During, "Postmodernism or Post-Colonialism Today"; essays in *Ariel* 20:4 (October 1989) by Graham Huggan, Linda Hutcheon, Simon During, and Stephen Slemon; Tiffin, "Post-Colonialism, Post-Modernism and the Rehabilitation of Post-Colonial History"; and Slemon, "Post-Colonial Allegory and the Transformation of History." Arjun Mukherjee strenuously critiques this school of thought, particularly as it is articulated in Tiffin, Ashcroft, and Griffiths's well-known *The Empire Writes Back: Theory and Practice in Post-Colonial Literatures;* see Mukherjee, "Whose Post-Colonialism and Postmodernism?"

50 It is important to note early in this study that I will not survey the vast literature of Euro-American modernist literary expatriation. There is no doubt that such canonical figures as Henry James, James Joyce, and Joseph Conrad deserve yet another careful examination, but I have chosen to proceed in a different fashion. I have selected literary histories that address groups of writers rather than distinct individuals as a way of moving past the celebration of individual authorship into social histories of literary/critical production.

51 Rosaldo, *Culture and Truth.*

1   "This Question of Moving": Modernist Exile/Postmodern Tourism

1   Baudelaire, *Paris Spleen,* 99–100.
2   Harvey, *The Condition of Postmodernity,* 25.
3   For a complex study of the structure and effects of tourism in modernity, see Valene Smith, *Hosts and Guests.* For a comprehensive study of exile, see Tabori, *The Anatomy of Exile.*
4   See McCarthy, "Exiles, Expatriates and Internal Emigres."
5   Aijaz Ahmad has written a passionate indictment of the appropriation of the term "exile" by elitist diasporic intellectuals in metropolitan locations: "Exile, immigration and professional preference become synonymous and, indeed, mutually indistinguishable." My discussion of "exile" in Euro-American modernist formations links the histories of such conflations of politics and art through modernist and postmodernist "international" cultures of professionalization. When exile becomes a form of "cultural capital," an inquiry into the terms of such commodification is in order. See Ahmad, *In Theory,* 85–87.
6   See Nixon, "London Calling."
7   Calinescu, *Five Faces of Modernity,* 5.
8   Meisel, *The Myth of the Modern,* 14.
9   Bradbury, "The Cities of Modernism," in *Modernism: 1890–1930,* ed. Malcolm Bradbury and James McFarlane, 101.
10   See, for example, Eagleton, *Exiles and Émigrés;* Steiner, *Extra-territorial;* Lamming, *The Pleasures of Exile;* and Tabori, *The Anatomy of Exile.*
11   In Bradbury and McFarlane's *Pelican Guide to Modernism,* the reference section of biographies of primary modernists contains only four entries on women out of one hundred: Dorothy Richardson, Edith Sodergran, Gertrude Stein, and Virginia Woolf. As for nationalities: French, Austrian, Danish, German, Russian, Italian, North American, Norwegian, Spanish, Irish, Swiss, Swedish, Belgian, Polish, English, and Finnish— apparently, this is the extent of "aesthetic internationalism" in this version of canon formation.
12   Anderson, *Imagined Communities,* 15.
13   Nixon, "London Calling," 2–3.
14   Williams, "Metropolitan Perceptions and the Emergence of Modernism," in *The Politics of Modernism,* 47.
15   Ibid.
16   Ibid., 45.
17   An approach that is echoed in some colonial and postcolonial writers, including Derek Walcott, George Lamming, Salman Rushdie, and Bharati Mukherjee. For critiques of the modernist cosmopolitanisms of sev-

eral of these writers, see Nixon, "London Calling"; Grewal, "Salman Rushdie"; and "Autobiographic Subjects and Diasporic Locations."

18 See Gilroy, *"There Ain't No Black in the Union Jack,"* 49–50.

19 Cited in Tabori, *The Anatomy of Exile,* 16.

20 Freud, "Mourning and Melancholia."

21 Rosaldo, *Culture and Truth,* 70–71.

22 Ibid., 71.

23 Ibid., 69–70.

24 Ibid., 3.

25 Berman, *All That Is Solid,* 5.

26 For a recent version of the privileging of expatriation as a mode of seeing and knowing, this time in a more "postmodern" mode, see Hartley, "Expatriation." Hartley writes: "The term expatriation not only extends, with varying degrees of approval, to all immigrants, emigrants and migrants, but it is also available as a metaphor for cultural studies. It's a term of displacement, a condition which is risky, unsettling, puzzling, invigorating—and normal—in the domain of knowledge" (451). It is precisely such a normalizing gesture of the metaphors of imperialism (exploration, uniqueness, etc.) that requires more historically precise deconstructions. It is my hope that "cultural studies" will not found itself as a set of emergent critical practices upon just such mystifications of the terms of displacement.

27 Wittlin, "Sorrow and Grandeur of Exile," 102.

28 Cowley, *Exile's Return,* 74. First published in the United States by Viking Press in 1951.

29 Levin, *Refractions,* 70.

30 Ibid., 65.

31 Ibid., 77.

32 Ibid., 81.

33 Ibid., 64.

34 In addition to the works discussed in more detail in this chapter, see Eagleton, *Exiles and Émigrés;* Steiner, *Extra-territorial;* Ilie, *Literature and Inner Exile;* and Griffiths, *A Double Exile.*

35 Seidel, *Exile and Narrative Imagination,* ix.

36 Ibid., x.

37 Ibid., xii.

38 Ibid.

39 See Newman, *Transgressions of Reading.*

40 Williams, *The Politics of Modernism,* 34.

41 Cowley, *Exile's Return,* 19.

42 Ibid., 61.

43 *Random House Dictionary,* s.v. "lost."
44 Cowley, *Exile's Return,* 8.
45 Ibid., 9.
46 See, for example, Benstock, *Women Writers of the Left Bank;* Hanscombe and Smyers, *Writing for Their Lives;* Broe and Ingram, *Women's Writing in Exile;* Jay, "The Outsider Among the Expatriates"; Scott, *The Gender of Modernism.*
47 Cowley, *Exile's Return,* 19.
48 Ibid., 5.
49 One useful overview of the social history of this period in the United States is Brier et al., *Who Built America?* vol. 2.
50 MacCannell, *The Tourist,* 34.
51 Cowley, *Exile's Return,* 61.
52 Ibid., 16.
53 MacCannell, *The Tourist,* 23.
54 Ibid.
55 Cowley, *Exile's Return,* 82.
56 Ibid., 62–63.
57 Ibid., 95–96.
58 MacCannell, *The Tourist,* 34.
59 Fussell, *Abroad,* vii.
60 See Mary Louise Pratt, *Imperial Eyes.*
61 Not unlike the flaneur, this masculine figure of travel predominates in Euro-American modernist cultural production. See Pollock, *Vision and Difference.* In the 1980s, historical recovery and theoretical analysis of the role of Euro-American and non-Western women travelers challenged the hegemony of the masculine, gentleman traveler: see Grewal, *Home and Harem;* Enloe, *Bananas, Beaches, and Bases;* Strobel, *European Women and the Second British Empire;* Chaudhuri and Strobel, *Western Women and Imperialism;* Donaldson, *Decolonizing Feminisms;* Ware, *Beyond the Pale;* Sharpe, *Allegories of Empire;* Shohat and Stam, *Unthinking Eurocentrism;* and my "'Getting to Know You,'" and "'A World Without Boundaries.'"
62 These citations appear on the back cover of the 1980 paperback edition.
63 Fussell, *Abroad,* 11.
64 Ibid., 24.
65 Contrast Iain Chambers's version of British expatriation during the same period: "The desire for another world was linked to the continuing refusal of industrial culture and urban life" (35). Chambers focuses on British national culture and its *resistance* to modernism as "foreign," "un-British," and "democratic." In this context, expatriation may favor artistic experimentation, but it is linked simultaneously to conservative,

class-specific, even protofascist movements as well. See Chambers, *Border Dialogues,* 30–37.

66 Fussell, *Abroad,* 36.

67 Ibid., 39.

68 See, for example, the work of Frantz Fanon, Aimé Césaire, Albert Memmi, Ngugi wa Tiongo, Homi Bhabha, Gayatri Spivak, Mary Louise Pratt, and Patrick Brantlinger.

69 Green, *Dreams of Adventure,* 3.

70 Ibid.

71 Fussell, *Abroad,* 39.

72 For discussions of the "truth-effect" of documentary and critiques of autobiographical genres, see my "Resisting Autobiography," and Foley, *Telling the Truth.*

73 In her biography of Freya Stark, Caroline Moorehead notes that while Stark was considered to be a major travel writer in Britain in the years just following World War II, Paul Fussell declined to include her in his study of the genre: "One of the few sour notes was cast only many years later by the American critic Paul Fussell, who, writing of travel books, chose not to include her works on the grounds that in order 'to write a distinguished travel book you have to be equally interested in (1) the travel and (2) the writing,' and that though Freya was unquestionably a traveller, 'the dimension of delight in language and disposition, in all the literary contrivances, isn't there.'" See Moorehead, *Freya Stark,* 125.

74 Fussell, *Abroad,* 42.

75 Pollock, *Vision and Difference,* 50–90.

76 Fussell, 43.

77 Ibid., 46.

78 See Arjun Appadurai's discussion of the construction of "natives" in "Putting Hierarchy in Its Place."

79 Fussell, *Abroad,* 46.

80 Ibid., 49.

81 Ibid.

82 Huyssen, *After the Great Divide,* vii.

83 Jonathan Culler has argued that the opposition between traveler and tourist is of fundamental interest to cultural criticism. His comments on MacCannell and Fussell provide a useful elaboration of the post-structuralist discourse on *travel* in the strictly Euro-American modernist/postmodernist arena. See Culler, "The Semiotics of Tourism."

84 For a particularly useful discussion of some of the limits of the "tourist," see Dennison Nash's important essay "Tourism as an Anthropological Subject" and the discussion that follows in *Current Anthropology* 22:5

(October 1981): 461–481. Another version of this essay, "Tourism as a Form of Imperialism," can be found in Smith, *Hosts and Guests*, 33–47. Outright denunciations of tourism and development policies are elaborated in John H. Bodley's *Victims of Progress* and Jamaica Kincaid's *A Small Place*. Within U.S. feminist contexts, see Jordan, "Report from the Bahamas"; Lorde, "Notes from a Trip to Russia," and "Grenada Revisited: An Interim Report," in *Sister Outsider: Essays and Speeches*, 13–35 and 176–190; and Davis, "Women in Egypt: A Personal View," in *Women, Culture, Politics*, 116–154.

85 Horne, *The Great Museum*, 45.

86 MacCannell, *The Tourist*, 1.

87 Ibid., 4.

88 Ibid., 8–9.

89 Ibid., 10.

90 Ibid., 13.

91 Horne, *The Great Museum*, 21.

92 MacCannell, *The Tourist*, 14.

93 Ibid., 101–102.

94 Horne, *The Great Museum*, 21.

95 Ibid., 11.

96 See Clifford, *The Predicament of Culture;* Clifford and Marcus, *Writing Culture;* Marcus and Fischer, *Anthropology as Cultural Critique;* and Asad, *Anthropology and the Colonial Encounter.*

97 Kincaid, *A Small Place*, 3. I discuss Kincaid's text in my "Reconfigurations of Geography and Historical Narrative."

98 Kincaid, *A Small Place*, 17.

99 Ibid., 18–19.

100 Horne, *The Great Museum*, 211.

101 Van Den Abbeele, "Sightseers," 13.

102 Morris, "At Henry Parkes Motel."

2 Becoming Nomad: Poststructuralist Deterritorializations

1 Eisenstein, "Through Theatre to Cinema," in *Film Form*, 3.

2 Baudrillard, *Cool Memories*, 233.

3 Eisenstein, "Through Theater to Cinema," 3.

4 Shohat, "Gender and Culture of Empire," 45. For related discussions see Shohat and Stam, *Unthinking Eurocentrism.*

5 Vis-à-vis the "dark continent," in addition to Shohat and Stam's work, see Christopher L. Miller, *Blank Darkness,* particularly introduction to part 1, 3–65.

6   See Jonathan Rutherford's autobiographical reference to his "identification" with "Lawrence of Arabia" and the "desert": "To the Western
European eye, the desert seems an uncanny space, its borders marking
out a margin between the habitable and the uninhabitable. Yet despite
its strangeness it holds a seductive fascination . . . In representing the
margins of our culture and the knowledge and values that underpin it,
it is also the place of their undoing. For Lawrence the desert left him
neither Arab nor English" ("A Place Called Home," 9–10).

7   I will refer to two key collections that suggest the profound seriousness
with which Deleuze and Guattari's notions of "deterritorialization" and
"nomadology" have been engaged in North American literary criticism:
JanMohamed and Lloyd, *The Nature and Context of Minority Discourse,*
and the two-volume special issue, "Post/Colonial Conditions: Exiles,
Migrations, and Nomadisms," *Yale French Studies* 82/83 (1993), edited
by Françoise Lionnet and Ronnie Scharfman. While these collections
hardly encompass the full range and number of vigorous responses to
Deleuze and Guattari's work, they serve as tangible examples, even emblems, of particular critical practices.

8   First published as *Amérique* (1986). All quotations from the text will refer
to the English-language edition through parenthetical notations to *A*
and the page number.

9   See, for example, Gane, *Baudrillard;* Kellner, *Jean Baudrillard;* Jameson,
"Postmodernism"; Best and Kellner, *Postmodern Theory;* Smart, *Modern
Conditions;* Connor, *Postmodernist Culture;* Harvey, *The Condition of Post-
modernity;* Chambers, *Border Dialogues;* Collins, *Uncommon Cultures;* Norris,
What's Wrong with Postmodernism; Callinicos, *Against Postmodernism;* and
McGowan, *Postmodernism and Its Critics.*

10   In this chapter I will focus on Deleuze and Guattari's primary texts in
English translation: *Anti-Oedipus; A Thousand Plateaus;* and *Kafka.*

11   I first made this argument in my dissertation, "The Poetics of Displacement: Exile, Immigration and Travel in Contemporary Autobiographical Writing." This early version of my critique of Deleuze and Guattari's
notion of "deterritorialization" has been published as "Deterritorializations: The Rewriting of Home and Exile in Western Feminist Discourse"
and reprinted in JanMohamed and Lloyd, *The Nature and Context of Minority Discourse,* 357–368.

12   Hoberman, "Lost in America," 15.

13   Throughout the 1980s, Baudrillard's work reached a larger European and
North American audience through a series of high-profile translations
and edited collections published by Columbia University Press and Stanford University Press. Periodicals devoted to poststructuralist theory also

published single issues on Baudrillard's work or became regular venues
for translated essays, for example, *Telos, October, Artforum, Semiotext(e),
Thesis Eleven,* and *The Canadian Journal of Political and Social Theory.*

14   See Ross, "The New Sentence," and "Baudrillard's Bad Attitude";
Aronowitz, "Postmodernism and Politics"; and Willis, *A Primer for Daily
Life.*

15   See, for example, Chang, "Mass, Media"; Chen, "The Masses and the
Media"; Hayward, "Implosive Critiques"; Kroker and Cook, *The Postmodern Scene;* and Kroker, *The Possessed Individual.*

16   Noteworthy exceptions include Gallop, "French Theory"; Braidotti, *Patterns of Dissonance;* and Morris, "Room 101," and "Great Moments." In
addition to Gallop's critique, see also Moore, "Getting a Bit of the
Other." A passing comment by Doreen Massey critiques Baudrillard's
virulent sexism in *America;* see her "Flexible Sexism" in *Space, Place, and
Gender,* 227. An excellent critique of masculinist proclivities in postmodern theory in general can be found in Bondi and Domosh, "Other
Figures in Other Places." Otherwise, most feminist commentators, if
they refer to Baudrillard at all, retreat from critique. For example, Rosi
Braidotti refers to Baudrillard as "an acute observer of contemporary
ideas" (122), while Lidia Curti cites Baudrillard in general terms in describing the postmodern context of cultural studies; see her "What is
Real and What is Not."

17   See, for example, Kroker, *The Possessed Individual;* Kellner, *Jean Baudril-
lard;* Hutcheon, *A Poetics of Postmodernism;* and Harvey, *The Postmodern
Condition.* Ed Cohen deftly critiques Baudrillard's devaluation of North
American popular culture, placing it within a tradition of European
privileging of "culture," particularly modernist variants. See his "The
'Hyperreal' vs. the 'Really Real.'"

18   Norris hits his shrillest note yet in *Uncritical Theory.*

19   Baudrillard's text follows a long line of European commentary on
North American particularity. Most recently, Michel Butor's *Mobile* and
Umberto Eco's *Travels in Hyperreality* have garnered critical attention and
acclaim.

20   Hoberman, "Lost in America," 16.

21   First published as *Cool Memories: 1980–1985* (1987). All further references
to the text will cite the English-language edition through parenthetical
notations to *CM* and the page number.

22   Kellner, *Jean Baudrillard,* 153.

23   Chris Turner, the translator of *America,* translates this French term as
"astral" or "sidereal." See translator's note on p. 5.

24   See Jean-Phillipe Mathy's discussion of the role of a return to animality

in Kojève's notion of posthistorical states of nature in general and the United States in particular. Mathy explicitly links Baudrillard to the French neo-Hegelian discourse on the end of history and the animalization of man (*Extrême-Occident*, 209–215).

25 Gane, *Baudrillard*, 182.

26 See, in particular, Said, *Orientalism;* Shohat and Stam, *Unthinking Eurocentrism;* Christopher L. Miller, *Blank Darkness;* and Hulme, *Colonial Encounters.*

27 In such a tossed-off comment as this, Baudrillard condenses several centuries of Euro-American "harem discourse," making the conventional misreading of a South Asian culture for a Middle Eastern one through the vehicle of the Western readers' preconceived stereotypes about secluded women, exotic sexuality, and other orientalist tropes. Such condensations of South Asian and Middle Eastern cultures through harem discourse abound: a recent example in popular culture occurred in the televised 1993 Oscar awards show that featured Debbie Allen's choreography to the soundtrack of *Aladdin*—"harem dancers" appeared in a stock "Middle Eastern" setting wearing "South Asian" (quasi-Hindu) apparel and hairstyles. An extensive critical literature has appeared within the last twelve years. For a general introduction, see Said, *Orientalism.*

28 See *De la séduction;* in translation, *Seduction.*

29 Gallop, "French Theory," 114.

30 David Morley and Kevin Robins trace this tradition to the 1930s in British culture, noting such sentiments in critics as diverse as Evelyn Waugh and George Orwell. In particular, the "feminization" of working-class tastes and habits was seen as a cause for concern. The popularity of American culture, it could be argued, contributed to a loosening of class divisions: "Perhaps the problem is not really about a brash and material American culture, but rather about a fake antique Europe? American culture repositions frontiers—social, cultural, psychic, linguistic, geographical. America is now within. America is now part of a European cultural repertoire, part of European identity" (Morley and Robins, "Spaces of Identity," 19–20).

31 Mathy, *Extrême-Occident,* 7.

32 Norton, "*America* by Jean Baudrillard," 169.

33 Brian Massumi identifies a nostalgic strain in Baudrillard's work: "He cannot see that all the things he says have crumbled were simulacra all along: simulacra produced by analyzable procedures of simulation that were as real as real, or actually realer than real, because they carried the real back to its principle of production and in so doing prepared their own rebirth in a new regime of simulation" ("Realer Than Real," 96).

34 Kellner, *Jean Baudrillard,* 182, 171.

35 Morley and Robins, "Spaces of Identity," 21.

36 Among the proliferating points of view and kinds of information on "Europe" in postmodernity, see Balibar, *"Es Gibt Keinen Staat in Europa;"* Hall, "The Local and the Global;" Gilroy, *"There Ain't No Black in the Union Jack"*; Kristeva, *Nations Without Nationalism;* Chakrabarty, "Provincializing Europe"; and "Shifting Territories: Feminisms and Europe," a special issue, *Feminist Review* 39 (Autumn 1991).

37 Deleuze and Guattari, *Kafka,* 26.

38 Among those who find much to praise in this oeuvre, see Patton, "Conceptual Politics," and "Marxism and Beyond"; Massumi, "Realer Than Real," and "Pleasures of Philosophy," translator's foreword to *A Thousand Plateaus,* by Deleuze and Guattari, ix–xv; Muecke, "The Discourse of Nomadology"; and Bogue, *Deleuze and Guattari.*

39 Deleuze and Guattari, *A Thousand Plateaus,* 25.

40 Deleuze and Guattari, *Kafka,* 18.

41 Ibid., 19.

42 Deleuze and Guattari, *A Thousand Plateaus,* 11.

43 Ibid., 382.

44 See Bloom, *Gender on Ice.*

45 Patton, "Conceptual Politics," 66.

46 Muecke, "The Discourse of Nomadology," 24.

47 Grisoni, introduction to *Politiques de la philosophie,* 11.

48 Braidotti, *Patterns of Dissonance,* 279. See also her *Nomadic Subjects.*

49 Braidotti, *Patterns of Dissonance,* 281.

50 Gabriel, "Thoughts on Nomadic Aesthetics," 63–64.

51 JanMohamed and Lloyd, preface to *The Nature and Context of Minority Discourse,* ix.

52 Rosaldo, "Politics, Patriarchs, and Laughter," 126.

53 Kaplan, "Deterritorializations," 361.

54 Woodhull, "Exile," 8.

55 Ibid., 9.

56 Raybaud, "Nomadism," 154.

57 Mehrez, "Azouz Begag," 28.

58 Lowe, "Literary Nomadics," 45.

59 Ibid., 47–48.

60 Spivak, "Can the Subaltern Speak?" 271.

61 Ibid., 272.

62 Ibid., 280.

63 Ibid., 273.

64 Ibid., 275.

65 Ibid., 280.

66 See "French Feminism in an International Frame" and "Scattered Speculations on the Question of Value" in *In Other Worlds,* 134–175; "The Political Economy of Women as Seen by a Literary Critic"; and with Rashmi
Bhatnagar, Lola Chatterjee, and Rajeshwari Sunder Rajan, "The Post-
Colonial Critic," in *The Post-Colonial Critic,* ed. Sarah Harasym, 67–74.

67 Radway, "Reception Study," 364.

68 Ibid., 368.

69 Grossberg, "Wandering Audiences," 377.

70 Ibid., 384.

71 Ibid., 385.

3   Traveling Theorists: Cosmopolitan Diasporas

1   Adorno, *Minima Moralia,* 127.

2   Said, "Movements and Migrations," in *Culture and Imperialism,* 332.

3   This figure, which is attributed to the United Nations, is quoted in
Jensen, "Death and Refugees," A17. See also *Refugees: Dynamics of Dis-
placement,* a report for the Independent Commission on International
Humanitarian Issues.

4   Jensen, "Death and Refugees," A17.

5   For the opening discussions, see Said, "Traveling Theory in *The World,
the Text, and the Critic*"; Clifford and Dhareshwar, "Traveling Theories,
Traveling Theorists"; Clifford, *The Predicament of Culture,* and "Traveling
Cultures."

6   Naficy, *The Making of Exile Cultures,* xvi.

7   Ibid.

8   Shohat, "Reflections of an Arab Jew," 42.

9   Ibid., 41–42.

10 Ibid., 40.

11 Ibid.

12 Ovid, *Tristia and Epistulae ex Ponto,* cited in Dahlie, *Varieties of Exile,* 2.

13 Farah, "A Country in Exile," 4.

14 Dahlie, *Varieties of Exile,* 3.

15 Hallvard Dahlie's study follows a rhetorical strategy of discussing the
definitional constraints of the term "exile" without resolving or historicizing the contradictions. See also, among many others, Seidel, *Exile
and the Narrative Imagination;* Eagleton, *Exiles and Émigrés;* Ilie, *Literature
and Inner Exile;* Griffiths, *A Double Exile;* and Newman, *Transgressions of
Reading.*

16 McCarthy, "Exiles, Expatriates and Internal Emigres," 706.

17 A roundtable critical discussion of *In Theory* including a response by Ahmad was published in *Public Culture* 6:1 (1993). See also Lazarus, "Post-colonialism and the Dilemma of Nationalism"; Lie, "Enough Said, Ahmad"; and Kaplan and Grewal, "Transnational Feminist Cultural Studies."

18 Ahmad, *In Theory*, 86.

19 Ibid.

20 Ibid., 85.

21 Ibid.

22 For a fuller discussion of the limits of masculinist Marxism, see Kaplan and Grewal, "Transnational Feminist Cultural Studies."

23 Ahmad, *In Theory*, 209.

24 On this very point, see Vivek Dhareshwar's critique of *In Theory*, "Marxism, Location Politics, and the Possibility of Change."

25 Chow, *Writing Diaspora*, 14.

26 Ibid.

27 Thiong'o, *Moving the Centre*, 104.

28 Ibid., 107.

29 Clifford, "On *Orientalism*," in *The Predicament of Culture*, 275–276.

30 For a useful collection of commentary on Said, see Sprinker, *Edward Said: A Critical Reader*. For examples of diverse viewpoints, see also Young, "Disorienting Orientalism," in *White Mythologies*, 119–140; Clifford, "On *Orientalism*," in *The Predicament of Culture*, 255–276; Mani and Frankenberg, "The Challenge of *Orientalism*"; Ahmad, "*Orientalism* and After," in *In Theory*, 159–220; Sivan, "Edward Said and His Arab Reviewers," in *Interpretations of Islam Past and Present*, 133–154; J. Hillis Miller, "Beginning With a Text"; Hayden White, "Criticism as Cultural Politics"; Robbins, "Homelessness and Worldliness," and "The East is a Career: Edward Said," in *Secular Vocations*, 152–179.

31 Said, *The World, the Text, and the Critic*, 2.

32 Ibid., 4.

33 Ibid., 8.

34 Ibid.

35 Ibid., 9.

36 Ibid., 15.

37 Ibid., 24.

38 Ibid.

39 Ibid., 35.

40 I am indebted to Inderpal Grewal for pointing out the limits of secularism in the context of different nationalist and transnational configurations.

41 Said, "The Mind of Winter," 49, 54.

42 Adorno, *Minima Moralia*, 33.

43 Ibid., 38–39.

44 Ibid., 87.

45 Said, "Reflections on Exile," 170.

46 Ibid., 159.

47 Cited in Said, "On Palestinian Identity," 66–67.

48 Said, "Reflections on Exile," 166.

49 Ibid., 161.

50 Ibid., 161.

51 Ibid., 160.

52 Said, "On Palestinian Identity," 69.

53 Said, "Movements and Migrations," in *Culture and Imperialism* 332–333.

54 Naficy, *The Making of Exile Cultures,* 2.

55 Ibid., 3.

56 Brennan, "Cosmopolitans and Celebrities," 2.

57 Ibid., 4.

58 Ibid.

59 Ibid., 6.

60 Ibid., 7.

61 Nixon, "London Calling," 2–3.

62 Ibid., 32.

63 Sivanandan, "The Enigma of the Colonised," 33.

64 Robbins, "Comparative Cosmopolitanism," 171.

65 Ibid., 173.

66 Ibid., 174.

67 Ibid., 183.

68 Clifford, "Tell About Your Trip: Michel Leiris," in *The Predicament of Culture,* 173.

69 Clifford, "A Politics of Neologism: Aimé Césaire," in *The Predicament of Culture,* 175.

70 Ibid., 177.

71 Ibid., 175.

72 One significant salvo fired against a general trend in anthropological studies, personified in part by Clifford, is the accusation that "postmodernism" is apolitical, it produces "obscure" texts that only specialists can read, and it erases important contributions to theory already made by Western "feminists." See Mascia-Lees, Sharpe, and Ballerino Cohen, "The Postmodernist Turn in Anthropology." See also Newton and Stacey, "Learning Not to Curse."

73 Clifford, "Notes on Theory and Travel," 179.

74   Ibid., 183. See also Said, "Traveling Theory."

75   Clifford, "Notes on Theory and Travel," 184–185.

76   Clifford, "Traveling Cultures," 101.

77   hooks, "Representations of Whiteness," in *Black Looks* 173.

78   Krupat, *Ethnocriticism*, 122–123.

79   Ibid., 116.

80   Clifford, "Traveling Cultures," 106.

81   hooks, "Representations of Whiteness," in *Black Looks* 173.

82   Clifford, "Traveling Cultures," 110.

83   Clifford, "Diasporas," 302.

84   Ibid.

85   For primary statements of the Birmingham School, see Centre for Contemporary Cultural Studies, *The Empire Strikes Back*. See also the writings of Stuart Hall, Paul Gilroy, Hazel Carby, Pratibha Parmar, Errol Lawrence, and Kobena Mercer. For an insightful critique of the school's theorization of opposition see Fox, *Class Fictions*.

86   It is worth mentioning that in spite of *The Black Atlantic*'s groundbreaking contributions to African diaspora cultural identities in general, it is less useful vis-à-vis female histories and practices. Gilroy's work does not address fully the implications of South American migrations and other versions of black diasporas, but it opens up an enormous field of study in an inventive and transformative manner.

87   Clifford, "Diasporas," 321.

88   Boyarin and Boyarin, "Diaspora," 701.

89   Ibid., 711.

90   I have a number of reservations about this essay. At times its "diasporic" sensibility seems to hail the poststructuralist deterritorialization imperative while at other moments it falls into a U.S.-style "multiculturalism" melting-pot format (Everybody do your own unique thing). I am also profoundly uncomfortable with the gendered nature of the argument: its reliance upon male circumcision as a privileged locus of identity as well as what I read as a rather patronizing attitude toward women's "special" characteristics. My reading, of course, does not necessarily reflect the authors' intentions, while it certainly reflects my scant knowledge of the rabbinic tradition and texts that form the substantial part of the analysis.

91   Clifford, "Diasporas," 321.

92   For a full discussion of these issues, see Grewal and Kaplan, *Scattered Hegemonies*.

93   Tölölyan, "The Nation-State and Its Others," 5.

94   Rouse, "Mexican Migration," 18.

95   Clifford, "Diasporas," 308.

96   Ibid., 328 n. 3.

97 In note 8, Clifford elaborates on this point: "Immigrants from Ireland and central, southern, and eastern Europe have been racialized. And anti-Semitism remains an often-latent, sometimes-explicit force. But generally speaking, European immigrants have come to participate as ethnic 'whites' in multicultural America. The same cannot be said, overall, of populations of color—although region of origin, shade of skin, culture, and class may attenuate racist exclusion." Although I ultimately agree with Clifford, it is worth pointing out that the phrase "have come to participate" collapses conflicts, tensions, and legal obstacles that have been part of the social construction of "race" for these migrants. Here, the end result of nationalist racism (the opposition between "white" and "nonwhite") is reproduced rather than deconstructed through an examination of how diasporic elements that would resist or support such racist ends contributed to the entry into "whiteness" rather than a consciousness of class, region, religion, and so on. While this task is not the one Clifford has chosen to undertake and it is unfair to expect him to discuss it at length, this is a project that needs more critical attention. See his "Diasporas," 329 n. 8.

98 Natarajan, "Reading Diaspora," introduction to *Writers of the Indian Diaspora*, xiv.

99 Ibid.

100 Chambers, *Migrancy, Culture, Identity*, 5.

101 Chow, *Writing Diaspora*, 171.

102 Chambers, *Migrancy, Culture, Identity*, 3.

4 Postmodern Geographies: Feminist Politics of Location

A section of this chapter was published in part as "The Politics of Location as Transnational Feminist Practice" in Inderpal Grewal and Caren Kaplan, editors. *Scattered Hegemonies: Postmodernity and Transnational Feminist Practices* (Minneapolis: University of Minnesota Press, 1994), 137–152.

1 Foucault, *Power/Knowledge*, 149.

2 Rich, "Notes Towards a Politics of Location," in *Blood, Bread, and Poetry*, 212.

3 Duncan and Ley, "Representing the Place of Culture," introduction to *Place/Culture/Representation*, 1.

4 Gregory, *Geographical Imaginations*, 7.

5 Ibid., 414.

6 Smith and Katz, "Grounding Metaphor," 80.

7 Jacques Rancière asks: "What makes the spatial representation—even when it is not exactly well-fitting—necessary to the formulation of political science?" His analysis of utopia and the operation of meta-

phor leads to an endorsement of deterritorialization or "learning to miss one's way"—reflecting the Euro-American theoretical endorsement of nomadic metaphors. See his "Discovering New Worlds."

8   Smith and Katz, "Grounding Metaphor," 68.

9   Ibid.

10 Keith and Pile, "The Place of Politics," introduction to part 2 in *Place and the Politics of Identity*, 37.

11 Lefebvre, *The Production of Space*, 21.

12 Harvey, *The Condition of Postmodernity*, 205.

13 Ibid., 201.

14 Ibid., 285.

15 Ibid., 201.

16 Ibid., 273.

17 Ibid., 271.

18 Ibid., 273.

19 Ibid., 275.

20 Ibid., 302.

21 Ibid., 303.

22 Soja, *Postmodern Geographies*, 2.

23 Ibid., 75. See also Jameson, "Cognitive Mapping."

24 For other critiques of sexism and masculinism in the field or considerations of gender issues in geography, see Spain, *Gendered Spaces;* Rose, *Feminism and Geography;* Women and Geography Study Group of the Institute of British Geographers, *Geography and Gender;* Bondi, "Progress in Geography and Gender"; Domosh, "Towards a Feminist Historiography of Geography"; Valentine, "Negotiating and Managing Multiple Sexual Identities"; Katz and Monk, *Full Circles;* and Blunt and Rose, *Writing Women and Space*. See also the new journal *Gender, Place, and Culture*.

25 Massey, "Flexible Sexism," in *Space, Place, and Gender* 225.

26 Ibid., 222.

27 Ibid., 233.

28 See Pollock, *Vision and Difference*, and Wolff, "The Invisible Flaneuse."

29 Massey, "A Place Called Home?" in *Space, Place, and Gender*, 164.

30 Massey, "A Global Sense of Place," in *Space, Place, and Gender*, 150.

31 Ibid., 235.

32 Ibid., 228.

33 Graham, "Fordism/Post-Fordism," 53.

34 See Neil Smith, *Uneven Development*.

35 Gregory, *Geographical Imaginations*, 414.

36 Hall, "The Local and the Global," 27.

37 Ibid., 29.

38 Morley and Robins, "Spaces of Identity," 22.

39 Cited in Robins, "Tradition and Translation," 27.

40 Ibid., 28.

41 Childers, "Colors on the Map," 8.

42 Ibid., 10.

43 Robins, "Tradition and Translation," 31.

44 Ibid., 36.

45 Hall, "The Local and the Global," 36.

46 Ibid., 38.

47 Mattelart and Piemme, "New Technologies, Decentralisation and Public Service," in *Communication and Class Struggle,* ed. Armand Mattelart and Seth Siegelaub (New York: International General, 1983), 2:415. Cited in Morley and Robins, "Spaces of Identity," 24–25.

48 Probyn, "Travels in the Postmodern," 178.

49 Ibid., 182.

50 Woolf, *Three Guineas,* 109.

51 Probyn, "Travels in the Postmodern," 176.

52 Mohanty, "Feminist Encounters," 31.

53 In the mid- to late '70s, Rich's position as a primary figure in women's studies was secured with the publication of her study of Western motherhood and female experience, *Of Woman Born,* as well as the collection of essays *On Lies, Secrets, and Silence.* Her most profound contributions to North American feminist thought and practice have pivoted around the issues of lesbian identity and relations among women of different races. Rich's editorial work for the lesbian-identified publication *Sinister Wisdom* and her increasing stature and visibility in the burgeoning field of women's studies throughout the '80s brought her work to the attention of a wide range of readers. In her work in the '80s, Rich continued to theorize Jewish American and lesbian identity, examine the politics of women's education and the history of women writers, and expand upon the ideas she had begun to explore in her 1978 essay, "Disloyal to Civilization: Feminism, Racism, Gynephobia." For Rich's prose writing see *Of Woman Born; On Lies, Secrets, and Silence; Blood, Bread, and Poetry;* and *What is Found There.*

54 Rich, *Blood, Bread, and Poetry,* 159.

55 Ibid., 216.

56 Ibid., 219.

57 Ibid., 225.

58 Ibid., 219.

59 For a useful introduction to this project see Weedon, *Feminist Practice and Poststructuralist Theory.*

60 Smith and Katz, "Grounding Metaphor," 77.

61 Mohanty, "Feminist Encounters."

62   I have discussed some of the readings of Rich's term that produce more relativist or managed diversity approaches in my essay, "The Politics of Location as Transnational Feminist Practices," in Grewal and Kaplan, *Scattered Hegemonies*, 137–154.

63   Mani, "Multiple Mediations," 4.

64   Clifford, "Notes on Theory and Travel," 179.

65   Ibid., 182.

66   Braidotti, *Nomadic Subjects*, 168.

67   Dhareshwar, "Marxism, Location Politics," 52.

68   Nicholson, introduction to *Feminism/Postmodernism*, 9.

69   The literature is quite extensive on this topic. Although I don't have space in this chapter to discuss the bulk of this work in depth, I would direct interested readers to the following key texts: Haraway, "Situated Knowledges"; in *Simians, Cyborgs, and Women*, 183–202; Braidotti, *Nomadic Subjects*; Anzaldúa, *Borderlands/La Frontera*; Ferguson, *The Man Question*; Davies, *Black Women, Writing, and Identity*; Bammer, *Displacements*; Ochoa and Teaiwa, "Enunciating Our Terms"; Taylor, "Re: Locations"; Bondi and Domosh, "Other Figures in Other Places"; Chen, "Voices from the Outside"; Santos-Febres, *The Translocal Papers*; and Lugones, "Playfulness, 'World'-Travelling, and Loving Perception." This is, of course, only a partial list of many provocative and insightful contributions to the debates around location, positionality, and identity.

70   See Hartsock, "Rethinking Modernism"; in the same volume, see also Christian, "The Race for Theory."

71   Hartsock, "Rethinking Modernism," 19.

72   Ibid., 25.

73   Ibid.

74   See Lorde, *Sister/Outsider*; Bulkin, Pratt, and Smith, *Yours in Struggle*; Bookman and Morgen, *Women and the Politics of Empowerment*; and Albrecht and Brewer, *Bridges of Power*.

75   Hartsock, "Rethinking Modernism," 25.

76   Reagon, "Coalition Politics," 358.

77   Ibid.

78   Ibid., 357.

79   Ibid., 367.

80   Ibid., 362.

81   Alarcón, "The Theoretical Subject(s)," 361.

82   Ibid., 364.

83   Grewal, "Autobiographic Subjects," 233.

84   Alarcón, "The Theoretical Subject(s)," 366.

85   Ibid., 356.

86 Ibid.

87 Grewal, "Autobiographic Subjects," 234.

88 Ibid., 235.

89 De Lauretis, *Alice Doesn't*. For other work by de Lauretis that is relevant here, see "Feminist Studies/Critical Studies"; *Technologies of Gender;* "The Essence of the Triangle"; and "Eccentric Subjects."

90 It is important to note that de Lauretis has significant differences with Alcoff and has addressed them at some length: "Why is it still necessary to set up two opposing categories, cultural feminism and poststructuralism, or essentialism and anti-essentialism, thesis and antithesis, when one has already achieved the vantage point of a theoretical position that overtakes them or sublates them?" See "Upping the Anti (sic) in Feminist Theory" (especially 261–264).

91 Alcoff, "Cultural Feminism," 115; first published in *Signs* 13:3 (Spring 1988): 419–436.

92 Ibid., 117.

93 Alarcón, "The Theoretical Subject(s)," 364.

94 See Grewal and Kaplan, "Transnational Feminist Practices."

95 Probyn, "Travels in the Postmodern," 186.

96 Massey, "A Global Sense of Place," in *Space, Place, and Gender,* 151–152.

97 Mohanty, "Feminist Encounters," 31.

98 Ibid., 41.

99 Ibid., 42.

100 For another influential theorization of "Third World feminism," see Sandoval, "U.S. Third World Feminism."

101 Mohanty, "Cartographies of Struggle," 7.

102 Ibid., 31.

103 See Fuentes and Ehrenreich, *Women in the Global Factory;* Ong, *Spirits of Resistance;* Ruiz and Tiano, *Women on the US-Mexican Border;* Fernandez-Kelly, *For We Are Sold;* Enloe, *Bananas, Beaches, and Bases;* and Kondo, *Crafting Selves.*

104 Mohanty, "Cartographies of Struggle," 13.

105 Ibid.

106 Anne McClintock also critiques the Eurocentrism of linear periodization and other temporal aspects of modernity and postmodernity vis-à-vis the term "postcolonial": "Orienting theory around the temporal axis colonial/postcolonial makes it easier *not* to see, and therefore harder to theorize, the continuities in international imbalances in *imperial* power" ("The Angel of Progress," 89). In the same issue, Ella Shohat argues for an examination of the "politics of location" of the term: "It is from my particular position as an academic Arab-Jew whose cultural topog-

raphies are (dis)located in Iraq, Israel/Palestine, and the U.S.A. that I would like to explore some of the theoretical and political ambiguities of the 'post-colonial'" ("Notes on the 'Post-Colonial,'" 99).

107   Frankenberg and Mani, "Crosscurrents, Crosstalk," 302.
108   Ibid., 307.
109   Ibid.
110   Ibid., 304.
111   Pratt and Hanson, "Geography and the Construction of Difference," 6.
112   Ibid., 9.
113   Ibid., 10–11.
114   Ibid., 11–12.
115   Ibid., 25.
116   Ibid., 26.
117   Shohat, "Columbus, Palestine, and Arab-Jews," msp. 2. See also the chapter "Ethnicities in Relation" in Shohat and Stam, *Unthinking Eurocentrism,* 220–247.

BIBLIOGRAPHY

Adorno, Theodor. *Minima Moralia: Reflections from a Damaged Life.* Trans. E. F. N. Jephcott. London: NLB, 1974.

Ahmad, Aijaz. "Postcolonialism: What's in a Name?" In *Late Imperial Culture,* ed. Román de la Campa, E. Ann Kaplan, and Michael Sprinker, 11–32. London: Verso, 1995.

————. *In Theory: Classes, Nations, Literatures.* London: Verso, 1992.

Alarcón, Norma. "The Theoretical Subject(s) of *This Bridge Called My Back* and Anglo-American Feminism." In *Making Face/Making Soul/Haciendo Caras: Creative and Critical Perspectives by Women of Color,* ed. Gloria Anzaldúa, 356–369. San Francisco: Aunt Lute Books, 1990.

————. "Traddutora, Traditora: A Paradigmatic Figure of Chicana Feminism." In *Scattered Hegemonies: Postmodernity and Transnational Feminist Practices,* ed. Inderpal Grewal and Caren Kaplan, 110–133. Minneapolis: University of Minnesota Press, 1994.

Albrecht, Lisa, and Rose M. Brewer, ed. *Bridges of Power: Women's Multicultural Alliances.* Philadelphia: New Society Publishers, 1990.

Alcoff, Linda. "Cultural Feminism versus Post-Structuralism: The Identity Crisis in Feminist Theory." In *A Reader in Contemporary Social Theory,* ed. Nicholas B. Dirks, George Ely, and Sherry B. Ortner, 96–122. Princeton: Princeton University Press, 1994.

Anderson, Benedict. *Imagined Communities: Reflections on the Origin and Spread of Nationalism.* London: Verso, 1983.

Anthias, Floya, and Nira Yuval-Davis. *Racialized Boundaries: Race, Nation, Gender, Colour and Class and the Anti-Racist Struggle.* London: Routledge, 1992.

Anzaldúa, Gloria. *Borderlands/La Frontera: The New Mestiza.* San Francisco: Spinsters/Aunt Lute Press, 1987.

Appadurai, Arjun. "Putting Hierarchy in Its Place." *Cultural Anthropology* 3.1 (1988): 36–49.

Appiah, Kwame Anthony. "Is the Post- in Postmodernism the Post- in Post-colonial?" *Critical Inquiry* 17.2 (Winter 1991): 336–357.

Arac, Jonathan, ed. *Postmodernism and Politics.* Minneapolis: University of Minnesota Press, 1986.

Aronowitz, Stanley. "Postmodernism and Politics." In *Universal Abandon?* ed. Andrew Ross, 46–62. Minneapolis: University of Minnesota Press, 1988.

Asad, Talal, ed. *Anthropology and the Colonial Encounter.* London: Ithaca Press, 1973.

Bachelard, Gaston. *The Poetics of Space.* Boston: Beacon Press, 1969.

Balibar, Etienne. "*Es Gibt Keinen Staat in Europa:* Racism and Politics in Europe Today." *New Left Review* 186 (March/April 1991): 5–19.

Balibar, Etienne, and Immanuel Wallerstein. *Race, Nation, Class: Ambiguous Identities.* London: Verso Books, 1991.

Bammer, Angelika, ed. *Displacements: Cultural Identities in Question.* Bloomington: Indiana University Press, 1994.

Basch, Linda, Nina Glick Schiller, and Cristina Szanton Blanc, eds. *Nations Unbound: Transnational Projects, Postcolonial Predicaments and Deterritorialized Nation-States.* Langhorne, PA: Gordon and Breach Publishers, 1994.

Baudelaire, Charles. *Paris Spleen.* New York: New Directions, trans. Louise Varese, 1970.

Baudrillard, Jean. *America.* Trans. Chris Turner. London: Verso, 1988. Originally published as *Amérique* (Paris: Bernard Grasset, 1986).

———. *Cool Memories.* Trans. Chris Turner. London: Verso, 1990. Originally published as *Cool Memories: 1980–1985* (Paris: Editions Galilée, 1987).

———. *Seduction.* New York: St. Martin's Press, 1990. Originally published as *De la séduction* (Paris: Denoel-Gonthier, 1979) trans. Brian Singer.

Behdad, Ali. *Belated Travelers: Orientalism in the Age of Colonial Dissolution.* Durham, NC: Duke University Press, 1994.

Benstock, Shari. *Women Writers of the Left Bank, Paris, 1900–1940.* Austin: University of Texas Press, 1986.

Berman, Marshall. *All That Is Solid Melts into Air: The Experience of Modernity.* Harmondsworth: Penguin Books, 1988.

Best, Steven, and Douglas Kellner. *Postmodern Theory: Critical Interrogations.* New York: Guilford Press, 1991.

Bhabha, Homi. *The Location of Culture.* London: Routledge, 1994.

———, ed. *Nation and Narration.* London: Routledge, 1990.

Bishop, Elizabeth. *The Complete Poems: 1927–1979.* New York: Farrar Straus Giroux. 1979.

Bloom, Lisa. *Gender on Ice: American Ideologies of Polar Expeditions.* Minneapolis: University of Minnesota Press, 1993.

Blunt, Alison, and Gillian Rose, eds. *Writing Women and Space: Colonial and Postcolonial Geographies.* New York: Guilford Press, 1994.

Boahen, A. Adu. *African Perspectives on Colonialism.* Baltimore: Johns Hopkins University Press, 1987.

Bodley, John H. *Victims of Progress.* Mountain View, CA: Mayfield Publishing Co., 1990.

Bogue, Ronald. *Deleuze and Guattari.* London: Routledge, 1989.

Bondi, Liz. "Progress in Geography and Gender: Feminism and Difference." *Progress in Human Geography* 14 (1990): 438–445.

Bondi, Liz, and Mona Domosh. "Other Figures in Other Places: On Feminism, Postmodernism and Geography." *Environment and Planning D: Society and Space* 10 (1992): 199–213.

Bookman, Ann, and Sandra Morgen, eds. *Women and the Politics of Empowerment.* Philadelphia: Temple University Press, 1988.

Boyarin, Daniel, and Jonathan Boyarin. "Diaspora: Generation and the Ground of Jewish Identity." *Critical Inquiry* 19.4 (Summer 1993): 693–725.

Bradbury, Malcolm, and James McFarlane, eds. *Modernism: 1890–1930.* Harmondsworth: Penguin Books, 1976.

Braidotti, Rosi. *Patterns of Dissonance: A Study of Women in Contemporary Philosophy.* Trans. Elizabeth Guild. New York: Routledge, 1991.

———. *Nomadic Subjects: Embodiment and Sexual Difference in Contemporary Feminist Theory.* New York: Columbia University Press, 1994.

Brennan, Tim. "Cosmopolitans and Celebrities." *Race and Class* 31.1 (1989): 1–20.

Brier, Stephen, et al., eds. *Who Built America? Working People and the Nation's Economy, Politics, Culture and Society.* New York: Pantheon Press, 1992.

Broe, Mary Lynn, and Angela Ingram, eds. *Women's Writing in Exile.* Chapel Hill: University of North Carolina Press, 1989.

Buell, Frederick. *National Culture and the New Global System.* Baltimore: Johns Hopkins University Press, 1994.

Bulkin, Elly, Minnie Bruce Pratt, and Barbara Smith. *Yours in Struggle: Three Feminist Perspectives on Anti-Semitism and Racism.* Brooklyn, NY: Long Haul Press, 1984.

Butor, Michel. *Mobile.* Paris: Gallimard, 1962.

Calinescu, Matei. *Five Faces of Modernity.* Durham, NC: Duke University Press, 1987.

Callinicos, Alex. *Against Postmodernism: A Marxist Critique.* Cambridge: Polity Press, 1989.

Campbell, Mary B. *The Witness and the Other World: Exotic European Travel Writing, 400–1600.* Ithaca: Cornell University Press, 1988.

Castles, Stephen. "Italians in Australia: Building a Multicultural Society on the Pacific Rim." *Diaspora* 1:1 (Spring 1991): 45–66.

Centre for Contemporary Cultural Studies, eds. *The Empire Strikes Back: Race and Racism in 70s Britain.* London: Hutchinson Press, 1982.

Chakrabarty, Dipesh. "Provincializing Europe: Postcoloniality and the Critique of History." *Cultural Studies* 6.3 (October 1992): 337–357.

Chambers, Iain. *Popular Culture: The Metropolitan Experience.* London: Routledge, 1988.

———. *Border Dialogues: Journeys in Postmodernism.* London: Routledge, 1990.

———. *Migrancy, Culture, Identity.* London: Routledge, 1994.

Chang, Briankle G. "Mass, Media, Mass Media-thon: Baudrillard's Implosive Critique of Modern Mass-Mediated Culture." *Current Perspectives in Social Theory* 17 (1986): 157–181.

Chatterjee, Partha. *Nationalist Thought and the Colonial World: A Derivative Discourse.* London: Zed Books, 1986.

———. *The Nation and Its Fragments: Colonial and Postcolonial Histories.* Princeton: Princeton University Press, 1993.

Chaudhuri, Nupur, and Margaret Strobel, eds. *Western Women and Imperialism: Complicity and Resistance.* Bloomington: University of Indiana Press, 1992.

Chen, Kuan-Hsing. "The Masses and the Media: Baudrillard's Implosive Post-Modernism." *Theory, Culture, and Society* 4 (1987): 71–88.

———. "Voices From the Outside: Towards a New Internationalist Localism." *Cultural Studies* 6.3 (October 1992): 476–484.

Childers, Peter. "Colors on the Map: Narrative, Geography, and the Multicultural Work of Target Marketing." Dept. of English, University of British Columbia, photocopy, 1994.

Chow, Rey. *Women and Chinese Modernity: The Politics of Reading Between West and East.* Minneapolis: University of Minnesota Press, 1991.

———. *Writing Diaspora: Tactics of Intervention in Contemporary Cultural Studies.* Bloomington: University of Indiana Press, 1993.

Christian, Barbara. "The Race for Theory." In *The Nature and Context of Minority Discourse,* ed. Abdul R. JanMohamed and David Lloyd, 37–49. New York: Oxford, 1990.

Clifford, James. *The Predicament of Culture: Twentieth-Century Ethnography, Literature, and Art.* Cambridge: Harvard University Press, 1988.

———. "Notes on Theory and Travel." *Inscriptions* 5 (1989): 177–188.

———. "Traveling Cultures." In *Cultural Studies,* ed. Lawrence Grossberg, Cary Nelson, and Paula Treichler, 96–112. New York: Routledge, 1992.

———. "Diasporas." *Cultural Anthropology* 9.3 (1994): 302–338.

Clifford, James, and Vivek Dhareshwar, eds. "Traveling Theories, Traveling Theorists." *Inscriptions* 5 (1989).

Clifford, James, and George Marcus, eds. *Writing Culture.* Berkeley: University of California Press, 1986.

Cohen, Ed. "The 'Hyperreal' vs. the 'Really Real': If European Intellectuals Stop Making Sense of American Culture Can We Still Dance?" *Cultural Studies* 3.1 (1989): 25–37.

Collins, Jim. *Uncommon Cultures: Popular Culture and Postmodernism.* New York: Routledge, 1989.

Colomina, Beatriz, ed. *Sexuality and Space.* New York: Princeton Architectural Press, 1992.

Connor, Steven. *Postmodernist Culture: An Introduction to Theories of the Contemporary.* New York: Basil Blackwell Press, 1989.

Cowley, Malcolm. *Exile's Return: A Literary Odyssey of the 1920s.* Harmondsworth: Penguin Books, 1982.

Crowley, Helen, et al., eds. "Shifting Territories: Feminism and Europe." *Feminist Review* 39 (1991).

Culler, Jonathan. "The Semiotics of Tourism." In *Framing the Sign: Criticism and Its Institutions,* 153–167. Norman: University of Oklahoma Press, 1988.

Curti, Lidia. "What is Real and What is Not: Female Fabulations in Cultural Analysis." In *Cultural Studies,* ed. Lawrence Grossberg, Cary Nelson, and Paula A. Treichler, 134–153. New York: Routledge, 1992.

Dahlie, Hallvard. *Varieties of Exile: The Canadian Experience.* Vancouver: University of British Columbia Press, 1986.

Davis, Angela. *Women, Culture, Politics.* New York: Vintage Books, 1990.

Davies, Carole Boyce. *Black Women, Writing, and Identity: Migrations of the Subject.* New York: Routledge, 1994.

de Lauretis, Teresa. *Alice Doesn't.* Bloomington: Indiana University Press, 1984.

———. "Feminist Studies/Critical Studies: Issues, Terms, and Contexts." In *Feminist Studies/Critical Studies,* ed. Teresa de Lauretis, 1–19. Bloomington: Indiana University Press, 1986.

———. *Technologies of Gender: Essays on Theory, Film, and Fiction.* Bloomington: Indiana University Press, 1987.

———. "The Essence of the Triangle, or, Taking the Risk of Essentialism Seriously: Feminist Theory in Italy, the U.S., and Britain." *Differences* 1.2 (Summer 1989): 3–37.

———. "Eccentric Subjects: Feminist Theory and Historical Consciousness." *Feminist Studies* 16.1 (Spring 1990): 115–149.

———. "Upping the Anti (sic) in Feminist Theory." In *Conflicts in Feminism,* ed. Marianne Hirsch and Evelyn Fox Keller, 255–270. New York: Routledge, 1990.

Deleuze, Gilles, and Félix Guattari. *Anti-Oedipus: Capitalism and Schizophrenia.* Trans. Robert Hurley, Mark Seem, and Helen R. Lane. Minneapolis: University of Minnesota Press, 1983. Originally published as *L'Anti-Oedipe: Capitalisme et schizophrénie I* (Paris: Minuit, 1972).

———. *Kafka: Toward a Minor Literature.* Trans. Dana Polan. Minneapolis: University of Minnesota Press, 1986. Originally published as *Kafka: Pour une littérature mineure* (Paris: Minuit, 1975).

———. *A Thousand Plateaus: Capitalism and Schizophrenia.* Trans. Brian Massumi. Minneapolis: University of Minnesota Press, 1987. Originally published as *Mille Plateaux: Capitalisme et schizophrénie II* (Paris: Minuit, 1980).

De Man, Paul. "Literary History and Literary Modernity." In *Blindness and Insight: Essays in the Rhetoric of Contemporary Criticism,* 142–165. London: Methuen, 1983.

Dhareshwar, Vivek. "Marxism, Location Politics, and the Possibility of Critique." *Public Culture* 6.1 (1993): 41–54.

di Leonardo, Micaela, ed. *Gender at the Crossroads of Knowledge: Feminist Anthropology in the Postmodern Era.* Berkeley: University of California Press, 1991.

Dirlik, Arif. "The Postcolonial Aura: Third World Criticism in the Age of Global Capitalism." *Critical Inquiry* 20 (Winter 1994): 328–356.

Domosh, Mona. "Towards a Feminist Historiography of Geography." *Transactions of the Institute of British Geographers* 16 (1991): 95–104.

Donaldson, Laura. *Decolonizing Feminisms: Race, Gender, and Empire-Building.* Chapel Hill: University of North Carolina Press, 1992.

Dowmunt, Tony, ed. *Channels of Resistance: Global Television and Local Empowerment.* London: BFI Publishing, 1993.

Drummond, Phillip, Richard Paterson, and Janet Willis, eds. *National Identity and Europe: The Television Revolution.* London: BFI Publishing, 1993.

Duncan, James, and David Ley, eds. *Place/Culture/Representation.* London: Routledge, 1993.

During, Simon. "Postmodernism or Post-Colonialism Today." *Textual Practice* 1.1 (Spring 1987): 32–47.

———, ed. *The Cultural Studies Reader.* London: Routledge, 1993.

Eagleton, Terry. *Exiles and Émigrés: Studies in Modern Literature.* New York: Schocken Books, 1970.

Eco, Umberto. *Travels in Hyperreality.* San Diego: Harvest Press, 1986.

Eisenstein, Sergei. *Film Form: Essays in Film Theory.* Trans. Jay Leyda. New York: Harcourt, Brace, Jovanovich, 1977.

Enloe, Cynthia. *Bananas, Beaches, and Bases: Making Feminist Sense of International Politics.* Berkeley: University of California Press, 1990.

Farah, Nurrudin. "A Country in Exile." *Transition* 57 (1992): 4–8.

Ferguson, Kathy E. *The Man Question: Visions of Subjectivity in Feminist Theory.* Berkeley: University of California Press, 1993.

Fernandez-Kelly, Patricia. *For We Are Sold, I and My People: Women and Industry on Mexico's Frontier.* Albany: State University of New York Press, 1983.

Foucault, Michel. *Power/Knowledge: Selected Interviews and Other Writings, 1972–1977.* New York: Pantheon Books, 1980.

———. "Of Other Spaces." Trans. Jay Miskowiec. *Diacritics* 16.1 (Spring 1986): 22–27.

Foley, Barbara. *Telling the Truth: The Theory and Practice of Documentary Fiction.* Ithaca: Cornell University Press, 1986.

Fox, Pamela. *Class Fictions: Shame and Resistance in the British Working-Class Novel, 1890–1945*. Durham, NC: Duke University Press, 1994.

Frankenberg, Ruth, and Lata Mani. "Crosscurrents, Crosstalk: Race, 'Postcoloniality' and the Politics of Location." *Cultural Studies* 7.2 (May 1993): 292–310.

Frankovits, André, ed. *Seduced and Abandoned: The Baudrillard Scene*. New York: Semiotext(e) Press, 1984.

Fraser, Nancy, and Linda Nicholson. "Social Criticism without Philosophy: An Encounter between Feminism and Postmodernism." In *Universal Abandon?* ed. Andrew Ross, 83–104. Minneapolis: University of Minnesota Press, 1988.

Freud, Sigmund. "Mourning and Melancholia." In *Metapsychology*, 245–268. Harmondsworth: Penguin Books, 1984.

Fuentes, Annette, and Barbara Ehrenreich. *Women in the Global Factory*. Boston: South End Press, 1983.

Fujikane, Candace. "Between Nationalisms: Hawaii's Local Nation and Its Troubled Racial Paradise." *Critical Mass: A Journal of Asian American Cultural Criticism* 1.2 (1994): 23–58.

Fusco, Coco. "About Locating Ourselves and Our Representations." *Framework* 36 (1989): 7–14.

Fussell, Paul. *Abroad: British Literary Traveling Between the Wars*. Oxford: Oxford University Press, 1980.

Gabriel, Teshome H. "Thoughts on Nomadic Aesthetics and the Black Independent Cinema." In *Blackframes: Critical Perspectives on Black Independent Cinema*, ed. Cham Mybe and Claire Watkins, 62–79. Cambridge: MIT Press, 1988.

Gallop, Jane. "French Theory and the Seduction of Feminism." In *Men in Feminism*, ed. Alice Jardine and Paul Smith, 111–115. New York: Methuen Press, 1987.

Gane, Mike. *Baudrillard: Critical and Fatal Theory*. London: Routledge, 1991.

Genesko, Gary. "Adventures in the Dromosphere." *border/lines* (Winter 1989/90): 34–36.

Gilroy, Paul. *"There Ain't No Black in the Union Jack": The Cultural Politics of Race and Nation*. Chicago: University of Chicago Press, 1991.

———. *The Black Atlantic: Modernity and Double Consciousness*. Cambridge: Harvard University Press, 1993.

Gonzalez, Jennifer A., and Michelle Habell-Pallan. "Heterotopias and Shared Methods of Resistance: Navigating Social Spaces and Spaces of Identity." *Inscriptions* 7 (1994): 80–104.

Gordon, Deborah, ed. "Feminism and the Critique of Colonial Discourses." *Inscriptions* 3.4 (1988): 1–5.

Graham, Julie. "Fordism/Post-Fordism, Marxism/Post-Marxism: The Second Cultural Divide?" *Rethinking Marxism* 4.1 (Spring 1991): 39–58.

Green, Martin. *Dreams of Adventure, Deeds of Empire*. New York: Basic Books, 1979.

Gregory, Derek. *Geographical Imaginations*. Cambridge, MA: Basil Blackwell Publishers, 1994.

Gregory, Derek, and John Urry, eds. *Social Relations and Spatial Structures*. New York: St. Martin's Press, 1985.

Grewal, Inderpal. "Salman Rushdie: Marginality, Women, and *Shame*." *Genders* 3 (Fall 1988): 24–42.

———. "The Guidebook and the Museum: Imperialism, Education and Nationalism in the British Museum." *Bucknell Review* (1990): 195–217.

———. "The Postcolonial, Ethnic Studies, and the Diaspora: The Contexts of Ethnic Immigrant/Migrant Cultural Studies in the US." *Socialist Review* 94.4 (1994): 45–74.

———. "Autobiographic Subjects and Diasporic Locations: *Meatless Days* and *Borderlands*." In *Scattered Hegemonies: Postmodernity and Transnational Feminist Practices,* ed. Inderpal Grewal and Caren Kaplan, 231–254. Minneapolis: University of Minnesota Press, 1994.

———. *Home and Harem: Imperialism, Nationalism, and the Culture of Travel*. Durham, NC: Duke University Press, 1996.

Grewal, Inderpal, and Caren Kaplan. "Transnational Feminist Practices and Questions of Postmodernity." Introduction to *Scattered Hegemonies: Postmodernity and Transnational Feminist Practices,* ed. Inderpal Grewal and Caren Kaplan, 1–33. Minneapolis: University of Minnesota Press, 1994.

Griffiths, Gareth. *A Double Exile: African and West Indian Writing Between Two Cultures*. London: Marion Boyars, 1978.

Grisoni, Dominique, ed. *Politiques de la philosophie*. Paris: Bernard Grasset, 1976.

Grossberg, Lawrence. "Wandering Audiences, Nomadic Critics." *Cultural Studies* 2.3 (1988): 377–389.

Grossberg, Lawrence, Cary Nelson, and Paula A. Treichler, eds. *Cultural Studies*. New York: Routledge, 1992.

Guha, Ranajit, and Gayatri Chakravorty Spivak, eds. *Selected Subaltern Studies*. New York: Oxford University Press, 1988.

Hall, Stuart. "The Local and the Global: Globalization and Ethnicity." In *Culture, Globalization and the World System: Contemporary Conditions for the Representation of Identity,* ed. Anthony D. King, 19–40. London: Macmillan, 1991.

Hannerz, Ulf. "The World in Creolisation." *Africa* 57.4 (1987): 546–558.

———. "Notes on the Global Ecumene." *Public Culture* 1.2 (Spring 1989): 66–75.

Hanscombe, Gillian, and Virginia L. Smyers. *Writing For Their Lives: The Modernist Women, 1910–1940.* London: The Women's Press, 1987.

Haraway, Donna. *Simians, Cyborgs, and Women: The Reinvention of Nature.* New York: Routledge, 1991.

Hartley, John. "Expatriation: Useful Astonishment as Cultural Studies." *Cultural Studies* 6.3 (October 1992): 449–467.

Hartsock, Nancy. "Rethinking Modernism: Minority vs. Majority Theories." In *The Nature and Context of Minority Discourse,* ed. Abdul R. JanMohamed and David Lloyd, 17–36. New York: Oxford University Press, 1990.

Harvey, David. *The Condition of Postmodernity.* Cambridge, MA: Basil Blackwell Press, 1990.

Hassan, Ihab. *Paracriticisms: Seven Speculations of the Times.* Urbana: University of Illinois Press, 1975.

Hayward, Philip. "Implosive Critiques." *Screen* 25 (1984): 128–133.

Helms, Mary W. *Ulysses' Sail: An Ethnographic Odyssey of Power, Knowledge, and Geographical Distance.* Princeton: Princeton University Press, 1988.

Hicks, D. Emily. *Border Writing: The Multidimensional Text.* Minneapolis: University of Minnesota Press, 1991.

Hidalgo, Cristina Pantoja. "Home and Exile in the Autobiographical Narratives of Filipino Women Writers." In *Philippine Post-Colonial Studies: Essays on Language and Literature,* ed. Cristina Pantoja Hidalgo and Priceline Pantajo-Legasto, 82–104. Diliman, Quezon City: University of the Philippines Press, 1993.

Hoberman, J. "Lost in America: Jean Baudrillard, Extraterrestrial." *Voice Literary Supplement* 34.72 (March 1989): 15–16.

Hobsbawn, E. J. *Nations and Nationalism Since 1780: Programme, Myth, Reality.* Cambridge: Cambridge University Press, 1991.

hooks, bell. *Yearning: Race, Gender, and Cultural Politics.* Boston: South End Press, 1990.

———. *Black Looks: Race and Representation.* Boston: South End Press, 1992.

Horne, Donald. *The Great Museum: The Re-Presentation of History.* London: Pluto Press, 1984.

Howe, Irving. *Decline of the New.* New York: Harcourt, Brace, Jovanovich, 1970.

Hulme, Peter. *Colonial Encounters: Europe and the Native Caribbean, 1492–1797.* London: Methuen, 1986.

Hunter, Diane, ed. *Seduction and Theory: Readings of Gender, Representation, and Rhetoric.* Urbana: University of Illinois Press, 1989.

Hutcheon, Linda. *A Poetics of Postmodernism: History, Theory, Fiction.* New York: Routledge, 1988.

Huyssen, Andreas. *After the Great Divide: Modernism, Mass Culture, Postmodernism.* Bloomington: Indiana University Press, 1986.

Ilie, Paul. *Literature and Inner Exile.* Baltimore: Johns Hopkins University Press, 1980.

Independent Commission on International Humanitarian Issues. *Refugees: Dynamics of Displacement.* London: Zed Books, 1986.

James, C. L. R. *Mariners, Renegades and Castaways: The Story of Herman Melville and the World We Live In.* London: Allison and Busby, 1985.

Jameson, Fredric. "Postmodernism, Or, The Cultural Logic of Late Capitalism." *New Left Review* 146 (1984): 53–92.

———. "Cognitive Mapping." In *Marxism and the Interpretation of Culture,* ed. Cary Nelson and Lawrence Goldberg, 347–357. Urbana: University of Illinois Press, 1988.

———. "Modernism and Imperialism." In *Nationalism, Colonialism, and Literature,* ed. Terry Eagleton, Fredric Jameson, and Edward W. Said, 43–68. Minneapolis: University of Minnesota Press, 1990.

JanMohamed, Abdul. "Worldliness-without-World, Homelessness-as-Home: Toward a Definition of the Secular Border Intellectual." In *Edward Said: A Critical Reader,* ed. Michael Sprinker, 96–120. Cambridge, MA: Blackwell Publishers, 1992.

JanMohamed, Abdul, and David Lloyd, eds. *The Nature and Context of Minority Discourse.* New York: Oxford University Press, 1990.

Jardine, Alice. "Woman in Limbo: Deleuze and His Br(others)." *SubStance* 44/45 (1984): 46–60.

Jardine, Alice, and Paul Smith, eds. *Men in Feminism.* New York: Methuen Press, 1987.

Jay, Karla. "The Outsider Among the Expatriates: Djuna Barnes's Satire on the Ladies of the *Almanack.*" In *Lesbian Texts and Contexts: Radical Revisions,* ed. Karla Jay and Joanne Glasgow, 204–216. New York: New York University Press, 1990.

Jayawardena, Kumari. *Feminism and Nationalism in the Third World.* London: Zed Books, 1986.

Jensen, Holger. "Death and Refugees, the Cost of Nonintervention." *San Francisco Examiner,* 31 July 1994, A17.

Jones, Kathleen B. "Identity, Action, and Locale: Thinking About Citizenship, Civic Action, and Feminism." *Social Politics: International Studies in Gender, State and Society* 1.3 (Fall 1994): 256–270.

Jordan, June. *On Call: Political Essays.* Boston: South End Press, 1985.

Kaplan, Caren. "The Poetics of Displacement: Exile, Immigration, and Travel in Autobiographical Writing." Ph.D. diss., University of California at Santa Cruz, 1987.

———. "The Poetics of Displacement in *Buenos Aires,*" *Discourse* 8 (Fall-Winter 1986–87): 84–102.

————. "Deterritorializations: The Rewriting of Home and Exile in Western Feminist Discourse." *Cultural Critique* 6 (Spring 1987): 187–198.

————. "Reconfigurations of Geography and Historical Narrative." *Public Culture* 3.1 (Fall 1990): 25–32.

————. "Resisting Autobiography: Out-Law Genres and Transnational Subjects." In *De/Colonizing the Subject: the Politics of Gender in Women's Autobiography,* ed. Sidonie Smith and Julia Watson, 115–138. Minneapolis: University of Minnesota Press, 1992.

————. " 'A World Without Boundaries': The Body Shop's Trans/National Geographics." *Social Text* 43 (June 1995): 45–66.

————. " 'Getting to Know You': Travel, Gender, and the Politics of Representation in *Anna and the King of Siam* and *The King and I.*" In *Late Imperial Culture,* ed. Román de la Campa, E. Ann Kaplan, and Michael Sprinker, 33–52. London: Verso, 1995.

Kaplan, Caren, and Inderpal Grewal. "Transnational Feminist Cultural Studies: Beyond the Marxism/Poststructuralist/Feminism Divides." *positions: east asia cultures critique* 2.2 (Fall 1994): 430–445.

Katz, Cindi, and Janice Monk, ed. *Full Circles: Geographies of Women Over the Life Course.* New York: Routledge, 1993.

Keith, Michael, and Steve Pile, eds. *Place and the Politics of Identity.* London: Routledge, 1993.

Kellner, Douglas. *Jean Baudrillard: From Marxism to Postmodernism.* Stanford: Stanford University Press, 1989.

Kern, Stephen. *The Culture of Time and Space, 1880–1918.* Cambridge: Harvard University Press, 1983.

Kincaid, Jamaica. *A Small Place.* New York: Farrar, Straus & Giroux, 1988.

King, Anthony D., ed. *Culture, Globalization and the World-System.* London: Macmillan Press, 1991.

Kondo, Dorinne K. *Crafting Selves: Power, Gender, and Discourses of Identity in a Japanese Workplace.* Chicago: University of Chicago Press, 1990.

Kristeva, Julia. *Nations Without Nationalism.* Trans. Leon S. Roudiez. New York: Columbia University Press, 1993.

Kroker, Arthur. *The Possessed Individual: Technology and the French Postmodern.* New York: St. Martin's Press, 1992.

Kroker, Arthur, and David Cook. *The Postmodern Scene: Excremental Culture and Hyper-Aesthetics.* New York: St. Martin's Press, 1986.

Krupat, Arnold. *Ethnocriticism: Ethnography, History, Literature.* Berkeley: University of California Press, 1992.

Laclau, Ernesto. "Politics and the Limits of Modernity." In *Universal Abandon?* ed. Andrew Ross, 63–82. Minneapolis: University of Minnesota Press, 1988.

Lamming, George. *The Pleasures of Exile*. London: Allison and Busby, 1984.

Larsen, Neil. *Modernism and Hegemony: A Materialist Critique of Aesthetic Agencies*. Minneapolis: University of Minnesota Press, 1990.

Lazarus, Neil. "Postcolonialism and the Dilemma of Nationalism: Aijaz Ahmad's Critique of Third-Worldism." *Diaspora* 2.3 (1993): 373–400.

Lefebvre, Henri. *The Production of Space*. Trans. Donald Nicholson-Smith. Cambridge, MA: Basil Blackwell Publishers, 1991.

Levin, Harry. *Refractions: Essays in Comparative Literature*. New York: Oxford University Press, 1966.

Lie, John. "Enough Said, Ahmad: Politics and Literary Theory." *positions: east asia cultures critique* 2.2 (Fall 1994): 417–429.

Lionnet, Françoise, and Ronnie Scharfman, eds. "Post/Colonial Conditions: Exile, Migrations, and Nomadisms." *Yale French Studies* 82/83 (1993).

Lorde, Audre. *Sister/Outsider: Essays and Speeches*. Trumansburg, NY: The Crossing Press, 1984.

Lowe, Lisa. *Critical Terrains: French and British Orientalisms*. Ithaca: Cornell University Press, 1991.

———. "Heterogeneity, Hybridity, Multiplicity: Marking Asian American Differences." *Diaspora* 1.1 (Spring 1991): 24–44.

———. "Literary Nomadics in Francophone Allegories of Postcolonialism: Pham Van Ky and Tahar Ben Jelloun." *Yale French Studies* 82 (1993): 43–61.

Lubiano, Wahneema. "Shuckin' Off the African-American Native Other: What's 'Po-Mo' Got to Do with It?" *Cultural Critique* 18 (Spring 1991): 149–186.

Lugones, Maria. "Playfulness, 'World'-Travelling, and Loving Perception." In *Making Face/Making Soul: Haciendo Caras,* ed. Gloria Anzeldúa, 390–402. San Francisco: Aunt Lute Books, 1990.

Lyotard, Jean-François. *The Postmodern Condition: A Report on Knowledge*. Trans. Geoff Bennington and Brian Massumi. Minneapolis: University of Minnesota Press, 1984.

MacCannell, Dean. *The Tourist: A New Theory of the Leisure Class*. New York: Schocken Books, 1976.

———. *Empty Meeting Grounds: The Tourist Papers*. London: Routledge, 1992.

McCarthy, Mary. "Exiles, Expatriates and Internal Emigres." *The Listener* (25 November 1971): 705–708.

McClintock, Anne. "The Angel of Progress: Pitfalls of the Term 'Post-Colonialism.'" *Social Text* 31/32 (1992): 84–98.

McGee, Patrick. *Telling the Other: The Question of Value in Modern and Postmodern Writing*. Ithaca: Cornell University Press, 1992.

McGowan, John. *Postmodernism and Its Critics*. Ithaca: Cornell University Press, 1991.

Mani, Lata. "Multiple Mediations: Feminist Scholarship in the Age of Multinational Reception." *Inscriptions* 5 (1989): 1–24.

Mani, Lata, and Ruth Frankenberg. "The Challenge of *Orientalism.*" *Economy and Society* 14.2 (1985): 174–192.

Marcus, George, and Michael Fischer, eds. *Anthropology as Cultural Critique.* Chicago: University of Chicago Press, 1986.

Martin, Susan Forbes. *Refugee Women.* London: Zed Books, 1991.

Mascia-Lees, Frances E., Patricia Sharpe, and Colleen Ballerino Cohen. "The Postmodernist Turn in Anthropology: Cautions from a Feminist Perspective." *Signs* 15.1 (1989): 7–33.

Massey, Doreen. *Space, Place, and Gender.* Minneapolis: University of Minnesota Press, 1994.

Massumi, Brian. "Realer Than Real: The Simulacrum According to Deleuze and Guattari." *Copyright* 1 (Fall 1987): 90–97.

Mathy, Jean-Phillipe. *Extrême-Occident: French Intellectuals and America.* Chicago: University of Chicago Press, 1993.

Mattelart, Armand. *Transnationals and the Third World: The Struggle for Culture.* South Hadley, MA: Bergin and Garvey Publishers, 1983.

———. *Mapping World Communication: War, Progress, Culture.* Minneapolis: University of Minnesota Press, 1994.

Mehrez, Samia. "Azouz Begag: *Un di zafras di bidoufile* or The *Beur* Writer: A Question of Territory." *Yale French Studies* 82 (1993): 25–42.

Meisel, Perry. *The Myth of the Modern: A Study in British Literature and Criticism after 1850.* New Haven: Yale University Press, 1987.

Mercer, Kobena. *Welcome to the Jungle: New Positions in Black Cultural Studies.* New York: Routledge, 1994.

Miller, Christopher L. *Blank Darkness: Africanist Discourse in French.* Chicago: University of Chicago Press, 1985.

Miller, J. Hillis. "Beginning with a Text." *Diacritics* 6.3 (Fall 1976): 2–7.

Miyoshi, Masao. "A Borderless World? From Colonialism to Transnationalism and the Decline of the Nation-State." *Critical Inquiry* 19.4 (Summer 1993): 726–751.

Mohanty, Chandra Talpade. "Feminist Encounters: Locating the Politics of Experience." *Copyright* 1 (Fall 1987): 30–44.

———. "Cartographies of Struggle: Third World Women and the Politics of Feminism." Introduction to *Third World Women and the Politics of Feminism,* ed. Chandra Talpade Mohanty, Ann Russo, and Lourdes Torres, 1–47. Bloomington: Indiana University Press, 1991.

———. "Under Western Eyes: Feminist Scholarship and Colonial Discourses." In *Third World Women and the Politics of Feminism,* ed. Chandra Talpade Mohanty, Ann Russo, and Lourdes Torres, 51–80. Bloomington: Indiana University Press, 1991.

Moore, Suzanne. "Getting a Bit of the Other—The Pimps of Postmodernism." In *Male Order,* ed. Rowena Chapman and Jonathan Rutherford, 165–192. London: Lawrence and Wishart Press, 1988.

Moorehead, Caroline. *Freya Stark.* Harmondsworth, England: Penguin, 1985.

Morley, David, and Kevin Robins. "Spaces of Identity: Communications Technologies and the Reconfiguration of Europe." *Screen* 30.4 (Autumn 1989): 10–34.

Morris, Meaghan. "Room 101 or a Few Worst Things in the World." In *Seduced and Abandoned: The Baudrillard Scene,* ed. André Frankovits, 91–117. New York: Semiotext(e) Press, 1984.

———. "At Henry Parkes Motel." *Cultural Studies* 2.1 (January 1988): 1–47.

———. "Things to Do With Shopping Centres." In *Grafts: Feminist Cultural Criticism,* ed. Susan Sheridan, 193–225. London: Verso, 1988.

———. "Great Moments in Social Climbing: King Kong and the Human Fly." In *Sexuality and Space,* ed. Beatriz Colomina, 1–51. New York: Princeton Architectural Press, 1992.

Muecke, Stephen. "The Discourse of Nomadology: Phylums in Flux." *Art and Text* 14 (1984): 24–40.

Mukherjee, Arjun. "Whose Post-Colonialism and Postmodernism?" *World Literature Written in English* 30.2 (August 1990): 1–9.

Naficy, Hamid. *The Making of Exile Cultures: Iranian Television in Los Angeles.* Minneapolis: University of Minnesota Press, 1993.

Nash, Catherine. "Remapping and Renaming: New Cartographies of Identity, Gender, and Landscape in Ireland." *Feminist Review* 44 (Summer 1993): 39–57.

Nash, Dennison. "Tourism as an Anthropological Subject." *Current Anthropology* 22.5 (October 1981): 461–481.

Natarajan, Nalini, ed. *Writers of the Indian Diaspora.* Westport, CT: Greenwood Publishers, 1993.

Nelson, Cary, and Lawrence Grossberg, eds. *Marxism and the Interpretation of Culture.* Urbana: University of Illinois Press, 1988.

Newman, Robert D. *Transgressions of Reading: Narrative Engagement as Exile and Return.* Durham, NC: Duke University Press, 1993.

Newton, Judith, and Judith Stacey. "Learning Not to Curse, or, Feminist Predicaments in Cultural Criticism by Men: Our Movie Date with James Clifford and Stephen Greenblatt." *Cultural Critique* 23 (Winter 1992–93): 51–82.

Ngugi wa Thiong'o. *Moving the Centre: The Struggle for Cultural Freedoms.* London: James Curry Press, 1993.

Nicholson, Linda J., ed. *Feminism/Postmodernism.* New York: Routledge, 1990.

Nixon, Robert. "London Calling: V. S. Naipaul and the License of Exile." *South Atlantic Quarterly* 87.1 (Winter 1988): 1–38.

Norris, Christopher. *What's Wrong with Postmodernism: Critical Theory and the Ends of Philosophy*. Baltimore: Johns Hopkins University Press, 1990.

——. *Uncritical Theory: Postmodernism, Intellectuals and the Gulf War*. Amherst: University of Massachusetts Press, 1992.

Norton, Jody. "*America* by Jean Baudrillard." *Discourse* 14.3 (Summer 1992): 167–173.

Ochoa, Maria, and Teresa Teaiwa, ed. "Enunciating Our Terms: Women of Color in Collaboration and Conflict." *Inscriptions* 7 (1994).

Ong, Aihwa. *Spirits of Resistance and Capitalist Discipline: Factory Women in Malaysia*. Albany: State University of New York Press, 1987.

——. "The Gender and Labor Politics of Postmodernity." *Annual Review of Anthropology* 20 (1991): 279–309.

Parker, Andrew, et al., eds. *Nationalisms and Sexualities*. New York: Routledge, 1992.

Partnoy, Alicia, ed. *You Can't Drown the Fire: Latin American Women Writing in Exile*. Pittsburgh: Cleis Press, 1988.

Patton, Paul. "Conceptual Politics and the War-Machine in *Mille Plateaux*." *SubStance* 44/45 (1984): 61–80.

——. "Marxism and Beyond: Strategies of Reterritorialization." In *Marxism and the Interpretation of Culture*, ed. Cary Nelson and Lawrence Grossberg, 123–136. Urbana: University of Illinois Press, 1988.

Peterson, Kirsten Holst, and Anna Rutherford, eds. *Displaced Persons*. Sydney: Dangaroo Press, 1988.

Pick, Zuzana M. "The Dialectical Wanderings of Exile," *Screen* 30.4 (Autumn 1989): 48–65.

Pollock, Griselda. *Vision and Difference: Femininity, Feminism, and the Histories of Art*. London: Routledge, 1988.

Potts, Lydia. *The World Labour Market: A History of Migration*. Trans. Terry Bond. London: Zed Books, 1990.

Prakash, Gyan, ed. *After Colonialism: Imperial Histories and Postcolonial Displacements*. Princeton: Princeton University Press, 1995.

Pratt, Geraldine, and Susan Hanson. "Geography and the Construction of Difference." *Gender, Place and Culture* 1.1 (1994): 5–29.

Pratt, Mary Louise. *Imperial Eyes: Travel Writing and Transculturation*. London: Routledge, 1992.

Pred, Allan, and Michael John Watts. *Reworking Modernity: Capitalisms and Symbolic Discontent*. New Brunswick, NJ: Rutgers University Press, 1992.

Probyn, Elspeth. "Travels in the Postmodern: Making Sense of the Local." In *Feminism/Postmodernism*, ed. Linda J. Nicholson, 176–189. New York: Routledge, 1990.

Radway, Janice. "Reception Study: Ethnography and the Problems of Dispersed Audiences and Nomadic Subjects." *Cultural Studies* 2.3 (1988): 359–376.

Rancière, Jacques. "Discovering New Worlds: Politics of Travel and Metaphors of Space." In *Traveller's Tales: Narratives of Home and Displacement,* ed. George Robertson et al., 29–37. London: Routledge, 1994.

Raybaud, Antoine. "Nomadism between the Archaic and the Modern." *Yale French Studies* 82 (1993): 146–158.

Reagon, Bernice Johnson. "Coalition Politics: Turning the Century." In *Home Girls: A Black Feminist Anthology,* ed. Barbara Smith, 356–369. New York: Kitchen Table: Women of Color Press, 1983.

Rich, Adrienne. *Of Woman Born: Motherhood as Experience and Institution.* New York: Norton, 1976.

———. *On Lies, Secrets, and Silence: Selected Prose, 1966–1978.* New York: Norton, 1979.

———. *Blood, Bread, and Poetry: Selected Prose, 1979–1985.* New York: Norton, 1986.

———. *An Atlas of the Difficult World.* New York: Norton, 1991.

———. *What is Found There: Notebooks on Poetry and Politics.* New York: Norton, 1993.

Richard, Nelly. "Postmodernism and Periphery." Trans. Nick Caistor. *Third Text* 2 (Winter 1987/88): 5–12.

Robbins, Bruce. "Homelessness and Worldliness." *Diacritics* 13.3 (Fall 1983): 69–77.

———. "Comparative Cosmopolitanism." *Social Text* 31/32 (1992): 169–186.

———. *Secular Vocations: Intellectuals, Professionalism, Culture.* London: Verso Press, 1993.

Robins, Kevin. "Tradition and Translation: National Culture in Its Global Context." In *Enterprise and Heritage: Crosscurrents of National Culture,* ed. John Connor and Sylvia Harvey, 21–44. London: Routledge, 1991.

Rosaldo, Renato. *Culture and Truth: The Remaking of Social Analysis.* Boston: Beacon Press, 1989.

———. "Politics, Patriarchs, and Laughter." In *The Nature and Context of Minority Discourse,* ed. Abdul JanMohamed and David Lloyd, 124–145. New York: Oxford University Press, 1990.

Rose, Gillian. *Feminism and Geography: The Limits of Geographical Knowledge.* Minneapolis: University of Minnesota Press, 1993.

Ross, Andrew. "Baudrillard's Bad Attitude." In *Seduction and Theory: Readings of Gender, Representation, and Rhetoric,* ed. Diane Hunter, 214–225. Urbana: University of Illinois Press, 1989.

———, ed. *Universal Abandon? The Politics of Postmodernism.* Minneapolis: University of Minnesota Press, 1988.

————. "The New Sentence and the Commodity Form: Recent American Writing." In *Marxism and the Interpretation of Culture*, ed. Cary Nelson and Lawrence Grossberg, 361–380. Urbana: University of Illinois Press, 1988.

Rouse, Roger. "Mexican Migration and the Social Space of Postmodernism." *Diaspora* 1.1 (Spring 1991): 8–23.

————. "Thinking Through Transnationalism: Notes on the Cultural Politics of Class Relations in the Contemporary United States." *Public Culture* 7.2 (Winter 1995): 353–402.

Ruiz, Vicki L., and Susan Tiano, eds. *Women on the U.S./Mexican Border: Response to Change*. Boston: George Allen and Unwin, 1987.

Rushdie, Salman. *Imaginary Homelands: Essays and Criticism, 1981–1991*. New York: Penguin Books, 1991.

Rutherford, Jonathan. "A Place Called Home: Identity and the Cultural Politics of Difference." In *Identity: Community, Culture, Difference*, ed. Jonathan Rutherford, 9–27. London: Lawrence and Wishart, 1990.

Sack, Robert David. *Place, Modernity, and the Consumer's World: A Relational Framework for Geographical Analysis*. Baltimore: Johns Hopkins University Press, 1992.

Safran, William. "Diasporas in Modern Societies: Myths of Homeland and Return." *Diaspora* 1.1 (Spring 1991): 83–99.

Said, Edward W. *Orientalism*. New York: Vintage Books, 1979.

————. "Zionism from the Standpoint of Its Victims." *Social Text* 1.1 (1979): 7–58.

————. *The World, the Text, and the Critic*. Cambridge: Harvard University Press, 1983.

————. "Reflections on Exile." *Granta* 13 (1984): 159–172.

————. "The Mind of Winter: Reflections on Life in Exile." *Harper's* (September 1984): 49–55.

————. "On Palestinian Identity: A Conversation with Salman Rushdie." *New Left Review* 160 (1986): 63–80.

————. "Intellectuals in the Post-Colonial World." *Salamagundi* 70–71 (Summer 1986): 44–64.

————. *After the Last Sky: Palestinian Lives*. New York: Pantheon Books, 1986.

————. "American Intellectuals and Middle East Politics: An Interview with Bruce Robbins." *Social Text* 19/20 (Fall 1988): 37–53.

————. "Edward Said: The Voice of a Palestinian in Exile." *Third Text* 3/4 (Spring/Summer 1988): 39–50.

————. "Yeats and Decolonization." In *Remaking History*, ed. Barbara Kruger and Phil Mariani, 3–30. Seattle, WA: Bay Press, 1989.

————. "Figures, Configurations, Transfigurations." *Race and Class* 32.1 (1990): 1–16.

————. *Culture and Imperialism*. New York: Alfred A. Knopf Publishers, 1993.

Sandoval, Chela. "U.S. Third World Feminism: The Theory and the Method of Oppositional Consciousness in the Postmodern World." *Genders* 10 (Spring 1991): 1–24.

Sangari, Kum Kum, and Sudesh Vaid, eds. *Recasting Women: Essays in Indian Colonial History.* New Brunswick, NJ: Rutgers University Press, 1990.

Santos-Febres, Mayra. *The Translocal Papers: Gender and Nation in Contemporary Puerto Rican Literature.* Ph.D. dissertation, Cornell University, 1991.

Schnapper, Aron. "A Host Country of Immigrants That Does Not Know Itself." *Diaspora* 1.3 (Winter 1993): 353–364.

Scott, Bonnie Kime. *The Gender of Modernism.* Bloomington: Indiana University Press, 1990.

Seidel, Michael. *Exile and Narrative Imagination.* New Haven: Yale University Press, 1986.

Sharpe, Jenny. *Allegories of Empire: The Figure of the Woman in the Colonial Text.* Minneapolis: University of Minnesota Press, 1993.

Shattuck, Roger. *The Banquet Years: The Origins of the Avant-Garde in France 1885 to World War I.* New York: Vintage Books, 1968.

Shohat, Ella. "Gender and the Culture of Empire: Toward a Feminist Ethnography of the Cinema." *Quarterly Review of Film and Video* 13.1–3 (1991): 45–84.

———. "Notes on the 'Post-Colonial'." *Social Text* 31/32 (1992): 99–113.

———. "Reflections of an Arab Jew." *Emergences* 3/4 (Fall 1992): 39–45.

———. "Columbus, Palestine, and Arab-Jews: Toward a Relational Approach to Community Identity." In *Reflections on the Work of Edward Said: Cultural Identity and the Gravity of History,* ed. Keith Ansell-Pearson, Benita Parry, and Judith Squires. London: Lawrence and Wishart, forthcoming 1996.

Shohat, Ella, and Robert Stam. *Unthinking Eurocentrism: Multi-Culturalism and the Media.* New York: Routledge, 1994.

Sivan, Emmanuel. *Interpretations of Islam Past and Present.* Princeton: Darwin Press, 1985.

Sivanandan, A. "New Circuits of Imperialism." *Race and Class* 30.4 (1989): 1–20.

———. "The Enigma of the Colonised: Reflections on Naipaul's Arrival." *Race and Class* 32.1 (1990): 33–44.

Sklair, Leslie. *Sociology of the Global System.* Baltimore: Johns Hopkins University Press, 1991.

Slemon, Stephen. "Post-Colonial Allegory and the Transformation of History." *Journal of Commonwealth Literature* 23.1 (1988): 157–168.

Smart, Barry. *Modern Conditions, Postmodern Controversies.* London: Routledge, 1992.

Smith, Neil. *Uneven Development: Nature, Capital, and the Production of Space.* New York: Blackwell Books, 1984.

Smith, Neil, and Cindi Katz. "Grounding Metaphor: Towards a Spatialized Politics." In *Place and the Politics of Identity,* ed. Michael Keith and Steve Pile, 67–83. London: Routledge, 1993.

Smith, Paul. "Visiting the Banana Republic." In *Universal Abandon?* ed. Andrew Ross, 128–148. Minneapolis: University of Minnesota Press, 1988.

Smith, Sidonie, and Julia Watson, eds. *De/Colonizing the Subject: The Politics of Gender in Women's Autobiography.* Minneapolis: University of Minnesota Press, 1992.

Smith, Valene, ed. *Hosts and Guests: The Anthropology of Tourism.* Philadelphia: University of Pennsylvania Press, 1977.

Smith, Valene, and William R. Eadington, eds. *Tourism Alternatives: Potentials and Problems in the Development of Tourism.* Philadelphia: University of Pennsylvania Press, 1992.

Soja, Edward. *Postmodern Geographies: The Reassertion of Space in Critical Social Theory.* London: Verso, 1989.

Spain, Daphne. *Gendered Spaces.* Chapel Hill: University of North Carolina Press, 1992.

Spivak, Gayatri Chakravorty. *In Other Worlds: Essays in Cultural Politics.* New York: Methuen Press, 1987.

———. "Can the Subaltern Speak?" In *Marxism and the Interpretation of Culture,* ed. Cary Nelson and Lawrence Grossberg, 271–313. Urbana: University of Illinois Press, 1988.

———. "The Political Economy of Women as Seen by a Literary Critic." In *Coming to Terms: Feminism, Theory, Politics,* ed. Elizabeth Weed, 218–229. New York: Routledge, 1989.

———. *The Post-Colonial Critic: Interviews, Strategies, Dialogues,* ed. Sarah Harasym. New York: Routledge, 1990.

———. *Outside in the Teaching Machine.* New York: Routledge, 1993.

Sprinker, Michael. "The National Question: Said, Ahmad, Jameson." *Public Culture* 6.1 (1993): 3–30.

———, ed. *Edward Said: A Critical Reader.* Cambridge, MA: Blackwell Publishers, 1992.

———. "Introduction." In *Late Imperial Culture,* ed. Román de la Campa, E. Ann Kaplan, and Michael Sprinker, 1–10. London: Verso, 1995.

Spurr, David. *The Rhetoric of Empire: Colonial Discourse in Journalism, Travel Writing, and Imperial Administration.* Durham, NC: Duke University Press, 1993.

Stafford, Barbara Maria. *Voyage into Substance: Art, Science, Nature and the Illustrated Travel Account, 1760–1840.* Cambridge: MIT Press, 1984.

Steiner, George. *Extra-territorial: Papers on Literature and the Language Revolution.* New York: Atheneum Press, 1971.

Strathern, Marilyn. "Or, Rather, On Not Collecting Clifford." *Social Analysis* 29 (January 1991): 88–95.

Strobel, Margaret. *European Women and the Second British Empire*. Bloomington: Indiana University Press, 1991.

Tabori, Paul. *The Anatomy of Exile: A Semantic and Historical Study*. London: Harrap, 1972.

Taylor, Jenny Bourne. "Re: Locations—From Bradford to Brighton." *New Formations* 17 (1992): 86–94.

Thomas, Nicholas. *Colonialism's Culture: Anthropology, Travel, and Government*. Princeton: Princeton University Press, 1994.

Tiffin, Helen. "Post-Colonialism, Post-Modernism and the Rehabilitation of Post-Colonial History." *Journal of Commonwealth Literature* 23.1 (1988): 169–181.

Tiffin, Helen, Bill Ashcroft, and Gareth Griffiths. *The Empire Writes Back: Theory and Practice in Post-Colonial Literatures*. London: Routledge, 1989.

Tölölyan, Khachig. "The Nation-State and Its Others: In Lieu of a Preface." *Diaspora* 1.1 (Spring 1991): 3–7.

Tomlinson, John. *Cultural Imperialism: A Critical Introduction*. Baltimore: Johns Hopkins University Press, 1991.

Trinh, Minh-ha T. *Woman/Native/Other: Writing, Postcoloniality and Feminism*. Bloomington: Indiana University Press, 1989.

———. *When the Moon Waxes Red: Representation, Gender, and Cultural Politics*. New York: Routledge, 1991.

Valentine, Gill. "Negotiating and Managing Multiple Sexual Identities: Lesbian Time-Space Strategies." *Transactions of the Institute of British Geographers* 18.2 (1993): 237–248.

Van Den Abbeele, George. "Sightseers: The Tourist as Theorist." *Diacritics* 10 (December 1980): 2–14.

———. *Travel as Metaphor: From Montaigne to Rousseau*. Minneapolis: University of Minnesota Press, 1992.

Wallace, Michele. "The Politics of Location: Cinema/Theory/Literature/Ethnicity/Sexuality/Me." *Framework* 36 (1989): 42–55.

———. "Modernism, Postmodernism and the Problem of the Visual in Afro-American Culture." In *Out There: Marginalization and Contemporary Cultures*, ed. Russell Ferguson, Martha Gever, Trinh T. Minh-ha, 39–50. Cambridge: MIT Press, 1990.

Ware, Vron. *Beyond the Pale: White Women, Racism, and History*. London: Verso, 1992.

Weedon, Chris. *Feminist Practice and Poststructuralist Theory*. Oxford: Basil Blackwell Ltd., 1987.

West, Cornel. "Postmodernity and Afro-America." *Art Papers* 10.1 (January/February 1986): 54.

White, Hayden. "Criticism as Cultural Politics." *Diacritics* 6.3 (1976): 8–23.

White, Jonathan, ed. *Recasting the World: Writing After Colonialism.* Baltimore: Johns Hopkins University Press, 1993.

Williams, Raymond. *The Politics of Modernism: Against the New Conformists.* London: Verso, 1989.

Williamson, Judith. "Woman is an Island: Femininity and Colonization." In *Studies in Entertainment,* ed. Tania Modleski, 99–118. Bloomington: Indiana University Press, 1986.

Willis, Susan. *A Primer for Daily Life.* New York: Routledge, 1991.

Wittlin, Joseph. "Sorrow and Grandeur of Exile." *The Polish Review* 11 (Spring-Summer 1957): 99–112.

Wolff, Janet. "The Invisible Flaneuse: Women and the Literature of Modernity." *Theory, Culture and Society* 2.3 (1985): 37–46.

———. "The Global and the Specific: Reconciling Conflicting Theories of Culture." In *Culture, Globalization and the World-System,* ed. Anthony D. King, 161–174. London: Macmillan Press, 1991.

———. "On the Road Again: Metaphors of Travel in Cultural Criticism." *Cultural Studies* 7 (1992): 224–239.

Women and Geography Study Group of the Institute of British Geographers. *Geography and Gender: An Introduction to Feminist Geography.* London: Hutchinson, 1984.

Woodhull, Winifred. "Exile." *Yale French Studies* 82 (1993): 7–24.

———. *Transfigurations of the Maghreb: Feminism, Decolonization, and Literatures.* Minneapolis: University of Minnesota Press, 1993.

Woolf, Virginia. *Three Guineas.* London: Harcourt Brace Jovanovich, 1938.

Young, Robert. *White Mythologies: Writing History and the West.* London: Routledge, 1990.

Yúdice, George. "Marginality and the Ethics of Survival." In *Universal Abandon? The Politics of Postmodernism,* ed. Andrew Ross, 214–236. Minneapolis: University of Minnesota Press, 1988.

———. "For a Practical Aesthetics." *Social Text* 25/26 (1990): 129–145.

———. "We Are *Not* the World." *Social Text* 31/32 (1992): 202–216.

Yúdice, George, Jean Franco, and Juan Flores, eds. *On Edge: The Crisis of Contemporary Latin American Culture.* Minneapolis: University of Minnesota Press, 1992.

INDEX

Theory, notion of, 76, 93, 130, 175; master narratives and, 17–18
Theroux, Paul, 50
Third World, 84, 88, 123; public voices of, 124–125; women, 162, 180–182
This Bridge Called My Back (Anzaldua and Moraga), 176–177
Thousand Plateaus, A (Deleuze and Guattari), 67, 87, 90
Todorov, Tzvetan, 53
Tölölyan, Khachig, 135
Tourism, 5; and angst, 56; counterdiscourses of, 62; and imperialism, 63; and modernity, 58; theoretical, 89, 93; and travel, 54–56. *See also* Travel
Tourist, 55; and antitourist, 55; and authenticity, 60; modern subject as, 57, 62
Tourist, The (MacCannell), 5
Transnationalism, effects of, 8; and critical practice, 10, 24
Travel, 22; hierarchy of, 56, 130; metaphors of, 1, 2, 4, 26; and modernism, 3; notion of, 130–133; real, 53; and tourism, 78–79, 85; and the traveler, 50; and the act of writing, 61
Traveling cultures, 130–132. *See also* Culture
Traveling theories, 5. *See also* Theory

Travel writing, 50–52, 54; golden age of, 53, 56
Triolet, Elsa, 33

United States, 79, 81, 84, 105. *See also* America
U.S. women of color, 166

Wallace, Michele, 13
Watts, Michael John, 20–21
West, Cornel, 12–13
Whiteness, 165
Williams, Judith, 15–16
Williams, Raymond, 31–33, 40
Wittlin, Joseph, 36–38
Wolff, Janet, 152
Woman, notion of, 75, 77–78, 162, 175–177; and desert, 77
Women, 76–77; of color, 181
Women's movement in the United States, 162–163
Woodhull, Winifred, 94–95
Woolf, Virginia, 161–162
World systems model, 20
World, the Text, and the Critic, The (Said), 5, 113–114
Writing Diaspora: Tactics of Invention in Contemporary Cultural Studies (Chow), 139

Yale French Studies, 94
Young, Robert, 9, 11

Caren Kaplan is Associate Professor in the Department of Women's Studies, University of California at
Berkeley. She is the co-editor (with Inderpal Grewal)
of *Scattered Hegemonies: Postmodernity and Transnational
Feminist Practices.*

Library of Congress Cataloging-in-Publication Data
Kaplan, Caren.
Questions of travel : postmodern discourses of displacement /
by Caren Kaplan.
(Post-contemporary interventions)
Includes bibliographical references and index.
ISBN 0-8223-1828-8. — ISBN 0-8223-1821-0 (pbk.)
1. Travel in literature.   2. Literature, Modern—History and criticism.
3. Postmodernism (Literature)   4. Modernism (Literature)
I. Title.
PN56.T7K37   1996
809'.93355—dc20